中国故事丛书

Understanding Modern China Series

（Editor-in-Chief: Feng Jun）

冯 俊◎主编

中国城镇化

New Analysis of Urbanization in China
By Chu Tianjiao, Wang Guoping, Zhu Yuan, et al

楚天骄 王国平 朱远 等◎著

人民出版社

总　序

　　中国国家的制度安排是怎样的？中国共产党为什么能够长期执政并带领全中国人民不断从胜利走向胜利？中国共产党执政的"秘诀"有哪些？中国的发展道路是什么？中国现阶段有哪些重大战略？中国下一步发展向何处去？中国经济为什么能够快速发展？诸如此类的问题，都是国际社会尤其是外国政党政要来华访问时思考和询问的问题。为了回答这些问题，让读者了解一个真实的中国和中国共产党，我们组织编写了《"中国故事"丛书》（以下简称《丛书》），作为介绍中国共产党，介绍中国发展道路、发展理论和发展经验的基本材料。

　　《丛书》以党的十八大以来习近平总书记提出的治国理政新理念新思想新战略为指导，着力体现"中国梦"的发展愿景和"两个一百年"的奋斗目标，着力体现协调推进"五位一体"的总体布局和统筹推进"四个全面"的战略布局，着力体现把握、适应和引领中国经济发展的新常态和贯彻落实"五大发展理念"，着力体现"一带一路"、京津冀协调发展、长江经济带等三大经济发展战略，在占有大量鲜活案例和经验的基础上,讲好中国故事,传播中国声音,分析中国问题,提供中国方案。

在编写过程中,《丛书》还努力注意把握好以下四个方面:一是在全面介绍中国改革开放以来取得的成就经验的基础上,注重阐释党的十八大以来全面深化改革的新举措、经济发展的新思路、对外工作的新理念等;二是在展示中国经济社会发展成果的同时,着重分析取得这些成果的原因、背后的运行逻辑、演进的过程;三是坚持问题导向、需求导向,不求大而全,不求系统完整,从国外受众需求出发,有针对性地释疑解惑;四是既讲中国"从何处来",更讲中国"向何处去",一方面引导读者了解认识中国历史发展进程,另一方面注重讲清楚中国如何把握过去、现在和未来的有机统一,继承与创新的有机结合,规划设计未来发展走向。

《丛书》在中共中央对外联络部的指导下,由中国浦东干部学院组织编写。

中共中央对外联络部(简称中联部)是中国共产党负责对外工作的职能部门。目前,中国共产党同世界上 160 多个国家和地区的 600 多个政党和政治组织有着不同形式的联系和交往,其中既有左翼政党,也有右翼政党;既有执政党,也有在野党。中国共产党的对外工作是党的事业的一条重要战线,也是国家总体外交的重要组成部分,其工作目标是通过政党交往促进国家与国家、人民与人民之间的了解与沟通。

中国浦东干部学院(CELAP)是中国国家级干部学院,作为中国开展国际合作培训交流的窗口,自 2005 年 3 月创立以来,坚持国际性、时代性、开放性的办学特色,大力开展国际合作培训,培训对象包括外国政党政要、企业高管、高级专家等各类国际领导人才。截至 2015 年年底,已经培训了来自 130 个国家和地区的学员 6000 余名,获得了培训国家和地区以及参训学员的广泛认可和普遍好评。

基于国外学员学习的需要,中国浦东干部学院于 2012 年年初启动《丛书》编写工作,历经 4 年的打磨精炼,数易其稿,于 2015 年年底定稿。《丛书》首批推出 10 册,分别是《中国治理新方略》、《中国共产党的建设》、《中国经济改革与开发区建设》、《中国政府架构与基本公共服务》、《中国城镇化》、《中国农业与农村发展》、《中国外交与和平发展》、《中国干部选拔任用》、《中国干部教育》、《中国改革开放的"排头兵"——上海》。丛书的作者主要来自中国浦东干部学院,此外还有上海市政府发展研究中心、上海国际问题研究院、杭州城市学研究中心的领导和专家。

《丛书》以中英文对照方式出版,英文翻译主要由上海外国语大学的资深教授主持,深致谢忱!人民出版社对《丛书》的出版予以大力支持,在编写和翻译过程中提出了诸多建设性意见,一并表示感谢!

编写供国外学员学习培训的系列化教材,在国内尚属首次。作为一种新的探索和尝试,难免有所疏漏、错谬,敬请指正。

《中国故事丛书》编写委员会
2016 年 9 月

目 录

导　言

城镇化是经济社会发展的必然趋势,是衡量国家和地区经济社会发展水平的标志之一。新中国成立 60 多年来,尤其是改革开放以来,城镇化水平显著提高。作为一个 13 亿多人口的大国,中国的城镇化对中国乃至世界的发展都将产生重大的影响。美国著名经济学家斯蒂格利茨指出,世界最大的发展中国家——中国的城市化与世界最大的发达国家——美国的高科技发展,将是深刻影响 21 世纪人类发展的两大重要课题。因此,中国城镇化发展道路及其经验无疑是世界城镇化的宝贵财富。

（一）本书目标

本书以中国城镇化为贯穿全书的主线,以时间为纵轴,以空间为横轴,动态讨论城镇化涉及的经济、社会、生态、文化的演变历程,全方位展示中国当前城镇化的显著特点,初步揭示中国城镇化的发展理念、发展路径和发展经验,使学员对中国道路、中国理念有更加深入的理解,进而帮助学员将中国城镇化经验因地制宜、因时制宜地运用到本国本地发展实践中。

(二)框 架 结 构

本书共包括七章内容。

第一章主要就中国城镇化的发展历程和现状特征进行描述,并针对中国城镇化存在的问题提出未来推进中国城镇化健康发展的政策方向。

第二章回顾中国城乡规划从无到有、从不完善到逐步完善的发展历程,总结城乡规划发展中的经验和教训,并概括介绍中国城乡规划行政体系和运作体系,以期反映中国特色城乡规划的全貌。

第三章描述了中国从计划经济体制向社会主义市场经济体制转型的过程中城市产业布局的演变,并重点介绍作为中国城市产业发展重要的空间载体的开发区建设和新城建设。

第四章介绍中国城市基础设施建设的主要成就、有效经验、重点问题和一般措施。

第五章描述了改革开放以来形成的中国城市土地有偿使用制度的基本框架,并着重介绍中国城市土地产权制度、城市土地利用管理和城市土地市场管理,以期概括中国城市土地制度的全貌。

第六章通过回顾中国城市社区管理体制的演化过程,描述中国社区管理体制的形成背景和鲜明特征,并介绍中国城市社区服务和城市社区自治的情况。

第七章按照中国历史文化遗产的分级保护体系,借助典型案例,扼要介绍中国的具体做法和经验体会。

(三)重 点 难 点

本书的重点在于通过回顾中国的城镇化历程,详细地描述中国的城市在改革开放以来发生的一系列重要变化,系统阐述中国政府在推动城镇化快速健康可持续发展方面构建的制度框架,帮助学员了解中国国情,为进一步深入探讨城镇化路径提供研究背景。

本书的难点在于如何切实把握外国学员的需求和兴趣,认真分析跨文化沟通的基本特点和要求,用平实生动的语言叙述国情,用鲜活的故事讲述中国城镇化走过的历程,为外国学员提供务实管用的教学材料,使学员看得懂、学得进、用得上。

（四）使　用　要　求

本书在教学内容、教学要求、呈现方式、编排风格等方面具有鲜明的开放性特点,是一本活的教材。教员应该树立开放的教学理念来充分利用开放的教材。本书中选择的教学内容反映了最基本、最基础的知识结构,具有一定的稳定性,以静态形式呈现的教材不可能即时呈现出中国城镇化的最新动态,这就需要教员在教学中主动寻找新的信息,不断学习,吸收新知识,激发学员的学习兴趣。而学员则应以教材为点,以现实社会为面,通过本书的学习之后,将课堂由室内延伸到课外,加深对中国经济社会发展的了解。

限于编写人员的知识水平和教学经验,本书的缺点和疏漏之处在所难免。因此,希望使用本书的教员和学员向编写人员提出宝贵意见。本书第一章、第二章、第三章、第五章由楚天骄撰写,第四章由楚天骄、朱远撰写,第六章由接栋正撰写,第七章由李明超、邵莹撰写。

（一）中国城镇化的历程与现状

所谓城镇化是指农业人口向非农业人口转移和生产、生活方式集约程度的提高[①]。中国城镇化是当前世界城镇化的重要组成部分，占世界发展中国家 1/4 总人口的中国城镇化进程将成为 21 世纪世界城镇化的主要力量。1975—2000 年，世界城镇人口总共增长了 13.17 亿人，年平均增长 5268 万人，其中发展中国家城镇人口总共增长 11.64 亿人，年平均增长 4652 万人。而 1978—2003 年中国城镇人口总共增长 3.52 亿人，年平均增长 1405 万人，占同期世界城镇人口年平均增长量的 1/4 左右，占同期发展中国家年平均城镇人口增长量的 1/3 左右。未来时期，中国城镇化的健康发展，将成为解决

[①] 周干峙：《探索中国特色的城市化之路》，《国际城市规划》2009 年第 S1 期。

中国一系列重大战略问题的路径,而中国城镇化特殊的世界历史意义,也决定了中国城镇化进程必定是 21 世纪人类发展的主题。

1. 中国城镇化的历程与现状

自 1949 年中华人民共和国成立以来,中国的城镇化可以划分为两个时期三个发展阶段。

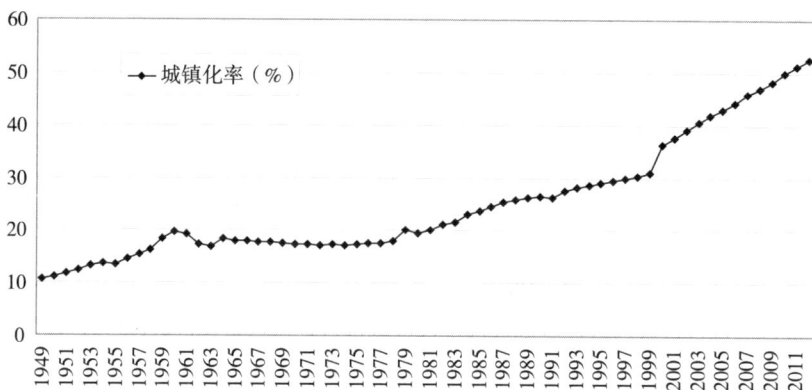

图 1-1　中国城镇化率(1949—2012 年)

①计划经济时期

——强调重工业发展阶段(1952—1965 年)

新中国成立之初,中国实行优先发展重工业的发展战略。在这种发展战略下,许多农村劳动力进入国有企业工作,工业城市,尤其是内陆的工业城市优先得到了发展。在此期间,城市人口增长速度超过了总人口的增长速度,中国的城镇化稳定发展。从 1952 年到 1965 年,城市人口由 7163 万增长到 13045 万,增长率为 82.1%,而同期全国总人口数从 57482 万增至 72538 万,增长率为 26.2%,比城市人口的增长慢得多。城市人口所占比重由 1952 年的 12.5%、1958 年的 16.3%一直提高到 1965 年的 18.0%。

中国从 1953 年开始实行第一个五年计划,大规模的工业建设吸收了大量从农村走出来的农民,工业化带动城镇化,城镇人口有计划地增长。全国城镇化水平从 1949 年的 10.60% 增长到 1958 年的 16.25%,平均每年增加 0.63 个百分点。在计划经济体制下,农村人口通过招工、招兵和招生等有限的途径有序地向城镇转移,到 1957 年城市人口达到 1 亿,城镇化水平达到 15.4%。

1958 年到 1965 年期间,中国城镇人口数量出现了大起大落的情形。1958 年到 1960 年上半年,由于中国政府实施了试图利用本国充裕的劳动力和蓬勃的群众热情在工业和农业上"跃进"的社会主义建设运动,搞虚幻的经济赶超,在农村大规模招工,3000 万农民进入城市,城镇化水平每年平均提高 1.45 个百分点,成为中国城镇化水平提升最快的年份。1963 年到 1965 年,由于粮食减产,城市口粮无法保证供应,又不得不将新进入城市的 2600 万人下放回农村,城镇化水平每年平均下降 1.0 个百分点,成为中国城镇化水平下降最快的年份。

——"文化大革命"期间(1966—1978 年)

1966—1977 年是中国"文化大革命"的十年动乱时期。在此期间城市的发展出现停滞甚至倒退。在"文化大革命"期间,一方面,为了解决城市中的就业问题,政府组织了 1000 多万城市中的年轻人移居到农村,数百万机关干部和知识分子也被下放到农村,使城镇人口净迁出 500 多万;另一方面,国家又把大量的资金用于内地工业化的发展,将许多军工企业和重工业企业从沿海地区迁往内地,工业建设大分散、小集中,工厂布点按照"靠山、分散、隐蔽"的原则来安排,而对城市建设的投资却微乎其微,导致新建的城市很少。1965—1975 年间,总人口的增长率高于城市人口增长率,城市人口所占比重不变甚至降低,1965 年为 18.0%,1970 年为 17.4%,1975 年为 17.3%,1978 年为 17.9%。

②走向市场经济时期

——改革开放,城镇化提升发展阶段(1978—1996 年)

1978 年起,中国不仅实行了开放政策和"社会主义市场经济",而且出台了鼓励城镇化的政策。许多县镇升级为市,城市数量迅猛增长,由 1978 年的 191 座增加为 1996 年的 666 座。与此同时,城市人口所占比重由 17.9% 增加到 29.4%,18 年间中国的城镇化率增长了 11.8

个百分点。

——深化改革、扩大开放,城镇化加速发展阶段(1996年以后)

1996年以后,中国的城镇化开始进入高速发展时期。近二十年的改革开放带来经济发展、资金积累和居民收入增长的同时,开发区和新区建设以及国际化大都市建设的热潮也使中国城镇化发展步入新的阶段。在这一时期,经济全球化浪潮提高了中国经济的开放性,中国的经济转型也加快了市场化的前进步伐,市场对城镇化的需求更加强烈。与此同时,政府的一系列制度创新不仅节约了城镇化的交易成本,还在降低风险的同时提高了城镇化的预期收益水平。在政府和市场的共同作用下,中国的城镇化水平步入加速发展阶段。城镇化率从1996年的29.4%提高到2012年的52.6%,增加了23.2个百分点,城镇总人口从3.59亿增加到7.1亿。

2. 中国城镇化现阶段的主要特征

(1)持续30多年的城镇化率高速度递增,为世界城镇化史上罕见

自1978年改革开放以来,中国城市迅速发展,小城镇迅速崛起,在此期间中国城镇化发展速度是同期世界城镇化平均速度的2倍左右。世界各国城镇化的进程各不相同(图1-2),从20%到40%的城镇化率,英国经历了120年,法国经历了100年,德国经历了80年,美国经历了40年,苏联经历了30年,日本经历了30年,而中国仅仅用了22年。目前中国城镇化仍然明显低于世界平均水平和同等工业化国家的水平。

(2)城镇人口的增长除了自然增长以外,主要来源于农村人口向城镇的转移,"候鸟型"流动人口与"定居型"流动人口将长期并存

改革开放以后,随着中国户籍管理制度的松动,大量农村劳动力涌入城市和沿海发达地区。这些农村劳动力的流动具有数量大、范围广、影响深刻的特点,是中国历史上最大规模的人口流动。农民工流动自1984年兴起,20世纪80年代末外出农民工只有3000万人,几经曲折,到2012年外出农民工已达到2.26亿人。由于城镇,特别是大城市的生活居住"门槛"过高、农民又拥有耕地的使用权和宅基地与自留地等

城市人口比重/%

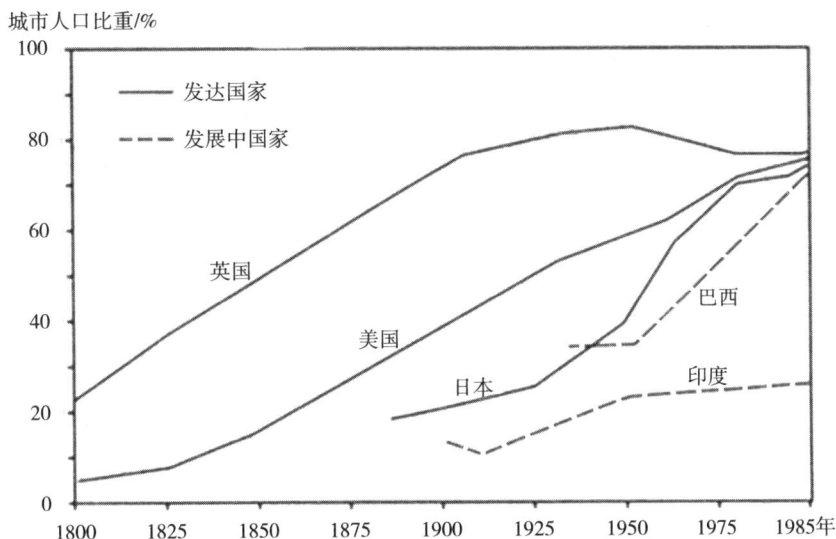

图1-2　部分国家城镇化率演变情况

原因,进城打工的人口中,只有17%在城镇定居,成为真正的城镇人口,83%是"候鸟型"流动人口。这同欧洲某些国家在城镇化早期依靠农民破产进城的情况有很大的不同。"候鸟型"流动人口虽然对送出地和接受地都有好处,但却不利于产业的技术成长和城镇化的质量提升。但是由于城市不可能在短期内接纳所有进城务工人员,"候鸟型"流动人口在相当长的时间内仍难以消除。

(3)中国正处在城镇化快速发展时期,今后的城镇化将主要由第二产业和它带起的第三产业驱动,并逐步过渡到主要由第三产业驱动

目前中国城镇化已进入中期发展阶段。世界城镇化的历史表明,一般说来,一个国家的城镇化水平在达到30%以后就进入快速城镇化阶段,达到70%以后发展就趋于缓慢。1978年,中国城镇人口比重只有17.92%。到1996年,这一比重就上升到30.48%。可以说,从此中国城镇化开始进入快速发展时期。到2006年,城镇人口比重上升到43.9%①。这10年间,城镇人口比重平均每年提升1.34个百分点,比1978—1996年间平均每年提升0.7个百分点快了近一倍。至2012年年底,全国城

---

① 《中国统计年鉴》(2007年),中国统计出版社2007年版,第105页。

镇人口比重已上升到 52.6%,从 2007 年到 2012 年的城镇化水平平均每年提升 1.54 个百分点。可见,目前中国城镇化正处于加速发展时期,城镇人口持续快速扩张,是这一阶段的基本特征(图 1-3)。

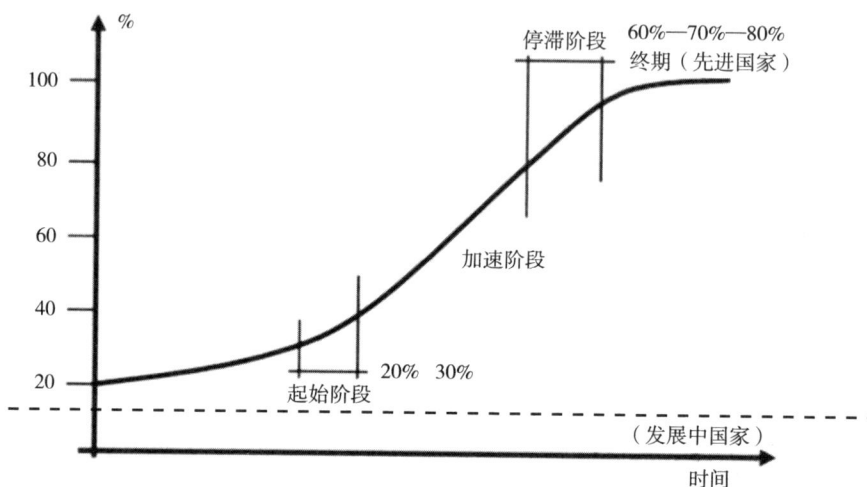

图 1-3　城镇化发展阶段示意图

工业一直是中国产业发展的支柱,是城市就业的主要保障,但今后第三产业在城镇化中的作用将进一步凸显。2012 年,中国产业结构中第一产业、第二产业和第三产业所占比重分别为 10.1%、45.3% 和 44.6%,工业占比重最大,第三产业次之。据《中国流动人口发展报告 2013》的资料,2013 年国家卫生计生委的调查数据显示,中国流动人口中,制造业从业人员比例为 33.3%,较 2011 年下降 4.1 个百分点。第三产业就业比例出现上升趋势,2013 年在批发零售和住宿餐饮行业就业的比例分别为 20.1% 和 11.3%,比 2011 年分别上升 2 个百分点和 1.4 个百分点。可见,今后中国的城镇化将主要由第二产业和它带起的第三产业驱动。

(4)政府主导与市场力量对城镇化进程的影响并存

1978 年以后,中国实行改革开放方针,一方面,政府为城镇化护航,如指出城镇化是解决"三农"问题的重要途径之一,在"十五"计划中明确提出推进城镇化的战略,以及调整部分限制和不利于农民进城的政策等,在"十一五"规划建议中又进一步提出促进城镇化健康发展;另一方面,在劳动力转移和就业、房地产开发、城镇基础设施建设等方面运用了市场机制,城镇化进程明显加快。2013年12月召开的中央城镇化工作会议明确指出,要以人为本,推进以人为核心的城镇化,提高城镇人口素质和居民生活质量,把促进有能力在城镇稳定就业和生活的常住人口有序实现市民化作为首要任务,并强调,推进城镇化,既要坚持使市场在资源配置中起决定性作用,又要更好地发挥政府在创造制度环境、编制发展规划、建设基础设施、提供公共服务、加强社会治理等方面的职能;中央制定大政方针、确定城镇化总体规划和战略布局,地方则从实际出发,贯彻落实总体规划,制定相应规划,创造性开展建设和管理工作。

(5)城镇化的地区差异很大

由于区域自然条件和社会经济条件的不同,中国的城镇化表现出明显的区域差异。2012年,东、中、西部(图1-4)的城镇化水平分别为56.4%、53.4%和44.9%。东部沿海地区的交通与对外开放之便,形成了以都市连绵区为标志的快速城镇化地区(图1-5);中部地区受资源开发导向的影响,沿路和沿江形成了较快的城镇化地区;西部因受经济、社会发展基础相对薄弱和生态环境脆弱的影响,城镇化进程较慢,仅在一些中心城市显示出较快的城镇化进程。此外,受原有城市规模大小的影响,城镇化进程的区域差异更加突出。

(6)城镇化与工业化、信息化、市场化、经济全球化同时推进,各类矛盾凸显

发达国家的城镇化是与工业化相伴而生的,历经几百年。同发达国家相比,中国的城镇化滞后150年。发达国家近200年完成的城镇化任务,中国要压缩到几十年完成,各类矛盾凸显并交织在一起。中国的城镇化不仅与工业化同步推进,还面临着信息化、市场化、经济全球化带来的诸多挑战。可以说,中国的城镇化就像是在一个高度压缩的时空反应釜中进行。尽管有幸发生于和平安定的环境中,有优越的社会主义制度作保障,但是,时空压缩下的"历时性矛盾共时性承受",也催化产生并堆积着大量可以预料和难以预料的问题、矛盾和风险。

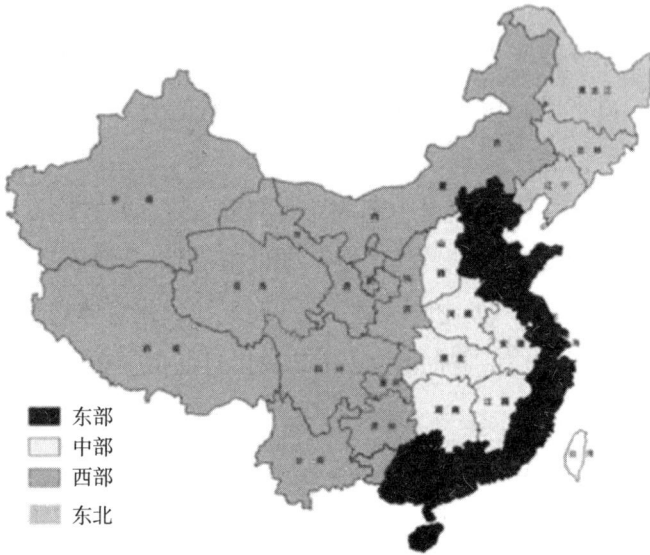

图1-4 中国东中西部范围示意图

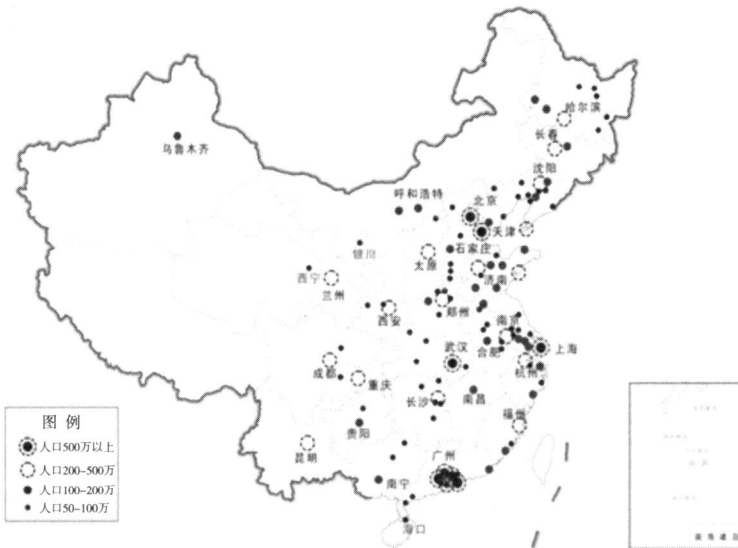

图1-5 中国都市连绵区分布示意图

（二）中国城镇化面临的挑战和问题

1. 中国城镇化面临的挑战

（1）资源与环境带来的挑战

①资源

资源危机已经成为中国城镇化发展的"瓶颈"，资源紧缺与资源浪费现象同时并存且严峻考验着中国城镇化的可持续发展。

这里提到的资源主要指在城镇化进程中所必需的水资源、土地资源、能源等。从水资源来看，中国人均淡水资源只有2290平方米，而且分布极不平均。随着城镇化人口的剧增，生产用水和生活用水大幅上升，加上江河湖泊等地表水及地下水质遭到严重污染，城市的空间布局与水资源承载能力不相适应的问题越来越突出。目前，全国655个城市中有近400个城市缺水，其中约200个城市严重缺水。全国城市日缺水量达1600万立方米，年缺水量达60亿立方米，以至于北方一些城市被迫限量供水。

从土地资源来看，城市用地数量的巨大需求与可供土地数量的严重短缺之间的矛盾日益尖锐，土地资源的稀缺性非常突出。随着中国城镇化进程的加快，土地资源尤其是耕地资源的短缺愈加凸显。始于2001年结束于2009年的第二次全国土地调查初步汇总发现，全国实际耕地面积为20.26亿亩，耕地面积越来越接近18亿亩"红线"（18亿亩耕地"红线"被认为是保证中国粮食安全的最基本耕地底线）。

中国土地利用形势十分严峻。一方面，城市建设用地的紧张成为不少城市发展中遇到的最大难题；另一方面，当前城市建设中土地浪费现象普遍存在，严重阻碍了城市综合质量的提高和功能的正常发挥，降低了城市的承载能力，影响了城镇化的健康发展。

从能源来看，中国城镇化发展面临的挑战主要是能源短缺和低效利用问题。能源短缺问题主要表现为城市需要的能源供给不足，尤其是石油和电力。随着城镇化进程的推进,重化工业、城市人口数量的增加和城市居民生活质量的提高,对能源需求大幅增加。2003 年以来,全国出现大面积"电荒",20 多个省(市)被迫限制用电。2009 年中国进口原油 2.04 亿吨,比上年增长 13.9%;同年,煤炭消费量 27.4 亿吨,比上年增长 3.0%。城市能源消耗快速增长的同时,还伴随着能源利用效率低下的问题。目前,全国综合能源利用效率约为 33%,比发达国家低 10%。

②生态环境

城镇化发展初期,中国主要是依靠工业化来推动城市化,再加上治污设施建设滞后,工业污染和城市污染物排放激增。城市化的快速发展,使得固体废弃物污染、水污染、空气污染等问题加剧,交通拥堵问题日渐严重。大多数城市工业、人口高度集中,狭小的区域内产生的大量废弃物远远超过了城市环境的自净化能力,导致城市污染日益严重,使得城市化陷入了巨大的生态困境。

2008 年全国工业固体废物产生量为 19.01 亿吨,比 2000 年增加近11 亿吨。城市生活垃圾产生量也呈直线增长态势,2008 年达到 1.54亿吨,而城市生活垃圾无害化处理率平均只有 66.8%。城市水污染主要来自工业废水和生活污水,而且城市生活污水不断增加逐渐成为城市水污染的主要原因,全国近一半的城镇饮用水源地水质不符合标准。城市大气污染严重,虽然大气污染总体较前几年有所改善,但形势仍很严峻。2008 年在监测的 519 个城市中,空气质量达到一级标准的城市有 21 个(占 4.0%),达到二级标准的城市有 378 个(占 72.8%),达到三级标准城市有 113 个(占 21.8%),低于三级标准城市有 7 个(占1.4%)。全国地级及以上城市,空气质量达标比例为 71.6%,县级市达标比例为 85.6%。北方城市,特大、超大型城市,产煤区的城市空气污染尤为突出。大城市交通拥堵问题也日渐严重,单位道路面积车辆逐年上升,市区平均行车速度逐年下降。

(2)扩大国内需求的挑战

"十二五"规划跟过去的规划相比,最大的不同就是强调以需求为主。"十一五"规划的重点是怎么增长得更好,怎么推进技术进步,发展新兴产业,思维的重点放在竞争力的角度、生产力的角度。"十二五"期间最重要的是创造内需。城镇化在这方面起着重要的作用。城市建设、基础设施建设、城市群的形成产生了大量的物质需求。再就是农民进城。城镇化进程的根本是农民进城。农民通过找到新的工作,找到更好的收入更高的工作,逐步成为中产阶级。城镇化是中产阶级逐渐扩大的过程,当农民真正在城市住下来,需求就会增加,除了工业可以更好地发展以外,服务业也可以发展。所以从开发需求的角度看,城镇化占有重要的地位。

（3）缓解社会矛盾的挑战

"十二五"期间的第二个大的主题延续了"十一五"的内容,更加强调缓解社会矛盾问题。"十二五"规划提出,居民收入增长和经济增长同步,其中重要的含义是缓解收入差距问题。围绕中国城镇化来扩大社会保障覆盖面,通过增加就业、调整公共政策、农民的市民化,一方面缩小收入本身的差距,另一方面缩小公共品供给上的差距。城镇化的进程应该是一方面就业增长,使农民工的收入有所增长,另一方面也使得公共品供给的差距缩小。这是解决中国社会问题的一个重要节点。

2. 中国城镇化面临的问题

（1）重点城镇群的国际竞争能力不强

从全球的范围进行比较,中国的重点城镇群中制造业比重仍较大,但又缺乏世界级的制造业企业。中心城市高端功能不足,发展质量不高。城市的制造业、社会服务业总体上还处于国际产业链条的低端,发展水平低。北京和上海第三产业比重虽然超过了50%,但国际性的金融、文化传媒等产业发展不足,在会计业、广告业等咨询服务领域的发展与世界城市差距较大,城市面向国际的基础设施建设依然不足,还不能满足高端人群居住与创业的需要。

（2）人居环境质量不高

居住条件有待进一步改善,城市低收入阶层和外来务工人员的住房条件普遍较差。城市棚户区、国有林场、农场等工矿区的改造任务艰巨,配套设施严重不足,设施老化问题普遍存在。

居民出行不便捷。一是大城市交通拥堵严重,且呈蔓延之势。特大城市主要路段全天的道路饱和度超过70%,城市中心地区高峰时段的平均车速普遍低于每小时20公里。上海城市中心区50%的车道在高峰时段道路饱和度达到95%,平均车速仅10公里/小时;2006年北京市民的平均通勤时间达43分钟。二是城镇群综合网络交通建设缓慢,枢纽布局不合理,各交通方式之间衔接不畅,交通运行效率低。三是区域轨道交通发展尚在初级阶段,城市之间、产业区与港口、机场间的联系主要依靠高速公路,高速公路建设规划与城镇群发展布局协调不够,所建线路流量差异很大,早期建设的线路因沿线城镇的发展,近乎成为城市内部快速路;大城市地铁线路不成网络,与公共交通、区域交通等缺乏有效的衔接,制约交通组织效率的提高。

社会服务设施建设难以满足需求。北京等中心城市教育、医疗资源丰富,但为周边地区提供服务的能力不足。与城市居民生活密切相关的社区级医院、文化馆、图书馆、体育设施、青少年活动中心、老年活动中心等设施匮乏,缺少日常维护和管理经费。社会设施服务水平难以满足广大人民日益增长的物质文化生活需求。城市外围和城乡结合部地区社会服务设施建设跟不上,布局不合理。

城市安全存在隐患。全国一半以上的城市存在缺水、供水系统老化等问题;全国城市生活垃圾累积堆存量已达60亿吨,并以平均每年4.8%的速度持续增长,城市周边存在大量"垃圾山";大气污染加剧,一多半城市的居民生活在三类及劣三类大气环境条件下;城市抵抗自然灾害的能力弱,因气候原因或人为事故造成城市功能瘫痪的事时有发生。

(3)小城镇承载能力偏低

城镇群中的小城镇总体上发展动力不足,特色经济不突出,人口集聚程度不高,规模偏小。据统计,县城的平均规模只有8万人,县城以外的建制镇,超过5万人的不足400个,占建制镇总数的不足3%。小城镇规划建设水平不高,基础设施建设滞后,公共服务水平低,难以形成较为完善的城镇供水、排污、供电等基础设施和商业、科技、教育等社会化服务体系,难以发挥相应的人口和产业的吸纳作用,更难以为周边农村服务。

(4)城乡统筹缺乏实质性的推进

城镇群地区城乡利益矛盾集中。城市扩张,失地农民难以很快地融入城市社会,城乡结合部是农村富裕劳动人口主要的聚居地,他们的居住、就业、子女教育、社会保障等还存在较多困难。

重城轻乡,在发展中对农村地区统筹考虑和扶持、反哺的力度依然不够。农村地区基础设施建设投入不足,公共服务网络不健全,社会保障欠缺。农村地区富余劳动力大量进城,造成留村农民人口老化、素质下降、基层组织薄弱,农村和农业缺乏发展活力。在新农村建设过程中,普遍存在研究村庄建设多,研究促进农村社会经济发展少的倾向,一些地区不顾本地实际,盲目提出大规模迁村并点的目标。

(5)发展思路有待转变

近些年来,中国的城镇群建设"遍地开花",在实际操作过程中存在一定盲目性。一些地区尽管经济社会发展水平不高,城市之间联系并不紧密,甚至在一些生态环境条件脆弱的地区,仅凭三两城市相邻或若干城市滨水,就急于"打造"城镇群。

城市建设追求奢华。一些城市在开发建设过程中有追求奢华的不良倾向。一些城市热衷于建设高标准、高耗能、大体量、造价昂贵的"标志性工程",这些项目维护费高、运营成本高、利用率低,与城市整体风貌也不甚协调。有不少城市喜欢造人工景观水面,甚至在西北缺水地区也大搞人工湖;山地城市不顾地形地貌限制搞大面积棋盘式城市布局,而与城乡居民生活密切相关的公益性服务和民生工程投入却不足,据中国人民大学的调查显示,虽然近些年各地在城市建设上加大了投入,也确实取得一些实效,但市民对城市的满意度却下降了。

工业开发区粗放扩张。一些城市在发展建设中热衷于扩张工业用地规模,工业开发区动辄占地上百平方公里。一些地方工业园区设立过多过滥,导致恶性竞争,人为压低企业发展成本,造成产能大量过剩。

（三）中国走新型城镇化道路的对策

党的十八大报告首次提出,新型城镇化是全面建设小康社会的载体和实现经济发展方式转变的重点。所谓新型城镇化,就是以科学发展观为统领,坚持以人为本和生态文明的理念与原则,工业化、信息化、城镇化、农业现代化"四化同步",全面提升城镇化质量和水平,城乡一体,区域协调发展,集约、智能、绿色、低碳的有中国特色的新型城镇化。

1.引导农村人口向城镇有序转移

乡村人口向城镇转移不完全是一个市场过程。要做到有序转移,就必须有政府政策的引导和干预,就必须有保证政策实施的工具。引导农村人口向城镇有序转移的政策可以从下列几个方面入手。

第一,分类引导人口进入城镇,对临时进城务工人员,继续实行亦工亦农、城乡双向流动的政策,在劳动报酬、劳动时间、法定假日和安全保护等方面依法保障其合法权益;对在城市已有稳定职业和住所的进城务工人员,要创造条件使之逐步转为城市居民,依法享有当地居民应有的权利,承担应尽的义务;对因城市建设承包地被征用、完全失去土地的农村人口,要转为城市居民,城市政府要负责提供就业援助、技能培训、失业保险和最低生活保障等。鼓励农村人口进入中小城市和小城镇定居,特大城市要从调整产业结构的源头入手,形成用经济办法等控制人口过快增长的机制。[①]

第二,加强职业需求预测和人口流动规律研究,建立国家和地方职业需求和人口迁移信息系统,根据工业化、经济发展、城镇化和增强国防建设的需要,提供职业需求指导性信息,并进行监控。

---

① 《中华人民共和国国民经济和社会发展第十一个五年规划纲要》,人民出版社 2006 年版。

第三,进一步改革户籍管理政策,逐步实行城乡统一的户籍管理制度。

第四,把人口迁移和产业结构调整结合起来,优化人口结构,调整人口分布的格局,实现人口、就业、资源、生态环境等多要素之间的协调和平衡。

2. 形成合理的城镇化空间格局

首先,让大城市充分发展,进一步增强大城市的综合辐射带动能力。大城市超前发展是城镇化的规律。在城镇化的初期和中期,大城市的规模扩张和充分发展对提高城镇化水平具有十分显著的贡献,是完成城镇化进程、形成相对完善的城镇体系的重要前提。没有经历大城市充分发展的过程,要率先实现中小城市和小城镇的大发展是超越发展阶段的设想,也难以取得预期的发展效果。

其次,要把城市群作为推进城镇化的主体形态,引导都市连绵区(Metropolitan region 或 Megalopolis)和城镇群的形成和发展,逐步形成以沿海及京广京哈线为纵轴,长江及陇海线为横轴,若干城市群为主体,其他城市和小城镇点状分布,永久耕地和生态功能区相间隔,高效协调可持续的城镇化空间格局。20 多年前出现的都市连绵区是城市发展的高级形态,是现代市场经济中引领经济增长的"发动机",处于财富聚集和创新的中心地位。都市连绵区是以一个或几个大城市为中心,周围聚集一批中小城市和小城镇,密集分布,地域可达几万平方公里的地区。1976 年,法国地理学家戈德曼(J.Gottmann)指出,全球已经形成 6 个世界级的都市连绵区,中国长江三角洲名列其中。这种态势至今仍在继续发展。现在,美国和日本的三大都市连绵区的 GDP 已分别占全国的 65% 和 69%。中国到 2020 年将有可能出现 12 个都市连绵区。目前,中国已形成城市群发展格局的有京津冀、长江三角洲和珠江三角洲等 3 大都市连绵区,其 GDP 只占全国的 38%。对于这三大城市群,要继续发挥其带动和辐射作用,加强城市群内各城市的分工协作和优势互补,增强城市群的整体竞争力。对于那些具备城市群发展条件的区域,要加强统筹规划,以特大城市和大城市为龙头,发挥中心城市作用,形成若干用地少、就业多、要素集聚能力强、人口分布合理的新城市群。

最后,引导中小城市和小城镇,根据自身的特点,发展特色产业,走集约化发展的道路,形成比较优势。人口分散、资源条件较差、不具备城市群发展条件的区域,要重点发展现有城市、县城及有条件的建制镇,成为本地区集聚经济、人口和提供公共服务的中心。虽然大城市引人注目,但是直到现在,世界上大多数城镇人口还是生活在中小城市和小城镇。因此,必须采取切实措施,扩大小城镇的规模,发挥聚集效应。

3. 高效利用和节约资源,保护生态环境

第一,加强建筑和交通等能源消耗重点领域的节能技术研究和政策引导。制定促进节能、节地、节水、节材、环保等标准体系和监督执行的措施;把节能省地型建筑纳入城乡建设用地指标框架体系;研究建立住宅小区和单体建筑的设计指标体系和农村住宅建设规划控制指标,并严格落实;对于既有建筑进行保温隔热系统改造,加快太阳能等可再生能源在建筑中的利用;建立和健全建筑全寿命成本核算和节能、节水、废弃物资源化的有效激励机制;加强对城市供水网络和家庭用水器具水的漏损情况调查研究,制定降低损漏率的措施;加大节能车辆研究和推广应用清洁能源、可再生能源;在单中心城市实施公交优先,鼓励合用汽车,建设快捷、方便、舒适的公共交通系统,包括专用公交车道;在特大和超大城市实行交通拥堵收费等;制定配套政策,在工业部门实行节能合作协议,从法律、电价和资金等方面支持在电力系统开展需求侧管理;建立可再生能源发电的市场保障机制,通过稳定、持续的市场保障措施推动对可再生能源投资和促进可再生能源开发利用的技术进步。

第二,倡导生态城市建设。将城镇作为一个“社会—经济—环境复合生态系统”进行规划、建设和管理。把生态成本纳入各级政府的经济分析与政策决策,把保护城镇生态系统、提高城镇环境质量和居民

生活质量列为城镇建设和地方政府业绩考核的主要指标。

第三,改变生产方式和消费模式。城市每天需要和排除的物质数量很大。以 2000 年珠海市为例,平均每天需要 5820 吨煤炭,1595 吨燃油,60 万吨水和 1127 吨食物;排放出 602 吨工业固体废物,30 万吨污水,1000 吨垃圾。单靠采用先进技术和建设基础设施,而不改变城市的生产方式和消费模式,资源浪费和环境污染问题依然不能解决。因此,需要制定产品回收利用政策,鼓励消费能源资源节约型产品,鼓励搭乘公共交通,宣传和鼓励节约能源,改变娱乐方式和生活习惯,把环境和卫生保护纳入经济发展规划和政策,运用市场机制和经济手段,建设卫生的、生态的城市。

第四,制定适应市场经济的规划和土地利用政策。例如:对工业用地,设定最高和最低容积率;在住宅用地中,对低容积率的土地开发和拥有多套住房者征收附加费用,以减小土地浪费和防止过量使用;根据一定时期城市经济和社会发展目标,通过调查研究和发展预测,提出与地面规划相协调的城市地下空间开发利用的方向和导则,确定城市地下空间开发的目标、功能、规模、布局,对各类地下设施进行综合部署和全面安排,在特大和超大城市率先制定地下空间利用规划。

第五,借鉴国外经验试行通过内部合同节约和回收节能投资。这项政策旨在解决启动资金和资金的有效回收机制问题,适于在大型单位内部实施。在大型单位里,上级单位审查节能项目的经济分析建议,认为合适时,就可以立项,并同下属实施单位签订内部合同。此后,节能项目资金进入节能项目。项目实施完成后,实施单位能源支出减少,并将节约的费用作为回转资金返回。此项政策可以用于供热控制、通风、采光、墙体和屋顶保温隔热、足球场保护、路灯、温度自动调节、节水以及热电联产等。它的特点是易于实施,不但解决了能源支出和投资来自不同渠道问题,而且用户支付的费用比过去减少。

4. 加强城市规划建设管理

第一,规划城市规模与布局,要符合当地水土资源、环境容量、地质构造等自然承载力,并与当地经济发展、就业空间、基础设施和公共服务供给能力相适应。

第二,提高城市规划和建设水平。加强城市水源地保护和供水设施建设。缺水城市要适度控制城市规模,禁止发展高耗水产业和建设高耗水景观。地下水超采城市要控制地下水开采,防止地面沉降。城市道路以及供排水、能源、环保、电信、有线电视等的建设,要破除部门和地方分割,在统一规划基础上协同建设,减少盲目填挖和拆建。加强城市综合防灾减灾和应急管理能力建设。稳步推进城市危旧住房和"城中村"改造,保障拆迁户合法权益。城市规划和建筑设计要延续历史,传承文化,突出特色,保护民族、文化遗产和风景名胜资源。强化城市规划实施的监管,推进城市综合管理,提高城市管理水平。

第三,改变规划的部门分割状态,急需调整和明确区域规划、土地利用规划、城市规划等主要空间规划之间的关系,在市域范围内,将城市规划与土地利用规划编制合二为一,并同经济社会发展规划整合,理顺相关部门的职能结构关系,加强法制建设,形成统一协调、调控有力的国家规划体系。

第四,依据《城乡规划法》,发挥城乡规划体制机制作用,推动主体功能区规划,开展跨区域的空间发展战略规划。

第五,根据农民进城后,村庄人员减少和搬迁、宅基地弃置等情况,重新整合乡村编制,合理布局居民点,促进进城农民所留宅基地依法流转,合理利用,节约土地。

5.贯彻落实工业反哺农业,城市支持农村的方针

城乡能否协调发展是实现可持续城镇化的关键之一。现在,中国政府明确提出了实施"工业反哺农业、城市支持农村,实现工业与农业、城市与农村协调发展"的全新的经济与社会发展思路。政府将下决心调整国民收入分配结构,在稳定现有各项农业投入的基础上,把新增财政支出和固定资产投资切实向农业、农村、农民倾斜,逐步建立稳定的农业投入增长机制。这意味着中国政府从此将结束把农业作为政

府收入来源、由农业向工业提供资本积累的工业化初期的发展道路,而将农业和农村领域作为政府支持的对象。

第一,坚持和强化对农村基础设施的投入,将农村中小型基础设施建设纳入各级政府基本建设投资的范围,加大对农田水利、乡村道路等小型农村基础设施建设的支持力度。

第二,完善以政府投入为主的农村义务教育经费保障机制;进一步增加对农村公共卫生体系的投入;完善对农村困难群体的救助体系,逐步提高农村社会保障覆盖面;大幅度增加对农业科研的投入,加强农业科技创新能力建设和技术推广体系建设;以提高农村的科技、教育、文化和医疗卫生水平,扩大农民的就业空间。

第三,研究制定城镇化进程中建设用地与农民土地之间的新的土地利用格局和配套政策,制定提高新增建设用地有偿使用费标准。在抓好土地出让金全程征收、管理与监督使用的同时,调整土地收益分配结构,允许被征地农民以土地承包经营权入股、租赁等形式参与项目合作,分享土地增值收益;在15%土地出让金返还用于农村基础设施和社会事业投资的基础上,逐步提高土地出让金的返还比例,用于投资农村基础设施和社会事业。

第四,改进城镇劳动就业政策,为农民进城就业创造更多的机会,对进城的农民工实施再就业培训,费用由政府和企业分担,逐步建立城乡统一的劳动力市场。积极探索多种形式,解决好进城务工人员子女就学、公共卫生、文化生活、社会保障等方面的实际问题。创造一个农民进得来、留得住的制度环境,逐步改变城乡二元结构。

思考题

1. 中国城镇化与世界城镇化是什么关系?

2. 从中国的城镇化历程与您所在国家的城镇化历程有什么不同?原因是什么?

3. 您怎么看待中国政府的城镇化政策对中国城镇化发展的作用?

参考文献

楚天骄、谭文柱:《快速城市化进程中的城市规划和城市管理》,北京:人民出版社,2012年。

周干峙:《探索中国特色的城市化之路》,《国际城市规划》2009年第S1期。

李京文:《中国城市化的重要发展趋势:城市群(圈)的出现及对投资的需求》,《创新》2008年第3期。

高新才、周毅、徐静:《中国城市化历史进程审视》,《学术交流》2010年第1期。

（一）新中国成立以来中国城乡
规划的回顾与总结

1949 年以后的中国现代城市规划的发展，同中国社会发展一样，也是坎坷曲折的。概括起来，大致以 1978 年为界，可分为前后两期。本节分改革开放前后两个时期、四个阶段对中国城市规划的发展进行回顾与总结。

1. 改革开放之前中国城乡规划发展历程及其特点

（1）城市规划的起步阶段（1949—1952 年）

1949 年以前的中国城市充分反映了半封建半殖民地社会中城市的特点。一方面，内地大多数城市工业基础十分薄弱，居住条件恶劣，城镇中根本没有现代工业，也没有现代的市政工程和公共设施。另一方面,沿海殖民地大城市商业高度繁华,局部地段已经有相当先进的市政设施,但城市社会集团的分割对立严重,贫民窟和洋楼区形成强烈的反差。比如在上海,20世纪30年代时,这座城市是世界第五大城市,也是世界上最繁荣的国际大都会之一,有"东方的巴黎"之称,车水马龙的外滩矗立着当时最时髦的西方建筑(图2-1),而与租界内的繁华和现代形成鲜明对比的是贫民百姓的居住场所。沿着当时上海的一条河道肇嘉浜形成了一个大的水上棚户区(图2-2),破烂不堪的棚户、"滚地龙"、"吊楼"(水上竹棚)、破船、桥洞窝棚里住着成千上万的贫民。

图2-1 20世纪30年代的上海外滩

在经济恢复时期,由于长期的战争创伤,城市工作的重点是恢复和发展生产,尽快恢复被破坏的工厂企业,同时重点扩建和新建了一些工业企业,如位于辽宁省的鞍山钢铁联合企业等。在城市建设方面,由于受经济能力的限制,仅在一些大城市内集中力量重点改建了一些劳动人民聚居的棚户区,改善了城市劳动阶层的居住和生活条件。比较著名的是北京龙须沟的治理。与上海的肇嘉浜棚户区一样,龙须沟是北

图 2-2　20 世纪 30 年代上海市肇嘉浜棚户区

京最穷的地区,穿过该地区的叫作龙须沟的水沟污染严重,常年散发着令人作呕的气味。新中国成立后,仅用了三个月的时间就完成了这个地区的改造工程。

随着城市建设的恢复与发展,城市规划工作也开始起步。从 1950 年开始,城市规划研究机构和建筑管理机构开始在大城市建立起来①。1952 年 9 月,中央政府召开了全国城市建设座谈会,正式提出要重视城市规划工作,并开始建立城市建设机构,加强对城市建设的领导。

经过三年的调整、恢复与发展,中国的城市规划与建设开始步入了一个以发展工业城市为目标进行规划建设的新阶段。

(2)"苏联模式"城市规划的引入与发展阶段(1953—1957 年)

这一时期也是中国的第一个国民经济五年计划时期。当时,为了配合苏联援助的 156 个重点工程为中心的大规模工业建设,并且处理好与原有城市的关系,国家急需建立城市规划体系。为此,引入了"苏联模式"的规划方式。

①　华揽洪:《重建中国:城市规划三十年》,李颖译,三联书店 2006 年版,第 28 页。

"苏联模式"的规划方式,就是把城市规划作为国民经济计划的具体化和延续。实际上,苏联当时的城市规划原理,就是把社会主义城市特征归结为生产性,认为城市的职能是工业生产,社会主义的城市及其规划的最主要优越性是生产的计划性和土地国有化。

新中国成立初期,中国城市规划编制方法,沿用的是一整套苏联的编制程序和方法。1956年中国第一个城市规划技术性法规——《城市规划编制暂行办法》(下称《暂行办法》)的编制与修订,也是当时的国家建设委员会顾问、苏联专家组组长、城市规划专家克拉夫秋克参与完成的。这个《暂行办法》影响着相当长时期的中国城市规划与建设,有的内容一直影响至今。

由于全面学习苏联,包括与计划体制相适应的一整套城市规划理论与方法,使中国当时的城市规划与建设,具有严格的计划经济体制特征,也带有一些"古典形式主义"的色彩。在城市规划中强调平面构图、立体轮廓,讲究轴线、对称、放射路、对景、双周边街坊街景等古典形式主义手法(图2-3);城市建设也一度出现了"规模过大、占地过多、求新求急、标准过高"等问题,忽视工程的经济效益。

(3)城市规划的动荡与中断阶段(1958—1977年)

这一时期长达20年。由于政治经济起伏波动较大,也带来了城市规划与建设的动荡甚至中断。尤其是1966年"文化大革命"开始后,城市规划工作受到严重的干扰和破坏,工作被迫停顿、机构被撤销、专业队伍被解散、高校城市规划专业停办、图纸资料被销毁,使本来就不强的城市规划专业队伍力量受到严重削弱。城市建设停滞不前,城市规划基本停滞,城市建设和管理呈现无政府状态,名胜古迹和园林绿地被侵占、破坏,违章建筑比比皆是,城市布局混乱,造成了许多无法挽回的损失,带来了大量的遗留问题。

2. 1978年以后中国城乡规划的发展历程及其特点

1976年年底"文化大革命"结束,中国进入了一个新的历史发展时期,特别是十一届三中全会的召开,使中国经济社会发生了深刻的变化,

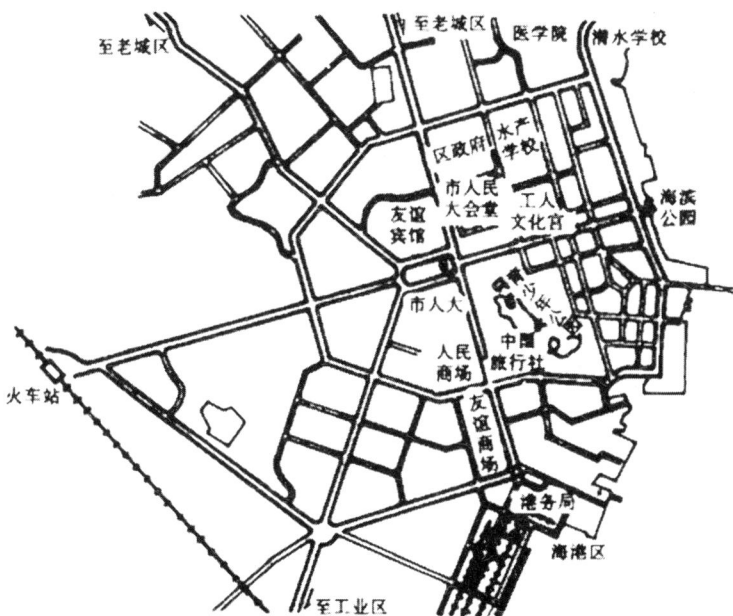

图2-3　湛江霞山新市区的环状布局结构图

资料来源:董鉴泓:《中国城市建设史》,中国建筑工业出版社2004年版,第390页。

城市规划与建设也步入了崭新的阶段。这个阶段又可以细分为四个时期。

（1）城市规划的恢复（1978—1980年）

1978年召开的第三次城市工作会议总结了过去30年城市规划工作的经验和教训,提出了恢复和加强城市规划工作问题。1980年10月,国家建委召开了全国城市规划工作会议,讨论了城市规划工作如何适应四个现代化的经济和社会发展目标,总结了城市规划在国家建设工作中的地位和作用,明确提出"市长的职责是把城市规划建设管理好",讨论通过了《城市规划法草案》,提出了"控制大城市规模、合理发展中等城市、积极发展小城市"的城市建设方针,要求全国各城市在1982年年底以前完成城市总体规划和详细规划的编制。这次会议端正了城市规划思想,在现代中国的城市规划事业发展历程中占有重要的地位。

（2）城市规划步入法制化（20世纪80年代）

20世纪80年代,中国各地普遍编制了城市总体规划,这些规划有利于加快城市建设步伐。截至 1986 年,全国已有 96% 的设市城市和 85% 的县镇编制完成了城市总体规划,其中,80% 的城市规划得到审批。第二轮城市规划的编制与审批,进一步表明中国城市进入了按照规划进行建设和发展的历史阶段①。

1989 年 12 月 26 日,七届全国人大常委会通过了《中华人民共和国城市规划法》,用法律形式肯定了城市规划在国家建设中的地位和作用,理顺了规划编制和管理过程中各方面的关系,明确了规划的内容和方法,强调了管理的程序和权限,使城市规划具有法律赋予的权威性和严肃性,为城市规划的编制和实施提供了法律保障。这是中国城市规划建设管理进程中一座重要的里程碑,标志着中国的城市规划与建设工作进入了以法治城的轨道。

专栏 2-1 第一部城市规划法

1989 年 12 月 26 日,全国人大通过了具有国家法律地位的《城市规划法》,成为中国第一部现代城市规划法。《城市规划法》共分 6 章 46 条,其内容组成为:(1)总则:规划法的使用范围、有关定义、机构等规定;(2)城市规划的制定:城市规划编制的组织、原则,编制城市规划的阶段、要求、审批和修改等;(3)城市新区建设和旧区改建:新区、旧区规划原则、部分重点设施的布点原则;(4)城市规划的实施:城市规划的公布、"一书两证"(相关内容请参阅本章第四节)、有关的开发控制;(5)法律责任;(6)附则。

——摘自董鉴泓:《中国城市建设史(第三版)》,中国建筑工业出版社 2004 年版,第 400—401 页。

(3)城市规划的变革(20 世纪 90 年代—2007 年)

进入 20 世纪 90 年代,特别是邓小平发表南巡讲话和党的十四大决定建设社会主义市场经济体制之后,城市建设进入一个更快的发展

---

① 董鉴泓:《中国城市建设史(第三版)》,中国建筑工业出版社 2004 年版,第 400 页。

阶段。同时,也出现了一些求大求洋现象,大工程、大项目、大广场、欧陆风比比皆是,很多城市都不切实际地提出了建设"国际性城市"的宏大目标,名目繁多的"别墅区"、"开发区"遍地开花,造成滥占土地、生态破坏、资金浪费,如同"规划法不在"。为了制止城市规划中的乱象,1996 年 5 月国务院颁发了《关于加强城市规划工作的通知》,指定非农业人口 50 万人以上的 80 个大城市的总体规划报国务院审批。建设部对新一轮城市总体规划进行了重要部署,要求严格控制城市规模,研究和确立现代化城市的发展目标,重视产业结构的优化,调整城市布局,加强宏观调控等。

至 20 世纪 90 年代末,全国第三轮设市城市总体规划编制工作基本结束。第三轮城市规划修订普遍运用了市场经济理论和规律,在实践中开始探索适应市场经济发展要求的城市规划编制方法。注重控制性详细规划对土地开发的引导和规划控制。深圳等地方建立了"法定图则"制度①,使城市规划技术文件通过法定程序批准成为地方性法规。城市规划开始从技术文件向公共政策转变。计算机、网络、遥感等新技术在城市规划编制和管理中得到普遍应用。这一时期,城市规划在社会主义市场经济条件下的地位和作用更加突出,也更加注重依法行政。

(4)城乡一体规划(2008 年以后)

改革开放以来,与飞速发展的城镇化进程相比,中国的城乡规划法律制度建设明显滞后。2008 年之前,中国的城乡规划法律制度可以用"一法一条例"来概括。"一法"是指《城市规划法》,"一条例"是指1993 年 6 月国务院发布的《村庄和集镇规划建设管理条例》。这种就城市论城市、就乡村论乡村的规划制定与实施模式,使城市规划和乡村

---

① 法定图则是由城市规划主管部门每年根据城市总体规划、分区规划的要求编制,对分区内各片区的土地利用性质、开发强度、配套设施、道路交通和城市设计等方面作出的详细规定。深圳在分区规划与详细规划编制之间增加了法定图则编制阶段。主要是对各片区土地利用性质、开发强度、配套设施等作进一步明确规划。法定图则经市规划委员会审批后具有法律效力,任何单位和个人不得擅自更改。深圳对法定图则进行公众意见征询,予以采纳的,则城市规划部门修改法定图则草案,增加了城市规划的透明性。法定图则强化了城市规划的法制精神,增强了公众对城市规划的了解和参与。

规划之间缺乏统筹协调,衔接不够,已经不适应中国经济社会迅速发展的新形势。随着城市的发展,不少村镇转变为建制镇,这些建制镇的规划管理前后却要适用两部法律法规,难以协调。即便是在中国经济比较发达的东部沿海地区,城乡规划的覆盖面也不宽,甚至存在不少规划空白区。城镇化的发展对完善原有的城乡规划法律制度提出了新的要求。

在总结《城市规划法》和《村庄和集镇规划建设管理条例》实施经验的基础上,结合改革开放以后中国城乡规划管理工作的经验,在科学发展观的指导下,2007年10月28日第十届全国人民代表大会常务委员会第三十次会议通过了《城乡规划法》,并于2008年1月1日起正式实施。《城乡规划法》对规划的制定、实施、修改、监督检查和法律责任作出了比较详细的规定,特别是对乡规划和村庄规划的制定和实施作了明确的规定。

专栏 2-2　《城乡规划法》比《城市规划法》的进步之处

中国住房和城乡建设部副部长仇保兴认为,与《城市规划法》相比,《城乡规划法》的进步主要体现在以下七个方面①:

第一,由《城市规划》到《城乡规划》一字之差,调整的对象即从城市走向城乡,从而将原来的城乡二元法律体系转变为城乡统筹的法律体系。

第二,从坚持的原则来看,《城市规划法》是"指导建设",而《城乡规划法》则是强调资源保护。《城乡规划法》从规划的编制到组织实施,始终贯穿着对耕地、自然资源、文化遗产资源、风景名胜资源的保护,而且对规划区内的各类资源进行多种形式的保护。

第三,从方法上看,《城市规划法》重规划的编制和审批,《城乡规划法》侧重规划的实施和监督。为了强化监督检查,《城乡规划法》专设了监督检查一章,完善了对规划的人大监督、公众监督、上级监督以及各项监督检查措施的落实。

---

① 这一部分内容主要参考了刘华:《仇保兴解读〈城乡规划法〉》,《中华建设》2008年第2期。

第四,以前违反规划后没有对责任主体的处罚,《城乡规划法》则有严格的责任追究,并把对城乡规划主管部门自身工作的约束摆到重要的位置。比如,对实施违法行为或者批准实施违法行为的直接负责的主管人员和其他直接责任人员,规定了相应的行政责任,对滥用职权、玩忽职守、徇私舞弊,构成犯罪的,还要依法追究刑事责任。

第五,《城市规划法》强调规划部门的作用,《城乡规划法》则强调公众参与社会监督。比如,根据《城乡规划法》,今后城乡规划在审批前应向社会公告,且时间不得少于30天。组织编制机关应当充分考虑专家和公众的意见,并在报送审批的材料中附具意见采纳情况及理由。村庄规划在报送审批前,还要经村民会议讨论同意。除法律、行政法规规定不得公开的内容之外,城乡规划经批准后应及时向社会公布。

第六,《城乡规划法》完善了对违章建筑的处理机制,依法设定了责令停止建设、限期改正、处以罚款、限期拆除、没收违法实物或者违法收入等各类行政处罚和行政强制措施。同时还规定当事人不停止建设或者逾期不拆除的,当地人民政府可以责成有关部门查封施工现场、强制拆除。

第七,在城市化快速发展阶段,规划必须有足够的弹性才能动态地适应城市的快速变化。为此,《城乡规划法》重视规划的修改,专门设立一章,明确城乡规划修改的条件和修改审批的程序。

(二)中国的城乡规划由谁制定和实施

城乡规划的行政体系涉及各级规划行政管理机构的设置及其在规划制定和规划实施两个阶段的权利和义务。

根据中国的《城乡规划法》,住房和城乡建设部作为国务院的城乡规划行政主管部门主管全国的城乡规划工作,县级以上地方政府的城乡规划行政主管部门主管相应行政区域内的城乡规划工作。各级城乡规划行政主管部门的职能主要体现在规划制定(包括编制和审批两个环节)和规划实施两个阶段。

1. 规划制定阶段的行政体制

(1)规划编制

①全国城镇体系规划由国务院主管部门会同国务院有关部门组织编制。

②省域城镇体系规划由省、自治区人民政府组织编制。

③城市总体规划由城市人民政府组织编制。

④县人民政府所在地镇的总体规划,由县人民政府组织编制;其他镇的总体规划由镇人民政府组织编制。

⑤城市的控制性详细规划由城市人民政府主管部门根据城市总体规划的要求组织编制。

⑥镇的控制性详细规划由镇人民政府根据镇总体规划的要求组织编制;县人民政府所在地镇的控制性详细规划,由县人民政府城乡规划主管部门根据镇总体规划的要求组织编制。

⑦重要地块的修建性详细规划,由城市、县人民政府城乡规划主管部门和镇人民政府组织编制。

⑧乡规划、村庄规划由乡、镇人民政府组织编制。

(2)规划审批

①全国城镇体系规划由国务院城乡主管部门报国务院审批。

②省域城镇体系规划由省、自治区人民政府报国务院审批。

③直辖市的城市总体规划由直辖市人民政府报国务院审批。省、自治区人民政府所在地的城市以及国务院确定的城市的总体规划,由省、自治区人民政府审查同意后,报国务院审批。其他城市的总体规划,由城市人民政府报省、自治区人民政府审批。

④县人民政府所在地镇的总体规划,由县人民政府报上一级人

民政府审批。其他镇的总体规划由镇人民政府报上一级人民政府审批。

⑤城市的控制性详细规划由城市人民政府主管部门组织编制完成后,经本级人民政府批准后,报本级人民代表大会常务委员会和上一级人民政府备案。

⑥镇的控制性详细规划由镇人民政府组织编制完成后,报上一级人民政府审批。县人民政府所在地镇的控制性详细规划,由县人民政府城乡规划主管部门组织编制完成后,经县人民政府批准后,报本级人民政府常务委员会和上一级人民政府备案。

⑦乡规划、村庄规划由乡、镇人民政府报上一级人民政府审批。村庄规划在报送审批前,应当经村民会议或者村民代表会议讨论同意。

⑧省、自治区人民政府组织编制的省域城镇体系规划,城市、县人民政府组织编制的总体规划,在报上一级人民政府审批前,应当先经本级人民代表大会常务委员会审议,常务委员会组成人员的审议意见交由本级人民政府研究处理。

镇人民政府组织编制的镇总体规划,在报上一级人民政府审批前,应当先经镇人民代表大会审议,代表的审议意见交由本级人民政府研究处理。

规划的组织编制机关报送审批省域城镇体系规划、城市总体规划或者镇总体规划,应当将本级人民政府代表大会常务委员会组成的人员或者镇人民代表大会代表的审议意见和根据审议意见修改规划的情况一并报送。

⑨城乡规划报送审批前,组织编制机关应当依法将城乡规划草案予以公告,并采取论证会、听证会或者其他方式征求专家和公众的意见。公告的时间不得少于 30 日。

2. 规划实施阶段的行政体制

在规划实施阶段,城市规划行政主管部门的职责涉及四个方面,分别是土地使用和建设工程的审批、竣工验收和监督检查、违法建设的处罚、行政复议。

《城乡规划法》授权各地的城乡规划行政主管部门对于城乡规划区内的土地使用和建设工程进行审批,各地城乡规划的行政主管部门可以参加城乡规划区内重要建设工程的竣工验收,并且有权对城乡规划区内的建设工程是否符合规划要求进行监督检查。

对于违法建设,各地规划行政主管部门依法进行处罚。如果当事方对于行政处罚不服,可以在规定期限内向上一级规划行政主管部门申请行政复议或直接向人民法院提出起诉。

因此,规划实施主要是当地的城乡规划行政主管部门的事务,上级规划行政主管部门只是受理行政复议。

专栏 2-3　城乡规划实施的监督检查

城乡规划监督检查贯穿于城乡规划制定和实施的全过程,是城乡规划管理工作的重要组成部分,也是保障城乡规划工作科学性与严肃性的重要手段。为了加强城乡规划实施监督,提高城乡规划的严肃性,《城乡规划法》专门设立了"监督检查"一章,强化对城乡规划工作的人大监督、公众监督、行政监督以及各项监督检查措施,从而从法律上明确城乡规划的监督管理制度,进一步强化城乡规划对城乡建设的引导和调控作用,促进城乡建设健康有序发展。

1. 城乡规划工作的行政监督

《城乡规划法》对城乡规划工作行政监督的规定包括两个层面的内容:

一是县级以上人民政府及其城乡规划主管部门对下级政府及其城乡规划主管部门执行城乡规划编制、审批、实施、修改情况的监督检查。也就是通常所说的政府层级监督检查。例如,建设部和四川、贵州等省(市)建立推广的城乡规划督察员制度,即由上级人民政府或其城乡规划主管部门向下级人民政府或其规划主管部门派驻规划督察员,对城乡规划的编制、审批、实施管理工作进行全面督查。

二是县级以上地方人民政府城乡规划主管部门对城乡规划实施情况进行的监督检查,即通常所说的对管理相对人的监督检查。

2. 人民代表大会对城乡规划工作的监督

《城乡规划法》第五十二条规定,地方各级人民代表大会应当向本级人民代表大会常务委员会或者乡、镇人民代表大会报告城乡规划的实施情况,并接受监督。

3. 公众对城乡规划工作的监督

《城乡规划法》规定,对城乡规划的监督检查情况和处理结果应当依法公开,供公众查阅和监督。

资料来源:全国人大常委会法制工作委员会经济法室、国务院法制办农业资源环保法制司、住房和城乡建设部城乡规划司、政策法规司编:《中华人民共和国城乡规划法解说》,知识产权出版社 2008年版。

(三) 中国的城乡规划如何编制、修改和实施

城乡规划的运作体系包括规划编制、修改和规划实施(在许多国家又分别称为发展规划和开发控制)两个阶段。

1. 城乡规划编制体制

各国的城乡规划编制体制虽然有所不同,但都可以分为两个基本层面,分别是城乡发展规划和开发控制规划。城乡发展规划是制定城乡发展的中长期目标,以及在土地利用、交通管理、设施配置和环境保护等方面的相应策略,为城市的各个地区的开发控制规划提供指导框架。开发控制规划作为规划实施的法定依据,规划编制的内容和程序都必须遵循相应的规划法规,因而在许多国家又称为法定规划。

中国对应于城乡发展规划的是城市总体规划（包括大、中城市的分区规划）和镇总体规划、乡规划和村庄规划，对应于开发控制规划的是控制性详细规划。各个层面的区域城镇体系规划为城市总体规划提供依据，而修建性详细规划只是作为特定情况下（如建设计划已经落实的重要地区）的开发控制依据。

2. 城乡规划的修改

为了体现城乡规划的科学性和严肃性，全过程把关，促进城乡建设的可持续发展，《城乡规划法》专门设立"城乡规划的修改"一章，以从法律上明确严格的规划修改制度，防止随意修改法定规划的问题。

（1）省域城镇体系规划、城市总体规划、镇总体规划的修改

《城乡规划法》第四十七条提出，有下列情形之一的，组织编制机关方可按照规定的权限和程序修改省域城镇体系规划、城市总体规划、镇总体规划：

①上级人民政府制定的城乡规划发生变更，提出修改规划要求的。

②行政区划调整确需修改规划的。

③因国务院批准重大建设工程确需修改规划的。

④经评估确需修改规划的。《城乡规划法》第四十六条提出，省域城镇体系规划、城市总体规划、镇总体规划的组织编制机关，应当组织有关部门和专家定期对规划实施情况进行评估，并采取论证会、听证会或者其他方式征求公众意见。组织编制机关应当向本级人民代表大会常务委员会、镇人民代表大会和原审批机关提出评估报告并附具征求意见的情况。

⑤城乡规划的审批机关认为应当修改规划的其他情形。

修改省域城镇体系规划、城市总体规划、镇总体规划前，组织编制机关应当对原规划的实施情况进行总结，并向原审批机关报告；修改涉及城市总体规划、镇总体规划强制性内容的，应当先向原审批计划提出专题报告，经同意后，方可编制修改方案。修改后的省域城镇体系规划、城市总体规划、镇总体规划应当按照规定的审批程序报批。

（2）近期建设规划的修改

控制性详细规划是城市、镇实施规划管理最直接的法律依据，更是国有土地使用权出让、开发和建设的法定前置条件（关于中国的建设用地管理请参见本书第五章），直接决定着土地的市场价值，决定着利益相关人员的切身利益。任何单位和个人，不得擅自修改控制性详细规划的内容。

修改控制性详细规划必须严格按法定程序进行。根据《城乡规划法》第四十八条的规定，修改控制性详细规划的，组织编制机关应当对修改的必要性进行论证，征求规划地段内利害关系人的意见，并向原审批机关提出专题报告，经原审批机关同意后，方可编制修改方案。控制性详细规划修改涉及城市总体规划、镇总体规划的强制性内容的，应当先修改总体规划。

3. 城乡规划实施体制

《城乡规划法》规定，中国城镇规划实施管理实行"一书两证"（选址意见书、建设用地规划许可证和建设工程规划许可证）的规划管理制度，中国乡村规划管理实行乡村建设规划许可证制度。法律规定的选址意见书、建设用地规划许可证、建设工程规划许可证、乡村建设规划许可证构成了中国城乡规划实施管理的主要法定手段和形式，其中核发选址意见书属于行政审批，建设用地规划许可、建设工程规划许可或乡村建设规划许可属于行政许可。

（1）建设项目选址规划管理

建设项目选址规划管理，是城乡规划行政主管部门根据城乡规划及其有关法律、法规对建设项目地址进行确认或选择，保证各项建设按照城乡规划安排，并核发建设项目选址意见书的行政管理工作。

《城乡规划法》明确提出了建设项目选址意见书的使用范围。《中华人民共和国城乡规划法》第三十六条规定："按照国家规定需要有关部门批准或者核准的建设项目，以划拨方式提供国有土地使用权的，建设单位在报送有关部门批准或者核准前，应当向城乡规划主管部门申请核发选址意见书。"

（2）建设用地规划管理

建设用地规划管理是城乡规划行政主管部门根据城乡规划法律规范及依法制定的城乡规划,确定建设用地定点、位置和范围,审核建设工程总平面,提供土地使用规划设计条件,并核发建设用地规划许可证的行政管理工作。

目前,中国建设单位的土地使用权获得方式主要有两种:土地使用权无偿划拨和有偿出让(参见专栏2-4)。以不同方式获得的建设用地,在规划管理上也有差异。

专栏2-4　中国建设用地土地使用权获得方式①

目前,中国建设单位的土地使用权获得方式主要有两种:土地使用权无偿划拨和有偿出让。

土地使用权划拨是指县级以上人民政府依法批准,在土地使用者缴纳补偿、安置等费用后将该幅土地交付其使用。划拨用地共包括四大类:国家机关用地和军事用地、城市基础设施用地和公益事业用地、国家重点扶持的能源、交通、水利等基础设施用地以及法律、行政法规规定的其他用地。

土地使用权出让,是指国家将国有土地使用权在一定年限内出让给土地使用者,由土地使用者向国家支付土地使用权出让金的行为。土地使用权出让可以采取招标、拍卖、挂牌出让或者双方协议的方式。根据现行法规政策规定,凡商业、旅游、娱乐和商品住宅等各类经营性用地,必须以招标、拍卖或者挂牌方式出让。

①在划拨用地的情况下,建设用地规划许可证的办理程序

在城市、镇规划区内以划拨方式提供国有土地使用权的建设项目,经有关部门批准、核准、备案后,建设单位应当向城市、县人民政府城乡

---

① 关于中国土地制度请参阅本书第五章。

规划主管部门提出建设用地规划许可申请,由城市、县人民政府城乡规划主管部门依据控制性详细规划核定建设用地的位置、面积、允许建设的范围,核发建设用地规划许可证。建设单位在取得建设用地规划许可证后,方可向县级以上地方人民政府土地主管部门申请用地,经县级以上人民政府审批后,由土地主管部门划拨土地。

②在土地有偿使用的情况下,建设用地规划许可证的办理程序

在城市、镇规划区内以出让方式提供国有土地使用权的,在国有土地使用权出让前,城市、县人民政府城乡规划主管部门应当依据控制性详细规划,提出出让地块的位置、使用性质、开发强度等规划条件,作为国有土地使用权出让合同的组成部分。

以出让方式取得国有土地使用权的建设项目,在签订国有土地使用权出让合同后,建设单位应当持建设项目的批准、核准、备案文件和国有土地使用权出让合同,向城市、县人民政府城乡规划主管部门领取建设用地规划许可证。

(3)建设工程规划管理

建设工程规划管理,是城乡规划行政主管部门根据依法制定的城乡规划及城乡规划有关法律规范和技术规范,对各类建设工程进行组织、控制、引导和协调,使其纳入城乡规划的轨道,并核发建设工程规划许可证的行政管理工作。

在城市、镇规划区内进行建筑物、构筑物、道路、管线和其他工程建设的,建设单位或者个人应当向城市、县人民政府城乡规划主管部门或者省、自治区、直辖市人民政府确定的镇人民政府申请办理建设工程规划许可证。

(4)乡村建设规划管理

在乡、村庄规划区内进行乡镇企业、乡村公共设施和公益事业建设的,建设单位或者个人应当向乡、镇人民政府提出申请,由乡、镇人民政府报城市、县人民政府城乡规划主管部门核发乡村建设规划许可证。

在乡、村庄规划区内进行乡镇企业、乡村公共设施和公益事业建设以及农村村民住宅建设,不得占用农用地;确需占用农用地的,应当依

照《中华人民共和国土地管理法》有关规定办理农用地转用审批手续后,由城市、县人民政府城乡规划主管部门核发乡村建设规划许可证。

建设单位或个人在取得乡村建设规划许可证后,方可办理用地审批手续。

思考题

1. 在快速城镇化的背景下,如何处理好城乡规划的刚性与弹性之间的关系?

2. 如何发挥城乡规划的作用,将多元化的资金引入城市建设领域?

3. 不同的政治经济体制对城乡规划的行政体系和运作体系有哪些影响?

参考文献

楚天骄、谭文柱:《快速城市化进程中的城市规划和城市管理》,北京:人民出版社,2012 年。

董鉴泓:《中国城市建设史(第三版)》,北京:中国建筑工业出版社,2004 年。

E.霍华德:《明日的田园城市》金经元译,北京:商务印书馆,2002 年。

耿毓修:《城市规划管理》,上海:上海科学技术文献出版社,1997 年。

李德华:《城市规划原理(第三版)》,北京:建筑工业出版社,2001 年。

（一）中国城市主导功能与产业布局

城市功能或职能是指城市在国家或区域经济发展中所起的作用①。随着城市由单一职能的小城镇成长为综合性职能的大城市，其起主导作用的功能也在发生变化。城市产业布局是城市功能的空间反映②，中国城市主导功能的发展变化是导致城市产业布局调整的基本原因。

1. 中国城市主导功能的发展变化

（1）改革开放前以生产功能为城市主导功能

---

① 于洪俊、宁越敏：《城市地理概论》，安徽科学技术出版社 1983 年版。

② 楚天骄：《城市转型中新加坡 CBD 的演化及其启示》，《现代城市研究》2011 年第 10 期。

中国有几千年的农业文明,新中国成立时仍处于前工业化社会时期,城市的生产功能不突出,主要是作为商品交换中心,及借助于军事手段行使政治统领、行政管辖等服务功能,消费属性大于生产属性。1952年,全国工业产值仅占国内生产总值的17.6%。城市依赖于农村提供农产品,却无法为自身及农村提供足够的工业品。在这种情况下,发展生产,变消费性城市为生产性城市,既是巩固新生人民政权、提高人民生活水平的手段,也是使中华民族屹立于世界民族之林的需要。因此,从"一五"计划起,中国就开始了围绕重点项目建设、以工业化为动力的城市化进程。

从20世纪50年代到70年代,在控制大城市、促进中小城市发展的城市发展战略指导下,中国城市化缓慢地波动式发展。在重点项目带动下,不仅老城市发展成为地区工业生产中心,而且建设了一批新城市;不仅首都、省会城市发展成综合程度和专门化程度不同的生产中心,而且多数县城也配套发展了五小工业①,形成全国不同等级、以生产功能为主的城市体系,全国第二产业产值占国内生产总值的比重不断攀升,到1980年达到48.5%。由于过分突出城市的生产功能,尤其是过分强调了城市作为工业生产基地的作用,导致重工业加速发展,而轻工业和服务业却发展缓慢,城市基础设施、生活服务设施和住宅供应严重不足②。在这一时期,农业劳动生产率和农产品供给能力的提高速度显著落后于城市工业的发展速度,加上户籍制度等种种约束,限制了农村剩余劳动力向城市非农产业的转移,使城市化严重滞后于工业

① 中国地方小型厂矿的总称。20世纪60年代一般指小钢铁厂、小煤矿、小电站、小化肥厂、小机械厂,后来又包括小水泥厂等。1970年的第四个"五年计划"中,中央政府要求各省区发展小煤矿、小钢铁厂、小化肥厂、小水泥厂和小机械厂,并决定中央财政拨出专项资金80亿元用于发展地方"五小"工业。"五小"工业的发展改变了我国工业经济的结构,扩大中小企业在工业企业中的比重,使中小企业能按照专业化和分工协作的原则,进行合理分工。中小企业可以为大企业起到补充作用;更重要的是小企业能更好地利用当地资源,不仅增强了地方经济实力,使县域经济面貌得以改善,从单一的农业经济转向农业生产为主,兼顾工业,适度提高农业外收入水平。但"五小"工业的这种快速发展有一定的盲目性,也带来一些不良的后果。
② 楚天骄:《城市化地域扩张的一般机制研究》,《经济地理》1998年第6期。

化的发展,因此,这一时期又被称为"没有城市化的工业化"时期。1949—1980 年,中国城市数目仅从 136 个增加到 193 个,年均增加 1.84 个,城镇非农人口和总人口比重仅分别从 9.1%和 10.6%提高到 13.7%和 19.4%[1]。

(2)改革开放后注重生产功能与服务功能的协调

从 20 世纪 80 年代中期开始,中国开始注重发挥大中城市对区域经济的带动作用,并积极支持城乡各种所有制企业、中小企业及农村乡镇企业的发展,大力发展小城市、小城镇,自下而上地促进城市与区域经济的互动式发展。大力发展小城市、小城镇使大量农村剩余劳动力就地向非农产业转移,减轻了对大中城市的人口迁移压力。

充分发挥大中城市对区域经济发展的带动作用,服务功能的发展是重要保障。20 世纪 80 年代以来中国城市基础设施建设和服务业取得长足进展,使城市经济结构得以调整,经济实力显著增强。各种所有制经济及乡镇企业的迅速发展,促进了中小城市和小城镇的迅速发展,不仅带来了 80 年代末至 90 年代初的设立城市高潮,而且在中国东部形成了几个城镇密集区。城市数量从 1980 年的 193 个增加到 1998 年的 668 个,年均增加 26.39 个。城镇非农人口和总人口比重分别从 13.7%和 19.4%提高到 23.97%和 30.4%。第三产业在经济发展中的作用受到普遍重视,并得到补偿性发展,占国民生产总值的比例从 1980 年的 21.4%,上升到 1998 年的 32.9%。同期第二产业产值比重仅从 48.5%提高到 48.7%,且工业产值比重从 44.2%下降为 42.1%。但工业产值仍高于第三产业,且 1997 年非农就业人员比重才超过农业,说明中国仍处于以工业化为动力的城市发展阶段[2]。

进入 20 世纪 90 年代,中国的城市开始从生产型城市向服务型城市[3]、生活型城市转变。一般来说,第三产业就业人员超过总就业人员

---

① 周一星:《城市地理学》,商务印书馆 1997 年版。

② 许学强:《中国城市化理论与实践》,科学出版社 2012 年版。

③ 中国城市规划设计研究院"中国城市规划发展趋势"课题组:《1997—1998 年中国城市规划发展趋势》,《城市规划汇刊》1998 年第 4 期。

的一半,被认为是一个国家从制造业经济转向服务性经济,进入后工业社会的重要标志之一。中国在 80 年代后期开始试点,90 年代开始全面展开的城市土地开发的有偿出让、国有企业改革和城市住房制度改革,促进了城市工业外迁①,使城市中心原有工业用地大量转为第三产业用地。房地产、金融保险、交通邮电等部门的迅速发展,第三产业的主导作用逐渐加强。在城市中心区,随着产业结构和用地结构的调整以及市民提高生活质量的需求的攀升,城市政府开始加大环境整治力度,改进城市基础设施和服务设施,建设公园绿地,改善居住条件等,开始了以北京、上海、广州、深圳等城市为代表的,从生产型城市向服务型、生活型城市的转变。这些城市不仅传统商业中心区、现代商务中心区的功能更为突出②,而且还在中心区外围形成不同规模的环境良好、设施较齐全、能适应不同收入层次居民需求的居住区和休闲娱乐区。

2. 城市主导功能变化与产业布局调整——以上海为例

20 世纪 80 年代以前,上海产业布局中一个极为突出的特征,是工业过于集中在中心城区。这与城市发展的历史以及计划经济体制时期城市功能单一有着直接的因果关系。由于上海工业是在解放前半殖民地的工业基础上发展起来的,很多工厂集中分布于市中心的租界内。解放后上海城市建设的指导思想,是建设成为生产性城市(图 3-1),过于强调发挥工业基地的作用,致使上海的城市功能趋于单一,工业的合理布局也没有得到足够的重视。

20 世纪 50 年代,上海先后在近郊建设了彭浦、北新泾等 8 个工业区,在远郊重点建设了闵行、吴泾、安亭等 7 个工业卫星城镇(图 3-2)。但是,随着中心城范围的不断向外扩展,到 80 年代,上海工业布局过于集中在中心城的空间格局并没有得到根本的改变。据统计,至 1987 年

---

① 楚天骄:《经济全球化背景下区域产业分工与合作的动力机制》,《中州学刊》2010 年第 2 期。

② 楚天骄:《外资寿险公司在中国的区位分布与区位选择研究》,《世界经济地理》2010 年第 1 期。

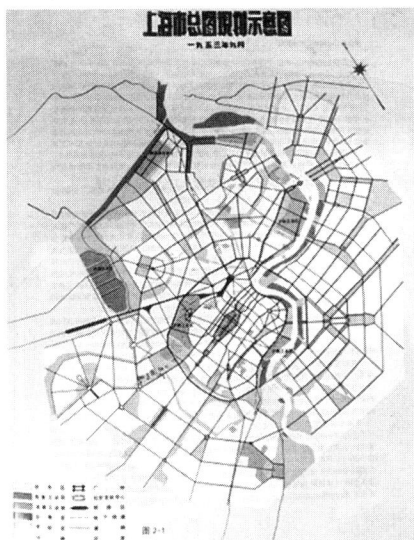

图 3-1　1953 年 9 月苏联城市
规划专家穆欣指导编制的
《上海市总图规划示意图》

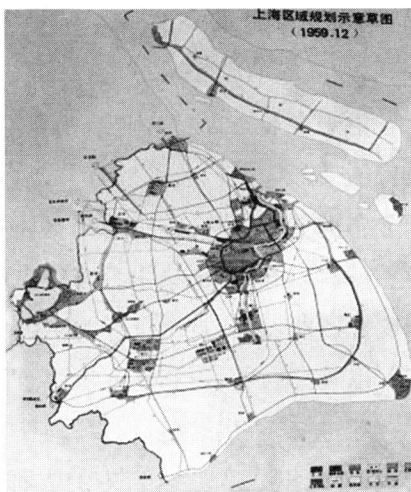

图 3-2　1959 年编制的
上海区域规划示意草图

年底,在 216 平方公里的中心城区范围内的工业企业数、职工数和工业总产值分别占全市工业的 47%、60% 和 66%,尤其是在中心城的 10 个区中,工业密度更高。直到 1990 年,中心城 10 个区的工业企业数仍占当时全市工业企业总数的 43.8%。工业过于集中于中心城区,不仅使工业企业用地紧张,城市交通运输压力加剧,"三废"污染严重,更使城市发展面临"空间危机"。由于工业占用城市用地过多,严重抑制了第三产业的发展和城市综合功能的发挥。

20 世纪 90 年代以后,上海对城市功能进行了重新定位,明确了建设国际经济、金融、贸易、航运中心的发展战略目标,并要求对城市产业结构进行战略性调整。按照城市发展目标的要求,整个 90 年代,上海的产业发展主要遵循了"二三产业并举"的产业发展方针,进行"优先发展第三产业,积极调整第二产业,稳定发展第一产业"的战略调整,形成了主要由第三、第二产业共同推动经济发展的格局。经过这一时期的产业结构调整,上海的第三产业占 GDP 比重从 1990 年的 31.9% 提高到 2000 年的 50.6%,第二产业占 GDP 比重从 1991 年的 61.7% 下降到 2000 年的 47.5%,第一产业占 GDP 的比重从 1991 年的 3.8%下降到 2000 年的 1.8%。

由于产业布局是产业结构在空间上的投影,上海的产业布局必须适应城市产业结构发展的方向,结合城市发展的总体规划,进行产业空间分布的重新安排:在中心市区重点布局了金融、贸易、商业等第三产业,并调整和搬迁了集中分布的大量传统工业企业;在郊区重点发展了以支柱产业、高新技术产业为主的工业区和产业基地,远郊区则重点发展了以种源农业、设施农业及生态为主的都市型农业。

经过 90 年代的产业布局调整,上海逐步形成了中心城以三次产业为主、郊区以二次产业为主的大都市产业布局构架。中心城(外环线以内约 600 平方公里)以发展第三产业为主,郊区(外环线以外 5700 余平方公里)主要发展第二产业及第一产业。其中,产业的具体分布是在市中心重点发展第三产业,并保留部分轻纺工业,构成中心城产业圈;在近郊区集中发展机械、电子、汽车、纺织以及新兴重化工业和市区配套工业,在城市边缘地区发展基础原材料工业,同时,还大力发展以生态、休闲、育种等功能为主的都市型农业,以形成郊区产业圈。通过产业布局的调整,到 2000 年,浦东新区和其他郊区(县)已经成为上海工业发展的重要支撑地区,工业企业数、从业人员、工业总产值等指标均已超过全市的 70%。

(二)开发区建设:新的产业空间

开发区是中国城镇化推进的重要空间载体,也是诱发城市产业空间重构的关键区域。要了解中国城市产业布局的演变,就不能不了解中国的开发区建设。1978 年以后中国城镇居民人口快速增加,如果只依靠原有城市的自然扩张,绝不可能提供容纳每年 1000 万左右新增城镇人口的条件,正是开发区建设为城镇人口扩容提供了空间载体和产业条件。在相当多的大型、特大型城市以及一大批老工业基地型城市的改造中,"退二进三"等战略之所以能够得以实施,在很大程度上依赖于开发区建设为产业结构调整和新产业形成提供了辗转腾挪的空间。

1. 开发区发展过程

开发区是以城市为依托,实行特殊经济政策和特殊管理体制的特定区域,是中国面对经济全球化和世界经济技术革命的战略选择。改革开放以来,中国开发区的建设走出了一条以园区为载体的中国特色新型工业化发展道路,成为中国经济发展最快、吸引外资最多、投资环境最优、技术水平最高的现代化产业集聚园区,是中国工业化、城镇化、国际化的重要平台和载体,是地方经济的重要增长极,发展成绩得到了党中央、国务院的肯定,也受到世界各国、特别是发展中国家的关注。截至 2006 年年底,中国共有 11568 个国家级开发区和省级开发区,总规划面积 7629 万平方公里,主要分布在沿海、沿(长)江、沿(陇海)路、沿边以及内地省会、首府和中心城市(图 3-3)。总结中国开发区的发展过程,可以将其划分为三个阶段。

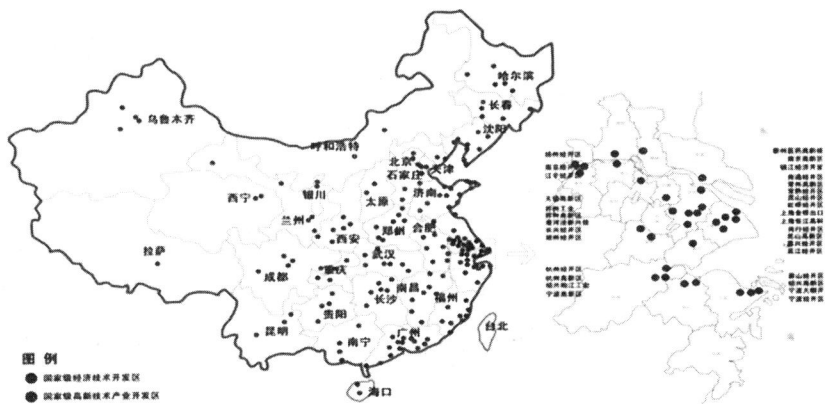

图 3-3 国家级经济技术开发区与国家级高新技术产业开发区布局示意图

(1)探索阶段(1984—1991 年)

中国改革开放是从兴办开发区开始的。在这一时期,开发区的建设主要是兴建国家经济技术开发区和建立国家高新技术产业开发区[1]。

---

[1] 顾朝林、王合生:《中国开发区的建设与发展》,载牛凤瑞、潘家华、刘治彦编:《中国城市发展 30 年》,社会科学文献出版社 2009 年版。

①兴建国家经济技术开发区

1984年党和政府决定开放大连、天津、广州等14个沿海港口城市,先后批准兴建大连、秦皇岛、宁波、青岛、烟台、湛江、广州、天津、南通、连云港、福州等11个经济技术开发区,以便"大力引进中国急需的先进技术,集中地举办中外合资、合作、外商独资企业和中外合作科研机构,发展合作生产、合作研究设计,开发新技术,研制高档产品,增加出口创汇,向内地提供新型材料和关键零部件,传播新工艺、新技术和科学的管理经验①"。1986年国务院又在上海批准建立虹桥、闵行两个经济技术开发区。这些国家级经济技术开发区成为中国最具活力的投资热土,在中国推进工业化、城市化和全面建设小康社会方面发挥了重要作用。

②建立国家高新技术产业开发区

为了推进科技创新和科技成果转化,1988年国家批准兴办国家高新技术产业开发区,在北京设立了中国第一个国家高新技术产业开发区——中关村科技园区。同年又在上海市原漕河泾仪表电子工业区和微电子工业区、生物工程基地的基础上建设了漕河泾新兴技术开发区。

(2)蓬勃发展阶段(1992—1996年)

中国经济经过1989年和1990两年的治理整顿②,1991年转入复苏和快速发展阶段,各类开发区得到了迅速发展,并成立了保税区和旅游度假区等新型开发区,中国的开发区建设进入蓬勃发展阶段。

这一时期,中国的开发区开始从沿海向沿江、从东部向中西部推进,各省、市也都在建设自己的开发区,在全国范围内掀起了"开发区热"。到1994年年底,全国共兴建国家和省市批准的开发区700多个,其中国家级的经济技术开发区32个,高新技术产业开发区52个,保税

---

① 国务院关于批转《沿海部分城市座谈会纪要》的通知,1984年5月4日。
② 1985—1988年,随着经济体制改革的推进,中国的经济过热问题一直没有得到有效遏制,通货膨胀呈明显加剧态势。1989—1990年,中国通过压缩社会总需求和坚持财政信贷双紧方针,积极调整经济结构,控制了通货膨胀,产业结构调整开始起步。

区 13 个,国家旅游度假区 11 个和新加坡苏州工业园区,另外,开发区中所有的保税区和 91.7% 的国家旅游度假区分布在东部沿海地带,其他类型和等级的开发区空间分布较为分散。

这一时期开发区的发展主要有三个特点:第一,利用外资的规模和质量都大幅度提高。跨国公司开始取代中小企业成为投资主体,有一定技术含量的项目大量引入,一些外资企业的研发中心也开始落户①,外商对华投资从试验性阶段进入实质性阶段。例如,1992 年美国摩托罗拉公司在天津开发区投资 11 亿美元,成为当时中国最大的外商独资企业。第二,经济实力、工业产值、税收、经济效益等方面都取得了前所未有的成绩。1996 年沿海 14 个经济技术开发区的工业产值比 1991 年增长了 858.2%,工业规模迅速扩大。第三,开发区的经济总量在其所在母城中所占份额越来越高。1996 年,广州开发区的工业产值占全市的 11.2%,天津开发区的工业产值占全市的 18%。开发区已成为城市经济的增长点②。

(3)稳定发展时期(1997 年——　)

1997 年亚洲金融危机爆发,中国的开发区吸引外资量骤减,发展外向型经济带来的巨大风险给开发区建设敲响了警钟,开发区开始进入调整和转型升级阶段。在这一时期,开发区建设的指导思想从单纯地引入外资调整为重视内外资共同引进、培育产业的根植性和促进产业结构的转型升级。与此同时,开发区的发展水平也在不断分化,一些开发区经济效益差、土地资源的浪费状况逐渐暴露了出来。2004 年,国家对各级各类开发区进行了较大力度的整顿,撤并了很多经济效益不好的开发区,进一步优化了开发区的结构。经过清理整顿,截至2007 年,通过审核的国家级开发区和省级开发区共 1568 个,其中国家级开发区 223 个(表 3-1)。这些通过审核的开发区在招商引资、进出

---

① 楚天骄、宋韬:《跨国公司在发展中国家 R&D 投资的空间格局及其成因研究》,《经济地理》2006 年第 1 期。

② 王峰玉、朱晓娟:《中国开发区的发展回顾与战略思考》,《云南地理环境研究》2006 年第 4 期。

口和工业发展方面在国民经济中占据着重要地位(表3-2),而国家级高新技术产业开发区也已经成为中国现代制造业的重要基地和高新技术产业化的重要基地。

表3-1　中国开发区类型与数量一览表(2007年)

等　级	类　型	数量	备　注
国家级开发区	合计	223	
	经济技术开发区	54	含享受国家级经济技术开发区政策的苏州工业园区、上海金桥出口加工区、宁波大榭经济技术开发区、厦门海沧台商投资区、海南洋浦开发区
	高新技术产业开发区	54	
	出口加工区	57	
	保税区	16	
	保税物流园区	6	
	台商投资区	4	
	海峡两岸科技工业园	2	
	边境经济合作区	14	
	边境互市贸易区	2	
	国家旅游度假区	12	
	跨境工业区	1	珠澳(珠海、澳门)跨境工业区是国内唯一跨越两个行政地域的国家级开发区
	金融贸易区	1	上海浦东陆家嘴金融贸易区是国内唯一的以"金融贸易"为主要功能的国家级开发区
省级开发区	合计	1345	
	经济开发区	810	
	工业园区(产业园区)	535	其中,高新技术产业园区64个
合　计		1568	

资料来源:根据国家发改委有关资料整理。

表 3-2　2006 年国家级经济技术产业开发区主要经济指标

指标	GDP（亿元）	工业增加值（亿元）	税收收入（亿元）	进出口总额（亿美元）	出口总额（亿美元）	进口总额（亿美元）	外商实际投资（亿美元）
开发区	10136.90	7414.24	1570.02	2830.96	1492.33	1338.63	147.12
全　国	209407	90351	37636	17607	9691	7916	630
开发区占全国比例	4.84%	8.21%	4.17%	16.08%	15.40%	16.91%	23.35%

资料来源:商务部。

进入 21 世纪,中国的开发区继续稳定增长。以国家级开发区为例。"十一五"期末,国家级开发区数量增加到 116 家,经济总量不断扩大,主要经济指标增速均高于全国平均水平,对国民经济贡献率持续提高。国家级开发区地区生产总值"十一五"期间年均增速达到 23%,占全国的比重提高到 7%,工业增加值所占比重达到 12%,出口总额占比为 16%,税收总收入占比为 6%,分别比"十五"期末提高了 2 个百分点、3 个百分点、0.5 个百分点和 1.5 个百分点。国家级开发区对所处区域的辐射带动能力增强,创造的地区生产总值占所在城市的比重超过 13%。

2. 开发区建设对中国城市产业空间重构的影响

中国设立开发区的初衷是吸引外资、发展高新技术产业和出口加工业,但是,随着时间的推移,开发区不仅成为所在城市强劲的经济增长点、外向型经济的主阵地、创新体系的核心区和改革开放的前沿,同时也成为城市化的重要动力和主要载体[1]。开发区不仅成为进城农民实现职业和生活方式转变的重要场所,也成为带动城市走向现代化的最重要区域之一。中国的许多城市通过开发区建设,不仅在较短时间内大量聚集了产业和人口,对促进所在城市的产业升级、城市空间组织

---

[1]　郑国:《中国开发区发展与城市空间重构:意义与历程》,《现代城市研究》2011 年第 5 期。

优化、城市功能的完善和提升,城市更新与新区建设等也具有非常重要的意义,因而,开发区被视为中国城镇化的重要载体。

中国的开发区与其所在城市的空间关系经历了两个阶段。

①开发区的"孤岛"阶段(1984年—20世纪90年代中期)

为了减少外资企业对中国经济体制的影响和干扰,中国最初设立的开发区大多距离城区有一定距离,并且用道路、河流等地理界线将其与所在城市分离开,从而在空间上形成一个"孤岛"。在这一时期,中国开发区的主要功能类似于国外的出口加工区,外资企业利用中国廉价的劳动力和优惠的政策投资设厂,投资规模较小,技术水平不高,企业的原料和市场都不在本地,与城市的经济联系不大。这个时期的开发区被视为城市的"孤岛"。

②开发区与城市融合发展阶段(20世纪90年代中期—　　)

20世纪90年代中期开始,中国出现了"开发区热",开发区的数量和规模快速增加,几乎所有的城市都规划建设了开发区。此外,1998年以后,开发区开始由只吸引外资转向中外资并重,外资企业的投资项目从出口导向逐渐转向出口与内销兼顾,开发区内企业之间、开发区与城市的企业之间的经济联系开始加强,开发区的增长极效应开始显现,对城市经济的带动作用明显增强。同时,城市基础设施建设规模的扩大使得城市面积进一步扩张,城市的整体布局开始从单中心城市向多中心城市过渡,开发区作为城市的一个组团或产业区,与城市之间的联系越来越密切。

由于开发区制造业的起点普遍较高,代表了城市制造业的发展方向,因此,在这一阶段,开发区在很大程度上主导着城市制造业空间的演化,并进而对城市其他产业空间、居住与社会空间和社会形态产生深远的影响。首先,开发区建设促进了城市制造业空间重构,促进了城市制造业空间结构形成新的扩散和新的集中,开发区成为城市制造业优势产业聚集地;其次,开发区的发展促进了城市人口郊区化和社会空间分异,这一阶段开发区内普遍形成了以富裕人群为主体的高档社区;最后,由于中国开发区规模普遍较大,而工业用地的扩展又是这一阶段中国城市发展的主导因素,是城市用地扩展的先导,因而开发区的发展在很大程度上主导了城市空间形态的重构①。

随着产业、人口和各种生产要素的集聚,结构和功能不断完善化,开发区人口密度、设施水平、功能类型等日益趋于一般意义上的城市化地区,开发区与城市其他区域之间有形和无形的"界线"日益模糊,开发区与城市之间不断融合,逐渐向一体化发展的方向演进。

(三)新城建设:城市的产业空间重构

在中国快速城市化的过程中,新城建设已经成为缓解中心城市人口和产业压力,优化大城市区域空间的必要政策和有效手段之一。21世纪初期,中国的很多大城市开始进行新城规划和建设,在新老城区之间形成更合理的产业分工格局,整个城市的产业空间得以优化。

1.中国新城建设的背景

中国的新城建设历史可以追溯到 20 世纪 50 年代的卫星城建设,该时期建设的卫星城,规模较小,工业门类单一,设施配套亦无法齐全,对居民的吸引力较低,在疏解中心城市人口和产业方面所起的作用极为有限。

20 世纪末期,在经济全球化及中国改革开放不断深入的背景下,中国的经济、社会和城市化呈现出了持续、快速发展的态势,而大城市的人口和经济社会活动过度密集已给城市的运行造成了巨大的压力,原有的城市结构若再不改变,就会成为城市发展的束缚。因而,拓展新的城市发展空间,优化城市结构,缓解老城的人口增长压力,提升城市的综合竞争能力,已成为大城市发展中的关键课题。越来越多的大城市开始采取建设"新城"的方式来拓展城市空间,目的是使产业和人口

---

① 郑国:《中国开发区发展与城市空间重构:意义与历程》,《现代城市研究》2011 年第 5 期。

能够合理布局,一方面,是为了转移中心城市的人口,疏解中心城市的人口和产业集聚压力,起到分流的作用;另一方面,是引导郊区城市化的集中发展,并期望对可能涌入中心城市的人口起到"截流"作用。

李贵文等总结了 2000 年以后中国新城建设大发展的深层次因素[①]。

第一,城市经济的发展带来了城市空间扩张的需要。改革开放以后,中国城市地区引领着经济的发展,这种极核式发展模式使得资源要素和人口不断向城市地区集聚。集聚与扩散是城市发展过程中的两种表现形式,尤其是发展到了一定阶段的大都市(如北京、上海、广州等城市),原有的城区由于资源和空间的限制,已经不能容纳过多的人口和产业,城市职能开始逐渐向外延伸和扩散,这种延伸和扩散的过程往往是形成老城的新城。

第二,土地制度改革的推进改变了城市产业的空间格局。改革开放以来,中国土地有偿使用制度的实施,以及土地市场的发育,都极大地促进了土地使用效率的提高,地价因素的作用使得城市的中心区成为商业、贸易和金融等高收益功能集聚地,工业、仓储等功能则向土地价格较低的郊区置换,大都市附近的新城就是功能置换的主要区域。

第三,住房制度改革使得城市居民具备了居住区位的选择权。从1998 年下半年起,全国城镇停止住房实物分配,实行住房的货币化分配。随着主城区住房价格的上涨,新区以住房价格低、房龄新等优势吸引了大量市民前去买房,从而带来了新城房地产的大开发以及新城住宅区的大发展。

第四,交通条件的改善为缩短新城与中心城之间的时空距离创造了必要条件。城市轨道交通和快速公交系统的发展,成为城市向外扩展的触角。到 2005 年年底,全国已开通城市轨道交通的城市有北京、

---

① 李桂文、张学勇、曾宇:《中国新城建设条件研究——以北京、上海、广州三市为例》,《华中建筑》2011 年第 2 期。

上海、天津、广州、长春、大连、重庆、武汉、深圳、南京等 10 个城市。在一个城市内,轨道交通的建设也从一条线逐步向网络化发展,轨道交通的建设可以将新城到大城市中心的行程时间缩短几倍,从而大大加强新城和中心区的联系,推动了新城的发展。

有别于 20 世纪 50 年代的工业卫星城,21 世纪以来中国兴建的这些新城具有更大的规模和更综合的功能,更具自我"平衡发展"的可能性。

2. 利用新城建设优化产业空间

(1)北京的新城体系

北京是中华人民共和国首都,也是中国最早进行卫星城建设的城市之一。21 世纪以来,促进和完善新城建设成为北京市疏散中心城区人口和产业的主要举措。根据《北京城市总体规划(2004 — 2020年)》,北京按照"两轴—两带—多中心"进行城市空间结构布局,形成"中心城—新城—镇"的结构,发展 11 个新城(图 3-4)。中心城是北京政治、文化等核心职能和重要经济功能集中体现的地区,面积约1085 平方公里。新城是在原有卫星城基础上,承担疏解中心城人口和功能、集聚新的产业,带动区域发展的规模化城市地区,具有相对独立性。规划中的 11 个新城中,通州、顺义和亦庄被确立为重点发展的 3个新城,规划人口规模为 70 万至 90 万人。

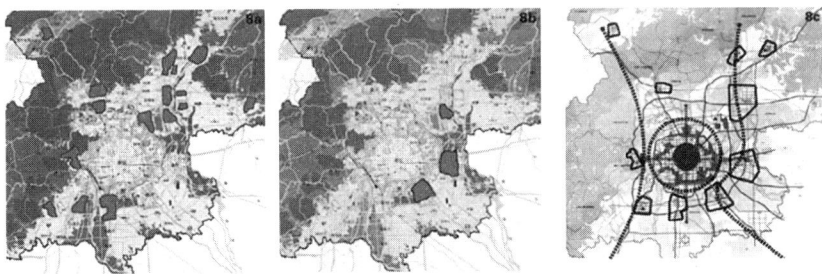

图 3-4 北京的新城分布图

a 重点建设的三个新城;   b 11 个新城分布图;   c 新城空间布局结构图

资料来源:北京市规划局。

（2）广州的多中心网络型城市

广州是中国第三大城市,改革开放以前,广州的城市发展主要集中于老城区。改革开放以后,"飞地"式地建设了广州经济技术开发区、南沙经济技术开发区、广州高新技术产业开发区及广州科学城四个具有初级新城属性的开发区。由于受到白云山和珠江的挟制,广州城市空间蔓延向东、北呈扇面展开。2000年,原番禺市和花都市撤市设区,为广州市建成区的空间增长创造了条件。在2000年制定的新的发展战略中,基本确定城市拓展方式为"点—轴"跨越式拓展方式,在向东和向南的拓展轴线上建设一系列新城。进入全面建设发展阶段的广州新城,其历史重任已经不仅是疏散广州的产业与人口,而是作为广州战略规划中所确定的城市发展轴线上的重要增长极,致力于促进改变城市拓展方式,促使城市空间结构发生调整,提高城市的综合区域竞争能力。

根据《广州城市总体规划纲要(2011—2020)》,至2020年,广州市城乡建设用地1772平方公里,常住人口1800万人。在城市空间布局上,形成"一个都会区、两个新城区、三个副中心"的多中心网络型城市空间结构(图3-5)。其中,都会区的定位是国家中心城市功能的主要承载地,重点发展现代商贸、金融保险、文化创意、医疗健康、商务与科技信息和总部经济等现代服务业,优化布局区域及城市高端功能;加强历史文化保护,提升都会区用地效益和环境品质。两个新城区分别是南沙滨海新城和东部山水新城,重点完善综合配套,提升综合服务功能,实现居住、就业、基本公共服务设施均衡协调及与产业同步发展,吸引人口加快集聚。三个副中心指花都、从化、增城。三个副中心,作为城乡统筹的重要载体,提升综合服务功能,承接都会区人口和功能的疏解,辐射带动镇、村整体联动、共同发展。

（3）宁波东部新城

浙江省宁波市中心城区的建设长期以来是以三江片为中心向外蔓延,这种建设模式不仅速度慢、成本高,而且导致老城区中心高度密集,城乡结合部杂乱不堪,无法满足宁波作为"长三角南翼经济中心"的发

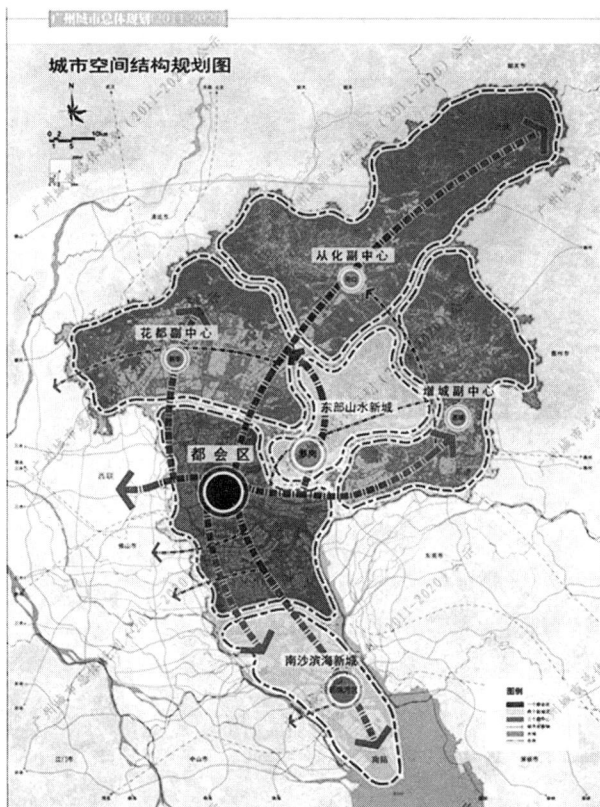

图 3-5　广州城市空间结构规划图

资料来源:广州市规划局。

展目标的空间要求。为了弥补老城区功能上的欠缺,缓解老城区面临的人口、住房、交通和环境等问题,宁波市政府决定开发建设新城。

按照《宁波城市总体规划(2004—2020)》,三江片以三产和生产居住为主,适当发展高科技或无污染的工业。三江片以市内的三条江——余姚江、奉化江、甬江为发展轴,沿江形成市级行政中心、商业中心、商务中心、文化中心和教育基地。城市内环以内以古城保护和旧城改造为主;中环以内发展第三产业及生活居住;中环与外环之间发展无污染的城市工业及生活居住(图3-6)。在老城区东部开发建设新城,拓展城市发展空间,缓解旧城压力,疏解老城区的人口和产业,置换城市中心区的部分原有功能,完善城市功能(图3-7)。

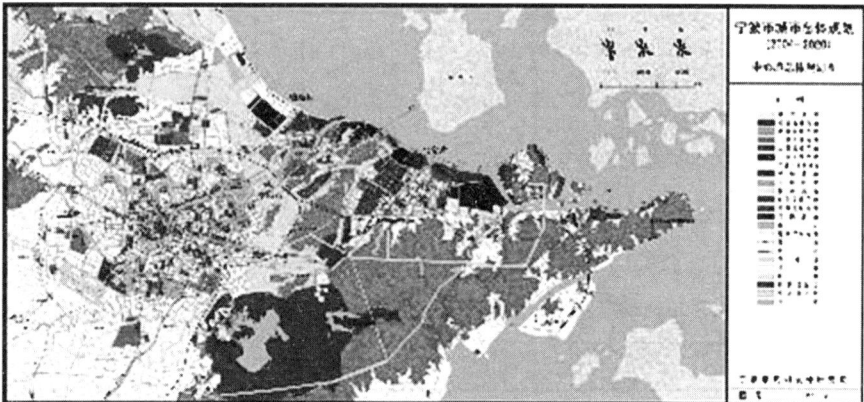

图 3-6　宁波城市总体规划(2004—2020)中心城总体规划图

资料来源:宁波市规划局。

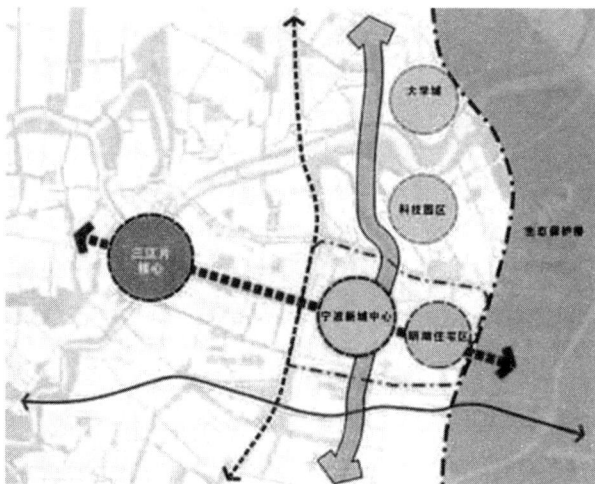

图 3-7　宁波东部新城与老城关系示意图

资料来源:宁波市规划局。

　　新城的城市功能主要包括行政中心功能,科技中心功能,技术中心功能,商务中心功能,信息、博览功能,生态休闲与生活居住功能,目标是成为宁波经济发展的中枢。按照这一功能定位,新城的人口规模为 20 万—30 万人,成为相对独立于中心城市的、综合功能完善的新城区。

思考题

1. 经济全球化对城市产业结构的空间布局会产生哪些影响?

2. 由政府主导的新城建设如何吸引多元资本参与?

3. 如何处理好新城发展与旧城功能提升之间的关系?

参考文献

楚天骄:《长三角地区制造业结构演化趋势研究》,《世界地理研究》2010 年第 3 期。

当代上海研究所:《当代上海城市发展研究》,上海:上海人民出版社,2008 年。

王峰玉、朱晓娟:《中国开发区的发展回顾与战略思考》,《云南地理环境研究》2006 年第 4 期。

于洪俊、宁越敏:《城市地理概论》,合肥:安徽科学技术出版社,1983 年。

郑国:《中国开发区发展与城市空间重构:意义与历程》,《现代城市研究》2011 年第 5 期。

（一）中国城市基础设施建设和发展的历程

城市基础设施是城市赖以生存和发展的基本条件。城市道路、交通、供水、排水、污水处理、供气、供热、供电、电信、园林绿化、环境卫生、城市防洪等设施，与各行各业千家万户有着密不可分的联系，城市中的一切经济活动和居民生活时刻离不开它们。中国的城市基础设施的大规模的建设和发展，主要还是从 20 个世纪 80 年代的改革开放以后开始的。可以说，中国的工业化和城市化极大地推动了中国的基础设施建设进步，最终使中国成为基础设施的大国甚至是强国。

基础设施是指在国民经济各行业中，为了满足生产、生活的需要而必须具备的一般条件的基础结构和公共设施。基础设施的建设是进行其他社会生产、生活等活动的基础,在整个社会中具有极其重要的地位。基础设施从不同的角度可以划分为不同的类型,其中最为主要的分类方法是从基础设施的构成与供给的角度可划分为经济基础设施和社会基础设施。按照世界银行的定义,经济基础设施包括公共事业、公共工程和其他交通设施三个部分。其中公用事业是指电力、通信、供水、环境卫生设施与排污、固体废弃物的收集与处理、管道煤气;公共工程包括公路、铁路、大坝、灌溉及排水用的渠道工程;其他交通设施是城市交通、海港、水运和航空等。社会基础设施包括文化、教育、医疗、保险等人力开发设施。本章讨论的主体仅限于经济基础设施。

1. 城市基础设施建设严重不足阶段(改革开放之前)

在新中国成立之后 20 多年的时间里,中国的基础设施的投资一直处于较低水平,"文革"期间还出现了较为严重的下降趋势。总体而言,全国的基础设施的建设投资占基本建设投资的比重一直维持在 2% 左右。建国之初,国家的经济发展计划偏重于工业,尤其是重工业,而忽视了城市发展,不重视基础设施的投入,致使基础设施严重滞后于工业和城市的经济发展。基础设施本身的不足和落后进一步加剧了在该领域的行政垄断,缺乏效率和公平;与此同时与基础设施相关的一系列规划、建设、运营和管理的法律法规和制度政策极为缺乏,存在大量空白;基础设施的企事业单位缺少自我发展的机制和动力[1]。

2. 基础设施投资建设逐步恢复阶段(1981—1990 年)

改革开放以后,中国各级政府和全社会开始认识到基础设施对社会经济发展的根本性作用,各地的经济和社会发展计划与固定资产投资开始向基础设施倾斜。与此同时,基础设施在投资、建设和管理体制初步进行了一些探索性的改革。在此十年间基础设施投资总额为640.17 亿元,是建国前 25 年的 5 倍,占固定资产投资总额的比例也由

---

[1] 蒋时节:《基础设施投资与城市化进程》,中国建筑工业出版社 2010 年版。

长期以来的 2%—3% 增加至 4%,中国的基础设施建设开始走出低谷①。

3.基础设施投资建设大发展阶段(20 世纪 90 年代—　)

在这一阶段,城市基础社会投资比例逐年上升(图 4-1),中国基础设施的建设取得了显著成绩(表 4-1)。各类基础设施均填补了历史的空白,并真正有了长足的进步。城市的基础设施开始走向健全,基础设施也有力地促进了中国各地的城市化。

表 4-1　中国城市基础设施水平基本情况

指　标	1990 年	1995 年	2000 年	2005 年	2010 年
城市建设					
建成区面积(平方公里)	12856	19264	22439	32521	40058
城市人口密度(人/平方公里)	279	322	442	870	2209
城市供水、燃气及集中供热					
全年供水总量(亿立方米)	382.3	481.6	469.0	502.1	507.9
生活用水量(亿立方米)	100.1	158.1	200.0	243.7	238.8
人均生活用水(吨)	67.9	71.3	95.5	74.5	62.6
用水普及率(%)	48.0	58.7	63.9	91.1	96.7
人工煤气年供气量(亿立方米)	174.7	126.7	152.4	255.8	296.5
家庭用量(亿立方米)	27.4	45.7	63.1	45.9	26.9
天然气年供气量(亿立方米)	64.2	67.3	82.1	210.5	487.6
家庭用量(亿立方米)	11.6	16.4	24.8	52.1	117.2
液化石油气年供应量(万吨)	219.0	488.7	1053.7	1222.0	1268.0
家庭用量(万吨)	142.8	370.2	532.3	706.5	633.9
供气管道长度(万公里)	2.4	4.4	8.9	16.2	30.9
燃气普及率(%)	19.1	34.3	45.4	82.1	92.0
集中供热面积(亿立方米)	2.1	6.5	11.1	25.2	43.6
城市市政设施					

① 蒋时节:《基础设施投资与城市化进程》,中国建筑工业出版社 2010 年版。

续表

指　　标	1990 年	1995 年	2000 年	2005 年	2010 年
年末实有道路长度(万公里)	9.5	13.0	16.0	24.7	29.4
每万人拥有道路长度(公里)	3.1	3.8	4.1	6.9	7.5
城市排水管道长度(万公里)	5.8	11.0	14.2	24.1	37.0
城市排水管道密度(公里/平方公里)	4.5	5.7	6.3	7.4	9.0
城市污水日处理能力(万立方米)				7989.7	13392.9
污水处理率(%)				51.95	82.31
城市公共交通					
年末公共交通运营数(万辆)	6.2	13.7	22.6	31.3	38.3
每万人拥有公交车辆(标台)	2.2	3.6	5.3	8.6	9.7
轨道交通运营线路总长度(公里)					1428.9
城市绿化和园林					
城市绿地面积(万公顷)	47.5	67.8	86.5	146.8	
人均公园绿地面积(平方米)	1.8	2.5	3.7	7.9	11.18
公园个数(个)	1970	3619	4455	7077	9955
公园面积(万公顷)	3.9	7.3	8.2	15.8	25.8
城市环境卫生					
生活垃圾清运量(万吨)	6767	10671	11819	15577	15805

资料来源:《中国统计年鉴 2007》、《中国建设年鉴 2011》。

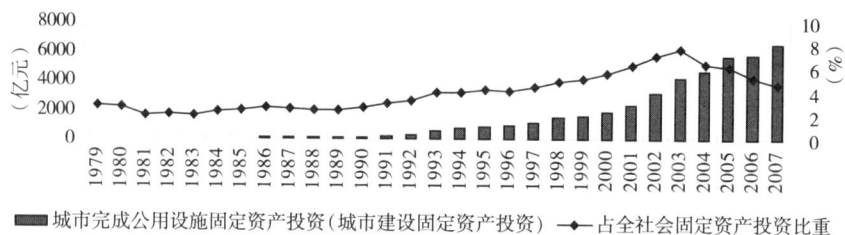

图 4-1　1979—2007 年城市基础设施投资比例

资料来源:根据《中国城市建设统计年鉴》整理。

　　从 2003 年开始,国家一方面积极采取措施加大政府对基础性产业和基础设施的投入,另一方面,鼓励外资和民营资本对基础产业和基础设施项目投资,使这一时期中国基础产业和基础设施水平又有了大幅提高。各地城市面貌、城市经济和社会发展水平和人民的生活质量有了显著的改善。从 2003 年至 2007 年这 5 年间,基础产业和基础设施建设投资总额达到 182703 亿元,是 1978—2002 年基本建设投资额的 1.6 倍,5 年中年均增长 24.9%,比同时期国民经济年均增长速度高 9.2 个百分点①。

在整个"十五"和"十一五"期间,全国大部分城市基础设施已经达到相当规模。据国家统计局统计,在"十一五"期间,中国城镇基础设施累计完成投资 22.1 万亿元。北京和上海等特大型城市抓住举办 2008 年夏季奥运会和 2010 年世博会等大型国际性活动的契机,进一步建设发展城市基础设施,提升城市功能。

在城市基础设施的硬件建设不断完善的同时,城市基础设施的软件建设也方兴未艾,基础设施领域的体制和机制的改革不断得到深化,其中最主要的改革主题是基础设施和市政公用事业领域的政企分开和市场化。近 20 年来,各类经济性质的企业主体和机构纷纷参与到城市基础设施的投资、建设和发展的大潮中,涌现了一大批有充分经营竞争实力的基础设施和市政公用事业专业企业。与此同时,中央和地方制定出台了一系列关于城市基础设施和公用事业的法律法规和政府规章,内容涉及投资、建设、运营和监管,初步形成了中国国家和地方关于城市基础设施和公用事业的法律体系(参见表 4-2)。

表 4-2 上海城市排水体制相关法律法规

颁布时间	法律、法规和文件名称	内容要点	其他说明
1995	《上海市排水设施使用费征收管理办法》及《实施细则》	排水费的目的、定义、适用范围、主管部门和征管单位,收费计算、标准、方式。	
1996	《上海市排水管理条例》	明确排水定义、排水费、水务局主管、各区县职责、排水公司职责、各级政府和相关部门在规划建设、运行管理和养护管理的职能。	1996 年首次颁布,历经三次修正,顺应政府水务管理体制改革

---

① 蒋时节:《基础设施投资与城市化进程》,中国建筑工业出版社 2010 年版。

续表

颁布时间	法律、法规和文件名称	内容要点	其他说明
2002	《市和区、县排水管理职责分工暂行规定》	明确市水务局在全市排水工作的职责:规划、监督、审批指导,管理市属市管排水设施;区县主管部门规划、监督、审批、上报,管理市属区管和区属区管设施。	顺应市区两级分工管理体制
2011	《上海市城市基础设施特许经营管理办法》	确定通过特许经营方式实施经营管理的基础设施和特许经营权竞争授予的方式。	将存量基础设施排除在外

（二）中国基础设施建设面临的问题

虽然中国在城市基础设施建设与发展取得了巨大的成就,广大人民也切切实实从城市基础设施的不断提升中享受到了生活品质的持续提高,但是,中国的城市基础设施的建设和发展还有很长的路要走,目前还存在大量的问题需要解决和完善。其中的主要问题简述如下:

1.城市基础设施建设发展的不均衡性

虽然中国城市基础设施的建设和发展有了很大的成绩,但是城市化进程的不断加快和城市居民不断增长的生活需要使城市基础设施建设步伐显得相对落后。目前,中国大部分类型的基础设施人均指标还远低于城市化发达国家的水平,有的还低于世界平均水平。城市基础设施建设发展还存在着较大的不均衡性。这种不均衡性简言之,一是指区域布局不均衡,中国的东、中、西部基础设施水平相差悬殊;二是指基础设施城乡分布不合理,存在显著的"重城市、轻农村"现象;三是指基础设施产业结构不合理,不同类型的基础设施发展情况差异很大。例如,在全国668个城市中,建成区有一半左右没有排水设施,且配套程度差,尤其是老城区大量存在有道路无上下水或者有上水无下水的状况,排水管网的普及率也只有60%左右①。

① 蒋时节:《基础设施投资与城市化进程》,中国建筑工业出版社2010年版。

2. 城市基础设施建设与发展依然面临严重的资金缺口

国务院发展研究中心的研究还表明,每增加一个城市人口,城市基础设施新增投资最保守估计需要 9 万元。联合国开发计划署研究认为,发展中国家城市基础设施投资一般占 GDP 的 3%—5%,如果处在城市化加速阶段,城市基础设施投资所占得 GDP 比重还应适度提高。亚洲开发银行、日本国际协力银行和世界银行在 2006 年共同研究成果《连接东亚:基础设施新框架》①中预测中国基础设施投资将达到年度 GDP 的 7% 左右(图 4-2)。据《2001—2002 年中国城市发展报告》估算,到 2050 年前后,要使中国城市化水平达到 70%,所需投入的基础设施建设资金大约要 40 万—50 万亿元,相当于每年投入 8000 亿—9000 亿元。巨额的基础设施投资资金如何筹措仍是未来中国基础设施建设亟须解决的一个关键问题。

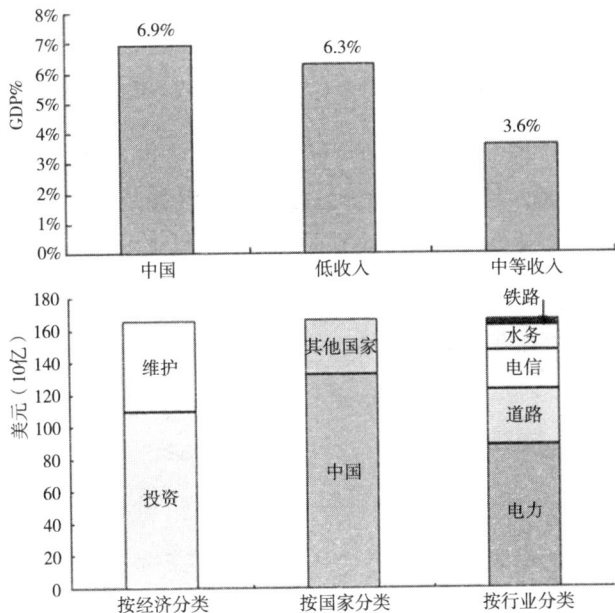

图 4-2　中国基础设施投资需求预测

资料来源:亚洲开发银行、日本国际协力银行和世界银行:《连接东亚:基础设施新框架》,世界银行出版社 2006 年版。

---

① 亚洲开发银行、日本国际协力银行和世界银行:《连接东亚:基础设施新框架》,世界银行出版社 2006 年版。

3. 城市基础设施体制机制需要进一步完善

1999 年以来,中国政府逐步放开城市基础设施市场,引入市场竞争机制,改革城市基础设施的投资、建设、运营和管理体制和机制,逐步形成资本多元化的格局①。

2004 年 7 月,国务院颁布的《关于投资体制改革的决定》提出鼓励和引导民营投资以独资、合作、联营、项目融资等方式参与经营性公益事业和基础设施项目。2005 年 2 月,国务院颁布的《关于鼓励和支持引导个体私营等非公有制经济发展的若干意见》,允许非公有资本进入公用事业和基础设施领域。加快完善政府特许经营制度,规范招投标行为,支持非公有资本积极参与城镇供水、供气、供热、公共交通、污水垃圾处理等市政公用事业和基础设施的投资、建设与运营。这一系列的框架性政策和制度推动了城市基础设施建设和投融资体制机制的改革不断深入,使得市场配置资源的基础性作用开始逐步发挥出应有的功效。

"十一五"以后,伴随着基础设施和公用事业市场化的快速发展,也出现了诸如政府监管不力等一些问题,也出现了"逆市场化"的种种思潮,但是,中央政府利用引入市场机制来促进基础设施和公用事业良性发展的立场始终没有改变,并一直对完善基础设施和公用事业的体制机制努力进行探索和改革。

4. 城市基础设施维护的需求巨大

长期以来,各地普遍存在对城市基础设施"重建设、轻维护"倾向。很多基础设施在建成之后,由于没有相应的维护制度保障,长期处于闲置状态。一些建好的基础设施往往由于没有维护资金保障机制而难以可持续利用。据调查,中国市级城市公共供水设施能力闲置达 20%以上,部分城市超过 50%;中国 668 座城市已建成的 709 座污水处理厂

---

① 廖茂林、黄育华:《中国城市基础设施建设投融资体制改革与发展》,载《中国城市发展30 年(1978—2008)》,社会科学文献出版社 2009 年版。

中,正常运行的只有 1/3,低负荷运行的约有 1/3,还有的 1/3 开开停停,有的甚至根本就不运行,等等。城市基础设施维护不足,就会使基础设施的效能不能有效发挥,难以正常运营,影响公共服务的提供。随着中国城市化进程的不断加速,城市基础设施建设的规模不断扩大,建成以后的城市基础设施的长期维护显然会存在巨大的需求。而应对这样的需求趋势,如果没有稳定的维护制度安排和经费保障,这些设施的运营就会受到严重影响,进一步造成巨大的损失和浪费。

(三)中国城市基础设施建设的探索

1.计划和市场的结合

中国原有的基础设施建设是由国家和政府包揽的完全的计划经济模式。在社会主义市场经济条件下,各地的城市基础设施建设和市政公用事业的发展依然离不开各级政府发挥的基础性作用。政府的基础性作用包括:利用财政资金承担基础设施部分或全部的资金;组织制定城市基础设施规划、行业发展规划和实施计划;制定和完善基础设施和市政公用行业市场化的体制、机制和法制;组织政府招标,实施政府采购和转移支付;组织市民听证、制定市政公共服务的价格;对市政公用行业实施政府监管,等等。

所以,中国的城市基础设施和市政公用行业积极探索在政府主导政策框架下进行有序的市场化,计划与市场有机结合。在这样的体制框架下,既能发挥政府的基础性和指导性作用,又能发挥市场的配置资源的功能,使企业在一个规范的市场上进行有效的竞争。中国的实践也反复表明,在基础设施领域,市场机制失灵的地方、市场企业无能为力的地方,也正是政府发挥重要作用的地方;等政府创造了良好的投资环境激发企业活力的时候,市场企业也会进一步投资和发展当地的基础设施和公用事业,最终使中国城市基础设施建设得到快速增长,从而加快中国各地的城市化进程和区域经济发展。

2. "软"和"硬"的结合

自从中国中央和地方政府在20世纪80年代初实施加快城市基础设施建设的战略以来,始终坚持因地制宜、因时制宜和与时俱进;政府部门不仅重视加快基础设施的硬件建设,也逐步认识到加快基础设施软环境建设的重要性,努力做到"软"和"硬"两手抓,两手都要硬的发展原则。基础设施的"软"环境的建设包括如下几个方面。

一是从重视城市基础设施外在形象建设向重视基础设施提供的公共服务的内涵转变。各地目前的政策重点已不仅仅是如何加快基础设施建设,而是在如何提升基础设施的公共服务水平,如何进一步透明公共服务的生产运营过程上下工夫,在全国水务领域推行成本公开就是一个例证。

二是在加快城市基础设施建设的同时,积极推进基础设施的一系列制度建设,其中遵循市场配置资源功能是一个主要的制度取向。首先,是推行基础设施领域的投融资体制改革,逐步开放市场、引入市场机制,使非市场资金被逐步进入基础设施建设领域;其次,是推动基础设施领域的行政体制改革,通过政企分开和特许经营制度,明确政府和企业在基础设施投资、建设和管理上的职责,使政府在基础设施和公用事业的定位从行政管理到行业监管的转变,逐步通过制定和运用产业政策、城市发展规划、法律法规等调控手段,从宏观上引导、从中观上管理与调节,充分调动各经济主体的积极性,从而促进城市基础设施的快速建设和发展;最后,是培育基础设施领域的市场产业化环境,鼓励各种经济性质的基础设施企业做强做大。政府在这方面的政策包括:通过鼓励上市等手段拓宽基础设施企业的融资渠道;通过政企分开改革消除政府对企业不合理的行政垄断;鼓励基础设施企业实施同行业兼并重组、整合资源;开放地区市场,鼓励基础设施企业跨区投资;等等。这一系列的政策表明,只有市场化的基础设施企业做强做大了,才能为地方城市政府和公众提供更多更好的公共服务。

三是基础设施建设与各地的城市化紧密结合。中国城市基础设施是为城市服务的,也是为快速的城市化服务的。脱离城市发展需求的基础设施是没有价值的,是一种极大的浪费。在中国的城市化进程中,始终坚持基础设施先行;在市场企业达不到的地方,始终坚持政府先行。这样,政府的城投公司从中就发挥了重要作用。城市基础设施投入的增加带动了城市经济生活的恢复,并形成了城市土地的级差地租,成为地方政府的主要财政来源,进一步加快了人口导入和地方城市经济的繁荣,从而使城市化反过来促进基础设施功能的提升和公共服务的优化。

3. 创新和现实的结合

因势利导、因地制宜、与时俱进、不失时机地推进基础设施领域的制度、体制和机制的改革与创新,坚持科技创新、管理和理念创新是中国城市基础设施建设与发展的重要法宝。但是,中国城市基础设施建设起步于经济与社会条件比较落后的社会主义初级阶段,各地发展水平也很不平衡,任何创新都要面对现实,与现实条件紧密结合,逐步推进、不能冒进,要"迈小步、不停步、不走回头路"。比如,上海的城市基础设施投融资体制改革并不是通过"顶层设计"而事先形成的,而是经过不断摸索、不断实践并伴随着中国社会主义市场经济体制改革的持续深化和金融与资本市场的日益完善以及上海城市自身的经济社会发展的需求而最终确定下来的,是经得起历史和实践检验的(参见专栏4-2)。相比之下,少数地区的城市不顾自身现实条件,盲目加快基础设施建设、扩大城市规模,形成基础设施投资泡沫,最终导致国家经济和社会资源的浪费,这也是违背中国城市基础设施建设和发展客观规律的。

专栏4-1:上海城市建设发展的基本经验[①]

在上海最近30年城市建设发展的历程中,上海人民坚持解放思想,实事求是,立足于社会主义初级阶段的基本国情,从实际出发、积极探索体现时代特征、联系上海实际并符合特大型城市特点的发展新路,形成和积累了一些成功经验和做法。主要有以下几点:

[①] 摘自陈士杰、冯小敏、罗世谦:《上海城市建设发展》,上海人民出版社2004年版。

一、始终坚持把城市建设放在突出的战略地位

20世纪90年代以来,上海坚持把城市建设放在突出的战略地位,作为一项关系上海改革和发展的全局性工作来抓,坚持经济发展和社会进步和城市建设同步发展、相互推进,坚持城市的规划、建设和管理统一部署、协调发展,始终保持城市建设的高强度投资、城建投资总量持续增长。城市建设成果不仅表现在城市面貌的巨变上,体现于城市供应能力,城市综合能力的发挥上,还全方位渗透于经济活动中。研究表明,城市建设是20世纪末和21世纪初的上海经济发展的主要推动力量之一。

二、科学规划、超前发展

以规划指导城市建设和管理,是上海的一条重要经验。上海坚持规划先行,很重要的一点是在城市总体规划后、专业规划(包括交通、环境、水务、能源、信息等)紧紧围绕展开,形成各行业超前发展的良性互动局面。所有这些规划的编制和政策研究成果,对专业基础设施的建设都起到了很好的指导作用。

三、改革创新、敢为人先

从根本上扭转城市基础设施落后的局面,上海坚持用改革和创新推动发展,把深化改革与创新体制放在统揽全局的地位。市场配置资源的基础性作用逐步增强,各个难题不断被破解,为加速发展提供了强大的制度支撑。

在城建管理体制变革与创新方面,高度集中的城建管理体制逐步被市区"两级政府、三级管理"和郊县"三级政府、三级管理"模式取代,管理重心下移。

在公用事业改革与创新方面,上海大规模推进城市建设的过程,也是大踏步地改革垄断行业的过程。从1996年至2000年,上海先后推进排水、公交、燃气和供水行业的体制、机制和费制的改革,形成了多家经营、多元投资和多种经营的市场化格局,并初步确立了全方位、全覆盖和全过程的行业管理体系。

在科技创新方面，上海在大规模推进城市建设的同时，十分重视发挥科技创新的作用，依靠科技进步提高城市建设的质量和效益。始终保持上海在建设科技的全国领先地位。同时及时制定相应的办法、标准和规程，把 GPS 信息管理、智能交通、生物环境工程等高科技成果引入城市管理和环境管理领域，提高了城市现代化管理水平。

在法制建设方面，1990 年至 2004 年，上海在城市建设和管理地方立法（包括制定和修订）近 200 件，其中 90% 左右是根据上海城市建设管理实际创设的。在立法过程中，注重立法规划、前期调研、充分论证和覆盖全面；在实际操作中，坚持从实际出发、逐步积累、循序渐进，保证立法的质量和可操作性，保证了地方法规的相对稳定性。行政主管部门坚持依法行政、依法管理，积极运用法律和经济手段，提高城市管理的效率和效益。

城建基础设施投融资体制改革是上海城市建设大规模推进的关键之举。通过利用外资、土地批租、发行股票和债券、向社会直接融资、开放房地产市场，向国内金融机构短期贷款，融通社会资金的方式，通过多元化和市场化的投融资模式，既成功破解了城建资金难题，又降低了融资成本和建设运营成本，提高了投资经济效益和社会效益。

四、社会参与、市民支持

上海城市建设的大规模推进，离不开社会方方面面的大力支持与协作，多元化融资就是社会参与城市建设的鲜明例证。广大市民识大体、顾大局、对承建的理解和支持是城市建设顺利实施的坚实基础。随着上海市政建设的逐步深入、市政工程拆迁面积越来越大，就迫切需要广大市民的理解、支持、配合。在工作指导思想上，坚持全心全意为人民服务的宗旨、关心群众疾苦、多办实事、办好实事，多一些雪中送炭。在具体工作中，坚持重大改革措施出台必须让群众"知情、了解、参与、支持"，把改革方针、政策和宣传落到实处，对一些涉及面较广、影响较大的改革方案，请大家出主意、想办法，取得人民群众的理解和支持。对于城市建设中出现的新情况、新问题，尤其是市民关心和议论较多的问题，及时摸清情况、予以梳理、指导，将可能激化的问题化解在萌芽状态。

思 考 题

1. 中国城市基础设施建设经历了哪些主要阶段？每个阶段的主要特征是什么？

2. 中国城市基础设施如何破解"资金难"的问题？通过哪些体制机制创新来解决？

3. 中国城市基础设施建设的做法给了您哪些启发和借鉴？

参考文献

柳学信：《中国基础设施产业市场化改革风险研究》，北京：科学出版社，2009 年。

蒋时节：《基础设施投资与城市化进程》，北京：中国建筑工业出版社，2010 年。

高坚、汪雄剑：《中国基础设施投资对策对经济增长的影响》，北京：北京大学出版社，2009 年。

（一）城市土地产权制度

　　土地所有制是指人们在一定社会条件下拥有土地的经济形式。它是整个土地制度的核心，是土地关系的基础。土地所有权是土地所有制的法律体现形式。土地所有权是土地所有者所拥有的、受到国家法律保护的排他性专有权利，这种权利可以细分为使用权、收益权、处分权等权能。《中华人民共和国土地管理法》规定："中华人民共和国实行土地的社会主义公有制，即全民所有制和劳动群众集体所有制"，并规定"城市市区的土地属于全民所有即国家所有。农村和城市郊区的土地，除法律规定属于国家所有的以外，属于集体所有；宅基地和自留山、自留地，属于集体所有"。

土地使用制是对土地使用的程序、条件和形式的规定,是土地制度的另一个重要组成部分。土地使用权是依法对土地进行利用、管理并取得收益的权利,是土地使用制的法律体现形式。中国土地产权制度改革主要集中在土地使用权制度的创新。

新中国成立以后,中国城市土地所有制经历一个从私有到国有的发展过程。旧中国实行土地私有制度,城市土地在国土面积中所占比重很小,分别由官僚资产阶级、封建地主、民族工商业者、个体劳动者和外国人所占有。新中国成立初期,各城市政府首先接管了一批国民党政府所有的城市土地,没收了帝国主义和官僚资产阶级在中国占有的大批城市地产;对那些民族工商业、个体劳动者、城市居民所拥有的私有土地仍给予承认。因此,在新中国城市成立初期,城市土地形成了国有与私有并存的格局。直到1956年,城市私有土地基本上可以买卖、出租、入股、典当、赠与和交换等。1956年1月18日,中共中央书记处出台的《关于目前城市私有房产基本情况及社会主义改造的意见》中规定:"一切私人占有的城市空地、街基地等地产,经过适当办法,一律收归国家",城市国有土地的使用"由当地政府无偿拨给使用,均不必再缴租金"①,从而在实现城市土地所有权全面国有化的同时,形成了城市国有土地无偿、无限期、无流动的城市土地使用制度。城市国有土地无偿划拨制度,将土地的所有权和使用权合为一体,完全置于国家控制之下②。

国有土地行政划拨制度与这一时期的计划经济发展模式是相适应的,但在实践中反映出来的弊端越来越明显:土地利用率低下,浪费土地现象严重;国家土地所有权在经济上得不到体现,国家在土地上的收益权和处分权实际上被严重削弱。

改革开放以后,随着中国经济体制改革和对外开放的发展,国家的经济体制发生了深刻的变化,原有的城市土地使用制度已经难以适应

---

① 转引自毕宝德:《中国地产市场研究》,中国人民大学出版社1994年版,第27页。

② 董黎明:《中国城市土地有偿使用的回顾与展望》,《云南地理环境研究》1992年第12期。

改革开放的要求,需要进行一系列土地使用制度的创新。这一时期中国城市土地使用制度创新主要表现为基于地租理论创建了城市土地有偿使用制度。具体表现在以下两个方面:

第一,征收土地使用费和土地使用税。

一是征收土地使用费。中国城市土地使用制度改革最早出现在中外合资企业的用地制度上。1979 年国务院颁布的《中华人民共和国中外合资经营企业法》规定:"中国合营者的投资可包括为合营企业经营期间提供的场地使用权。如果场地使用权未作为中国合营者投资的一部分,合营企业应向中国政府交纳使用费。"1980 年 7 月 26 日,国务院《关于中外合营企业建设用地的暂行规定》指出,"中外合营企业用地,不论新征用土地,还是利用原有企业的场地,都应计收场地使用费。"这些法律政策改变了中国城市土地无偿使用状况,拉开了城市土地使用制度改革的序幕。1982 年,深圳开始征收土地使用费。至 1988 年,全国已有 100 多个城市先后开征城市土地使用费。

二是征收土地使用税。按照 1988 年 9 月 7 日国务院发布的《中华人民共和国城镇土地使用税暂行条例》,从 1988 年 11 月 1 日起开始对城镇土地征收土地使用税,对国内的土地使用者由中央统一征收,对外商投资企业和外国企业在华机构由各地区、各城市收取。至此,中国城市土地在法律上正式步入了有偿使用的轨道。

第二,建立城市土地流转制度。

收取土地使用费的实践打破了过去土地无偿使用制度,为土地使用制度改革提供了宝贵经验,但尚未涉及土地市场机制的变革。随着城市建设规模的加大,土地资源的有效配置问题日益得到国家的重视。由于土地使用费征收标准低,收取的使用费远远不能适应城市基础设施建设的需求。一方面,开发企业靠土地收益迅速致富;另一方面,政府作为国有土地所有者的代表,其所有权在经济上得不到体现。另外,单靠征收少量的土地使用权费,并不能促进土地资源的合理配置和城市土地的高效利用。行政划拨供地虽然力求初次配置的合理性,但因缺乏必要的竞争和经济杠杆,加之土地使用权不能进入市场进行合法转让、抵押,缺乏流动机制,土地不能按照市场信号高效使用。因此,进行更深程度、更大规模的土地使用制度改革势在必行。

深圳市率先进行了土地使用制度改革的探索,尝试把土地所有权与土地使用权分离,在明确城市土地属国家所有的前提下,政府采取公开竞标和招标的方式,出让城市土地使用权。1987 年 9 月 9 日、9 月 29 日、12 月 1 日,深圳市分别以协议、公开招标和公开拍卖的方式,出让了三宗国有土地使用权,突破了国有土地使用权不允许转让的法律禁区,开全国市场配置土地资源的先河。1987 年 11 月,国务院批准确定在深圳、上海、天津、广州、厦门和福州进行土地使用改革试点,改革的核心思路是:变原来的行政划拨土地使用权无偿、无限期、无流动为有偿、有限期、有流动的使用制度。

实践的发展促进了相关法律的修改。1988 年 4 月,全国人民代表大会对《宪法》进行了修改,将原《宪法》中有关土地不得转让的规定修改为"土地的使用权可以依照法律的规定转让"。随后,《土地管理法》也做了相应的修改,从而为国有土地使用权的出让和转让提供了法律依据。1990 年 5 月国务院发布了《中华人民共和国城镇土地使用权出让和转让暂行条例》,对国有土地使用权出让、转让、出租、抵押、终止等问题作出了明确的规定。1994 年《城市房地产管理法》出台,明确规定:"国家依法实行国有土地有偿、有限期使用制度。"1998 年新《土地管理法》进一步明确规定:土地使用权可以依法转让,国家依法实行国有土地有偿使用制度,建设单位使用国有土地应当以出让等有偿方式取得。这些法律法规的颁布实施,形成了由《物权法》《土地管理法》、《城市房地产管理法》、《农村土地承包法》、《招标拍卖挂牌出让国有土地使用权规定》等一系列法律规范构筑而成的土地权利体系,并基本确立了国有土地市场运行的基本制度框架,建立了具有中国特色的土地产权制度。

（二）城市土地利用管理

土地利用管理是国家为了合理组织土地利用,对各种土地利用过程实行国家干预措施。中国的土地利用管理的主要内容包括土地利用计划管理、土地利用规划管理、土地整理、用途管制等。改革开放之后,根据国情,中国建立了独具特色的土地利用管理制度。

1. 严格的耕地保护制度

保护耕地是中国土地管理的首要任务,更是土地利用管理的重点。1986 年 3 月,中共中央、国务院《关于加强土地管理、制止乱占耕地的通知》,首次明确提出"十分珍惜和合理利用每寸土地,切实保护耕地"的基本国策。1994 年 8 月,国务院颁布《基本农田保护条例》,标志着中国基本农田保护步入法制轨道。1999 年修订的《土地管理法》确立了中国耕地保护的两大政策框架:耕地占补平衡制度和用途管制制度。这两大政策明确了土地管理工作从保障建设用地供应转到切实保护耕地;从分级限额审批制度(参见专栏 5-2)转到用途管制制度①。

①建立严格的土地用途管制制度

土地用途管制制度是目前世界上土地管理制度较为完善的国家和地区广泛采用的土地管理制度。所谓土地用途管制制度,是指国家为保证土地资源的合理利用,促进经济、社会和环境的协调发展,通过编制土地利用规划,规定土地用途,明确土地使用条件,并要求土地所有

---

① 土地用途管制制度是指各级政府编制土地利用总体规划,规定土地用途,将土地分为农用地、建设用地和未利用地,土地所有者和使用者应当严格按照国家确定的用途利用土地。土地用途管制制度是我国土地管理制度的核心。国家严格限制农用地转为建设用地,控制建设用地总量,对耕地实行特殊保护。实施农业结构调整和发展设施农业,应尽量利用荒山、荒坡、滩涂等未利用地和低效闲置的土地,不占或少占耕地,严禁占用基本农田。

者、使用者必须严格按照规划确定的用途和条件使用土地的制度。中国希望通过土地用途管制制度实现对耕地的严格保护。

②强化耕地占补平衡制度

耕地占补平衡也可叫做耕地总量动态平衡,是指通过采取各种措施,保证耕地总面积在一定时期内满足社会和经济发展的需要,是保证耕地总量不减少的重要制度。《中华人民共和国土地管理法》第三十一条明确规定:国家实行占有耕地补偿制度。非农业建设经批准占用耕地的,按照"占多少,垦多少"的原则,由占用耕地的单位负责开垦与所占用耕地的数量和质量相当的耕地。保持耕地总量动态平衡实行省级政府负责制。如果某一省级行政区域内耕地总量减少,则由国务院责令在规定期限内组织开垦与所减少耕地的数量与质量相当的耕地,并由国务院土地管理部门会同农业行政部门验收。

除了以上两项措施外,中国还从严格控制城镇用地规模、大力开展土地整理提高耕地质量、建立耕地动态保护监测系统等方面加强耕地保护管理工作。

2. 土地利用规划及其实施体系

1986 年 6 月发布的《土地管理法》明确要求"各级政府组织有关部门编制土地利用总体规划"。按照《土地管理法》的要求,中国重新构建了土地分类体系,并进行了规划期分别为 2000 年、2010 年和 2020 年的三轮全国性土地总体规划,形成了以全国、省、市、县、乡五级土地利用总体规划体系,完成了对全国土地利用规模结构、空间布局、强度和时序的优化配置,实现了各类用地的平衡,保护了耕地,促进了存量低效和未利用土地资源的开发利用,保障了建设用地需求。同时,全面开展了基本农田保护规划、土地整理规划、土地整治规划、开发复垦规划等各项规划;通过两上两下方式编制了年度土地利用计划(含非农建设用地占地指标)(参见专栏 5-1)、土地用途管制等规划实施制度。

专栏 5-1　土地利用计划管理

土地利用计划管理是国家对土地利用活动进行宏观控制的一项措施,即国家通过编制计划和下达控制指标,宏观地指导和约束人们有计划地合理组织土地利用,把土地利用纳入国家计划管理轨道的一项宏观调控措施。土地利用计划管理主要包括计划编制、指标下达和计划实施三部分内容。计划包括土地利用的中长期计划和年度建设用地计划;指标主要指国家每年下达的各项建设占有耕地的指标和其他各项用地指标;计划实施包括计划的执行、检查和总结三部分。即由地方各级土地管理部门提出用地指标建议数,然后逐级上报,由国家土地管理部门和国家计划部门进行平衡后,提出计划草案,并把用地指标分解到各省、然后逐级下达控制指标;地方土地管理部门依据下达的用地控制指标,修改原用地指标建议数,然后再逐级上报,最后经中央批准后,按隶属系统逐级下达计划指标。

3. 建设用地管理制度

建设用地,是指人们通过一定的物质投入和工程措施,使其具备专一用途的建设条件,用来进行工程营造和资源开发的土地。建设用地按其利用方式不同,又分为农业建设用地和非农业建设用地,非农业建设用地根据土地权属性质、投入资金来源和土地利用类型的不同,又可以分为国家建设用地、乡(镇)村建设用地和外商投资企业用地三种类型。城市建设用地主要包括国家建设用地和外商投资企业用地。

国家建设用地是指国家进行经济、文化、国防以及兴办社会公共事业所需要的建设用地,包括城镇建设用地、工矿区用地、运输用地、水利用地和特殊用地。

外商投资企业用地,是指中外合资企业、中外合作经营企业、外资企业进行生产经营和工程建设所需用地。

（1）国家建设项目用地管理

国家建设用地的来源主要有两个途径：征用农村集体土地和划拨国有土地。此外，国家建设用地还可以通过有偿出让、转让的方式获得。

土地征用是国家根据经济、文化、国防建设及兴办社会公益事业的需要，依法将集体所有的土地转为国有土地的过程。

土地使用权划拨是指县级以上人民政府依法批准，在土地使用者缴纳补偿、安置等费用后，将该幅土地交其使用，或者将土地使用权无偿交付给土地使用者使用的行为。

土地使用权出让是指国家将国有土地使用权在一定年限内出让给土地使用者，由土地使用者向国家支付土地使用权出让金的行为。通过出让方式取得土地使用权的用地者，在规定的使用年限内，有转让、出租、抵押土地使用权或从事其他经营活动的权利。

根据《中华人民共和国土地管理法实施条例》的规定，国家建设用地审批程序基本由以下几个部分组成：

其一，建设单位持经批准的设计任务书或者初步设计、年度基本建设计划等有关文件，向被征用土地所在地的县级以上地方人民政府土地管理部门申请建设用地。

其二，县级以上地方人民政府土地管理部门对建设用地申请进行审核，划定用地范围，并组织建设单位与被征地单位以及有关单位依法商定征用土地的补偿、安置方案，报县级以上人民政府批准。

其三，建设用地的申请，依照法定批准权限，经县级以上人民政府批准后，由被征用土地所在地县级以上人民政府发给建设用地批准书，土地管理部门根据建设进度，一次或者分期划拨建设用地。

其四，建设项目竣工后，建设项目主管部门组织有关部门验收时，由县级以上人民政府土地管理部门核查实际用地（城市规划区内的建设项目竣工后，由城市规划行政主管部门会同土地管理部门核查实际用地），经认可后依照有关规定，办理土地登记手续，核发国有土地使用证。

（2）外商投资企业建设用地管理

目前,外商投资企业用地取得的主要方式有有偿出让国有土地使用权、划拨土地使用权、以土地使用权作为合作条件和租赁房屋及场地等。

①出让国有土地使用权

出让国有土地使用权,是国家将国有土地使用权在一定年限内出让给外商投资企业,由外商投资企业一次性支付土地使用权出让金。土地使用权出让一般采取拍卖、招标或者双方协议的方式。从事房地产开发、商业、旅游、娱乐和豪华住宅等经营性项目的外商投资企业用地,许多地方规定必须通过出让方式取得土地使用权。

②划拨土地使用权

由县级以上人民政府依法批准后,所在地市、县土地管理部门与外商投资企业签订土地使用合同,并按规定缴纳土地使用费,办理登记手续,颁发土地使用证,外商投资企业即取得土地使用权,但不得转让、抵押和出租。

③以土地使用权作为合作条件

按国家有关规定,中方企业可以把企业拥有的厂房及设备连同土地使用权作价入股作为合作条件与外商合资组成合作经营企业。但中方企业要到县级以上土地管理部门办理用地手续。如果属于行政划拨土地使用权作为合作条件的,其合资合作企业的中方须每年按规定缴纳土地使用费。

④租赁房屋及场地

外商投资企业直接向国有、集体、乡镇企业、部队、集体经济组织租赁房屋或场地,外商投资企业依照租赁合同按年或按月向出租者缴纳租金。

4. 产业用地管理制度

为促进经济发展,中国形成了特有的开发区制度和政策,集中和高效配置二次产业用地。但各地为了招商引资,低价甚至零地价出让土地,造成产业盲目上马、层级低、土地资源浪费与土地资产流失等问题。为此,2004年10月,国务院发布了《关于深化改革严格土地管理的决定》,指出工业用地也要创造条件逐步实行招标、拍卖、挂牌方式出让,推进土地资源市场化配置。在此政策出台前,工业用地一直采用"先立项后供地"模式,用地规模是按照工程项目建设用地指标或工程设计规范予以确定的。2006年9月,《国务院关于加强土地调控有关问题的通知》强调了工业土地使用权的出让必须执行工业用地出让最低价标准,并且一律采取招标、拍卖、挂牌的方式出让,确立了"先土地后项目"的模式。2007年起,《全国工业用地出让最低价标准》的实施,明确了工业用地出让的最低价标准。2009年10月1日,国土资源部颁布的《限制用地项目目录(2006年增补本)》和《禁止用地项目目录(2006年增补本)》,进一步贯彻了《国务院批转发改委等部门关于抑制部分行业产能过剩和重复建设引导产业健康发展若干意见》,促进产业结构调整和节约集约利用土地。有些地区如上海市先后制定颁布了《上海市建设项目审批中用地规模控制管理试行办法》、《上海产业用地指南》(2004年版、2006年版),《上海工业产业导向及布局指南》、《上海工业供地导则(试行)》、《上海工业用地的出让价格标准》等相关各类实施细则和管理标准,进一步完善了产业用地管理制度。

专栏5-2　上虞市建设多层标准厂房,提高产业用地效率

浙江省上虞市大力推行工业标准厂房用地公开出让和标准厂房建设,走出了一条集约节约用地的创新之路。2005年,上虞市为解决土地对经济发展的瓶颈制约,决定把标准厂房建设作为解决工业用地的途径,以集约用地的方式为中小企业搭建平台。政府规定,凡用地10亩以下、投资1000万元以下的项目不再单独供地,全部用标准厂房解决。从2005年至2007年4月底,上虞市共公开出让标准厂房用地1567.8亩,建成多层标准厂房面积117.6万平方米,入住中小企业145家。

　　为促进标准厂房建设和鼓励中小企业入住标准厂房,上虞市政府采取以下激励政策:第一,优先办理标准厂房项目;第二,对标准厂房建设企业给予奖励和补助;第三,对入住企业给予奖励和补助。

　　上虞市规划建设的标准厂房建筑物均在 4 层以上,容积率在 1.3以上,建筑密度在 35% 以上,投资强度达每亩 135 万元以上,绿地率控制在 15% 以内,行政办公和生活设施占地比例控制在 7% 以内,行政办公和生活设施建筑面积控制在 15% 以内。标准厂房建设大大提高了土地集约利用水平。

　　资料来源:李风,裘建勇:《"一号工程"两赢——上虞市推进多层标准厂房建设透视》,《中国土地》2007 年第 6 期。

（三）城市土地市场管理

1. 城市土地市场现状

中国的土地市场目前主要是土地使用权出让和转让市场。

（1）土地使用权出让市场

　　又称土地批租市场。指国家把土地的使用权有偿出让给土地使用者的过程。在土地批租市场上,土地所有者,即国家可通过协议、招标或拍卖等方式,将土地使用权出让给机关、企业、事业单位或个人。交易的并非是土地所有权,而是有一定使用期限的使用权,并且是地面的使用权,地下的自然资源、矿产及埋藏物、隐藏物等不在交易之列,当试用期满时,除非双方续签协议,否则,土地所有者将把土地使用权和地上建筑物收归自己所有。土地批租市场的交易方式有两种:第一种是土地的长期批租,适用于长期用地需要,批租年期可根据生产行业和经营项目的营利情况及实际需要确定。中国现行各类用地最长出让年限分别为:居住用地 70 年;工业用地 50 年;教育、科技、文化、卫生、体育用地 50 年;商业、旅游、娱乐用地 40 年;综合或者其他用地 50 年。以上是国务院规定的法定最高出让年限,各地在实施过程中又做了各自不同的具体规定。第二种是土地使用权的短期批租,又称土地租赁,适用于一些临时、短期用地需要,一般为 1 年至 10 年。

在土地批租上,土地使用权的批租一般要附加一系列的规定和限制条件。这些规定和限制使城市政府按照社会经济发展的总体设想和土地利用规划制定时,主要通过具有法律效力的批租契约加以规定和实施。批租契约是土地所有者与承租者签订的合同。契约的内容应包括承租者享受的权利、应承担的责任和遵守的事项,如租地期限、租地用途、开发形式、建筑高度、建筑密度、建筑容积率、最低投资额及公共设施建设的要求;土地用途改变必须经政府批准并补交土地差价的规定;在出让期内土地使用权再转让必须进行变更登记的规定;政府对违反契约规定的惩处权利的规定。

土地批租市场特征表现在:第一,这是一种土地使用权的买卖市场,买卖成交后,买者付出地价,获得了一定时期的土地使用权,卖者获得地价,失去了土地使用权,但所有权并没有丧失。第二,土地价格是一定时期的土地使用权的购买价格,其构成基础包括绝对地租、级差地租及土地资本利息。第三,这是一种垄断竞争型市场,土地使用权的出让者是国家,由国家土地管理部门代表政府垄断这一土地市场的土地供给活动;众多的土地使用者可在土地需求方面展开竞争,运用各种竞争手段取得土地的使用权。

(2)土地使用权转让市场

土地使用权转让市场是指土地使用权在土地使用者之间转让的市场。获得土地使用权的原用地单位若要将土地使用权再转让出去,仅限于原用地者与土地所有者所签订协议规定的期限内。这种土地使用权的转让必须在政府土地管理部门的管理下进行,否则就是非法交易,必须依法制裁。

土地使用权的转让,是原土地使用者将一定时期的土地使用权完全转卖给新的使用者,彻底脱离与土地所有者的关系。其与土地所有者之间的权利、义务关系,也随之转由新的土地使用者承担。这种交易遵循"认地不认人"原则,该原则的基本含义是,当某单位或个人买入土地使用权或房产,其不仅享受土地、房产的权益,也同时把出售土地、房地产的责任承担下来。实行"认地不认人"原则,就可以保证政府和其他单位、个人的权利不受土地使用权、房产的多次转让而受到影响。土地使用权转让必须向国家缴纳土地增值税。

土地使用权转让市场的特征表现为:第一,经济法律关系更为复杂,不仅涉及用地者与用地者之间,而且涉及用地者与所有者之间的经济法律关系。第二,交易的结果是土地使用权的横向流动,有助于克服土地批租市场上土地使用权纵向流动的局限性,克服土地闲置现象,提高土地使用效益,有助于土地资源的合理配置。第三,这是一种有管理的竞争型市场。在这一市场上,土地使用权在供给方面展开竞争,而需求者在获得土地使用权方面展开竞争,土地使用权的买卖价格或租赁价格受价值规律和土地供求规律的调节更为明显。

土地使用权出让市场和土地使用权转让市场相互补充、有机结合,共同构成中国的总体土地市场模型。

2. 城市土地市场管理的内容和方式

(1)城市土地市场管理的基本内容和方式

土地是重要的生产要素之一,也是政府可以调控的一种重要资源。政府从社会经济发展的总体目标出发,综合运用经济手段和行政手段对城市土地市场进行干预,以达到抑制土地投机、维护土地市场稳定、优化土地资源管理、合理分配土地收益的目的。

①土地市场的宏观管理

土地市场宏观调控,是指国家从社会经济发展的总体和长远目标出发,通过经济手段(主要包括产业政策、财政信贷政策和税收政策)和行政手段(主要包括规划和计划),对城市土地市场进行干预,以达到抑制土地投机、维护土地市场稳定、优化土地资源配置、合理分配土地收益的目的。土地市场宏观管理包括土地市场供需管理和土地市场价格管理两个方面。

②土地市场的微观管理

所谓土地市场的微观管理,是指国家通过法律、行政等手段对土地市场运行进行统一的规范与管理,保证市场主体公平交易、平等竞争,以发挥土地市场机制的正常调节功能。

(2)土地市场供需调控与管理

土地市场供需调控有利于稳定地价和房价,有利于土地利用结构的调整和优化,是优化土地资源配置、合理分配土地收益的重要手段。

①土地市场供需调控的主要内容

——土地市场供需调控的方向。供需调控的方向包括两方面的内容:一是选择调控目标;二是确定调控措施的作用方向。选择调控目标的确定依据是一定时期内土地市场发展目标。确定调控措施的作用方向则需要在明确调控目标的基础上,对当前土地市场的运行状态和变化趋势进行分析。作用方向大致可分为两类:一类是刺激土地市场发展的措施,其作用方向是向上,如减免税收、降低贷款利率等;另一类是抑制土地市场发展的措施,其作用方向是向下,控制贷款规模、限制土地供给量等。一般来说,在土地市场景气循环的萧条阶段和复苏阶段,采用作用方向向上的调控措施;在土地市场出现"过热"预兆时,采用作用方向向下的调控措施。

——土地市场供需调控的时间。确定供需调控时间,也就是要确定何时开始调控,调控时间应持续多长。在确定土地市场供需调控的时间问题上,必须考虑以下三个方面:供需调控措施的决策时间;供需调控效应的滞后时间;调控效应的惯性。城市土地市场的供需调控必须与完善的土地市场监测预警系统相结合。

——土地市场供需调控的力度。供需调控力度大小与作为调控手段的变量的变化大小相关。土地市场供需调控的力度要考虑如下因素:土地经济波动的幅度;调控手段从使用到产生效应的滞后时间;调控效应惯性大小;调控环境。

②土地市场供需调控的措施

——发展计划和规划土地利用计划,特别是年度计划,是把握土地入市环节,调控土地市场的有效手段。土地利用规划是政府控制土地供给量,协调供求关系,调节和稳定土地价格的重要手段,对土地市场具有宏观调控作用。

——财政政策。应用土地市场供需调控的财政政策主要有地租政策、税收政策和财政投资政策,这些政策在调节土地市场发展速度和供求关系上发挥着重要的作用。税收政策作为财政收入政策对土地市场的供需调控作用体现在两个方面:第一,通过对土地市场运行过程中不同环节进行征税实现对土地市场的调控;第二,通过减免税实现对土地市场的调控。财政投资政策对土地市场的调控作用主要体现在财政投资的导向作用上,利用财政投资引导社会投资,以调整产业结构和调节地区差异。

——金融政策。国家金融政策是政府对土地市场供需进行调控的重要手段。金融政策对土地市场的调控可分为直接调控和间接调控。直接调控是指政府通过制定土地金融政策依靠中央银行直接干预土地信用业务的质和量。间接调控是指国家通过利率和贷款成数等金融杠杆来调节货币供应量和需求量,进而调控土地市场供需。

(3)城市土地市场宏观调控与管理创新——土地储备制度

所谓土地储备制度是指政府依法运用市场机制,通过收购土地所有权或使用权,按照土地利用总体规划和城市规划,对土地进行前期开发整理与储备,以供应或者调控城市建设用地需求的城市土地管理制度和运行机制。

土地收购储备制度的运作主要包括土地收购、土地储备和土地供应三个程序。

①土地收购。土地收购是指根据市政府授权和土地储备计划,土地储备机构收购或收回市区范围内国有土地使用权的活动。其工作程序是申请收购、权属核查、征询意见、费用测算、方案报批、收购补偿、权属变更、交付土地。土地收购补偿费一般按被收购土地的开发成本计

算。对于以出让方式取得的土地使用权,收购补偿费还应包括对土地使用权人已支付的土地出让金的补偿,但应扣除原土地使用权人已实际使用土地期间应付出的出让金部分。

②土地储备。对于进入土地储备体系的土地,在出让给新的土地使用单位以前,由土地储备中心负责组织前期开发和经营管理。

③土地供应。对进入土地储备体系的土地,由土地储备机构根据城市发展需要和土地市场需求制定土地供应计划,有计划地统一向用地单位供应土地。根据现行土地管理规定,储备土地的供应方式可分为招标拍卖挂牌出让和协议出让两种类型。

为配合企业改制,盘活城市存量土地资产,优化土地资源配置,有利于政府对土地市场实施调控,2001 年 4 月,国务院发布《关于加强国有土地资产管理的通知》,其指出:为增强政府对土地市场的调控能力,有条件的地方政府要对建设用地试行收购储备制度。市、县人民政府可划出部分土地收益用于收购土地,金融机构要依法提供信贷支持。随后全国大部分城市开始建立土地储备机构,推行土地储备制度。中国城市土地储备主要有三种模式:

①市场主导型模式。土地收购储备机构根据收购计划和政府要求,对拟收购地块先行评估,再与原土地使用者协商确定土地收购价格,或者约定土地收益分成,然后由土地储备机构支付购买金,取得土地,按现行规定办理过户手续。储备机构负责对土地进行拆迁、平整和相关基础设施配套,然后由土地管理部门适时出让给新的土地使用者。

②政府主导型模式。土地收购的范围由政府行政法规规定,规定范围内的土地统一由土地储备机构受政府委托按计划进行收购、储备、开发,土地管理部门根据用地需求采用招标、拍卖、挂牌等方式对储备土地实行统一出让。

③政府主导与市场运作相结合的模式。主要针对国有企业改革中原划拨土地的收购储备。对于经政府批准可进行公开交易,已补交土地出让金,且用途调整符合规划的原划拨土地,可以由土地收购储备机构进行收购,也可以在土地市场公开交易。

思考题

1. 您怎样评价中国的土地产权制度?

2. 土地市场供需调控有哪些方法?土地市场供需调控政策怎样与金融政策和财政政策相协调,才能实现理想的调控效果?

3. 如何提高城市土地的利用效率?

参考文献

毕宝德:《中国地产市场研究》,北京:中国人民大学出版社,1994年。

楚天骄:《土地流转模式及其规范化研究》,《上海综合经济》2002年第4期。

何芳:《中国特色的土地制度发展与创新》,《上海土地资源》2012年第3期。

（一）中国城市社区管理体制的演化

中国的城市社区建设已经走过了 20 多年的历程，不仅在满足人民群众生活基本需要、化解改革进程中的社会矛盾、倡导良好的社会风尚、保障改革顺利进行等方面发挥了不可替代的作用，而且也为构建社会主义和谐社会提供了有益经验。新中国成立以后，城市社区管理体制经历了两个时期。

1. 计划经济体制下的街居管理体制

（1）计划经济体制下街居制的产生

新中国成立后，中国共产党迅速地建立了以单位制为核心的城市社会管理体制，把绝大多数城市市民掌控在单位中，余下的一些社会闲散人员、民政救济对象、社会优抚对象、家庭妇女等"无单位人员"依靠街道和居民委员会(简称"居委会")进行管理。这样,单位制与街居制相辅相成,构成了城市社会管理体制的总体框架。政府利用单位制和街居制对城市居民实行分类管理,两种体制均对政府负责,前者管理有单位的人员,后者管理无单位的人员。

街居制就是以街道办事处和居民委员会为载体管理基层的一种社会管理组织形式。街道办事处和居民委员会的产生可以追溯到新中国成立之初。当时,政府在城市基层社区的行政组织首先是以街政府或街公所体制为主,即街道是城市的基层政权,是接管城市时的一种基层政府机关,这是由"接管委员会办事处"演化而来的。1953 年,时任北京市市长的彭真同志向中央提交了《关于城市街道办事处、居民委员会组织和经费问题的报告》,建议"街道的居委会必须建立,它是群众自治组织,不是政权组织,也不是政权组织下面的脚,城市街道不属于一级政府,但为了把很多不属于工厂、企业、机关、学校的无组织的街道居民组织起来,为了减轻区政府和公安派出所的负担,还需要设立市或区政府的派出机关——街道办事处"①。该报告经中央同意后,1954 年全国人大常委会制定并颁布了《城市街道办事处组织条例》和《城市居民委员会组织条例》,对街道办事处和居民委员会的性质、地位、作用、职责、组织结构、与有关部门和单位的关系以及经费来源作出了明确规定,由此,中国城市基层管理体制的街居制制度建立起来了。

需要注意的是,在单位制下,由于特殊的原因形成了类似于居民委员会的家属委员会(简称"家委会")。由于单位要承担职工的生活管理职责,因此,绝大多数单位都以自己的居住地为中心,建立了大小不一的集宿舍和各种服务设施于一地的生活区,在这些生活区中,通常都有由单位直接领导的家委会的建制。与居委会一样,家委会也是改革前城市最基层的、属于群众自治性质的社会管理组织,但是多数家委会并不接受所在街道的"地方"领导,也不与其发生联系,仅是单位内部

---

① 王振耀、白益华:《街道工作与居民委员会建设》,中国社会出版社 1996 年版,第 179——181 页。

的管理组织。

（2）计划经济体制下街居的职能变迁

①街道办事处职能的变迁

街道办事处设立之初，管辖范围不大，人口不多，任务比较单一。1954年颁布的《城市街道办事处组织条例》规定，街道办事处有三项任务：一是办理市或市辖区政府有关居民工作的交办事项；二是指导居民委员会的工作；三是反映居民的意见和要求。实际上，当时街道办事处的工作对象仅限于单位制以外的老弱病残，工作内容也仅包括户政、调解、救济、市容卫生等，在整个社会管理中起着拾遗补缺的作用。

20世纪90年代以来，城市街道办事处的作用不断加强，逐渐承担起相当于一级政府的作用。目前街道办事处至少承担着10个方面的任务：第一，发展街道经济；第二，城市管理，包括辖区市容、环境卫生、市政设施和园林绿化管理；第三，民政工作，包括举办社会公共福利事业、做好优抚救济、拥军优属、婚姻登记；第四，社区服务，包括开展老年人服务、残疾人服务、精神卫生服务、便民利民服务、民俗改革服务；第五，人口管理，包括辖区内居民计划生育、劳动人口就业、暂住人口管理；第六，社会治安综合治理，包括做好普法宣传、人民调解、治安保卫、维护社会秩序；第七，开展社会主义精神文明建设，包括发展社区文化、社区教育、社区科技、社区体育、卫生保健等；第八，行政管理和办理区政府交办的有关事项；第九，指导居民委员会工作，反映居民的意见和要求；第十，加强街道党的建设。

②居民委员会职能的变迁

1954年颁布的《城市居民委员会组织条例》明确了居民委员会的任务：办理有关居民的公共福利事业；向当地人民政府或者它的派出机关反映居民的意见和要求；动员居民响应政府号召并遵守法律；领导群众性的治安保卫工作，调解居民间的纠纷。20世纪80年代后期，居民委员会的职能有所增加。根据1989年颁布的《城市居民委员会组织法》，居民委员会的任务包括：第一，宣传宪法、法律、法规和国家政策，维护居民的合法权益，教育居民履行依法应尽的义务，爱护公共财产，开展多种形式的社会主义精神文明建设活动;第二,办理本居住地区居民的公共事务和公益事业;第三,调解民间纠纷;第四,协助维护社会治安;第五,协助人民政府或者它的派出机关做好与居民利益有关的公共卫生、计划生育、优抚救济、青少年教育等工作;第六,向人民政府或者它的派出机关反映居民的意见、要求并提出建议。

（3）计划经济体制下街居制的主要特征

街居制产生于计划经济"强国家、弱社会"体制之下,是单位制的辅助体制,因而在很多方面具有独特性质,其中最突出的是政府的绝对控制以及组织管理城市居民的"剩余性"特点①。

①政府的绝对控制

同计划经济体制下的单位制"统得过死"的特征相联系,国家对街道、居委会采取的是绝对控制,即在人事任免权和财政权上没有留下半点空间,法律形同虚设。1954 年颁布的《城市街道办事处组织条例》规定,"街道办事处的主任、副主任、干事都由市辖区、不设区的市的人民委员会委派"。实际上,1958 年以后成立的街道办事处的主要领导都是由上级机关任命的。1954 年颁布的《城市居民委员会组织条例》规定,"由居民小组各选派委员 1 人,并且由委员互推主任副主任人选",但事实上都是由街道委派或者内定的。对于财政权,《城市街道办事处组织条例》规定:"街道办事处的办公经费及工作人员的工资,由省、直辖市的人民委员会统一拨发";《城市居民委员会组织条例》规定,"居民委员会的公杂费和居民委员会的生活补助,由省、直辖市的人民委员会统一拨发"。这样,上级政府通过控制人事权和财政权,对街道办事处和居委会进行掌控。

②辅助剩余性特点

20 世纪 50 年代中期以后,中国政府主要借助单位制来实现对社会的控制和整合。街道办事处和居民委员会的产生是由于单位制之外

---

① 雷洁琼:《转型中的城市基层社区组织——北京市基层社区组织与社区发展研究》,北京大学出版社 2001 年版,第 35、197—198 页。

还有部分人没有纳入单位之中加以管理,因此,街居制可以视为单位制的辅助体制。街居制的辅助剩余性主要表现在两个方面:其一,是服务管理对象的非主体性。街居制的主要对象是没有进入到单位的居民,他们大多是老弱病残、家庭妇女等。这些人不是政府管理的主要对象,属于城市的非劳动人口。其二,是所管事务的相对次要性。居民委员会产生之际,只承担维持秩序、社会治安、打扫卫生、解决矛盾纠纷等职能,这些事务既非生产性任务,也非政治性任务,与单位制承担的政治、经济、文化、教育、动员、管理等职能相比,街居制处于城市全部社会生活的边缘。

尽管街居制只是单位制的辅助体制,但在当时的计划经济体制下,以街道和居委会为基本组织形式的城市基层组织在维护城市秩序、发动居民、发展便民服务、发展基层经济、扩大就业等方面仍然发挥了重要的作用。伴随着改革的深入和社会的转型,这种基层管理体制的缺陷越来越多地暴露了出来,已经不能适应形势发展的需要,亟须进行改革。

2. 市场经济体制下的社区管理体制

(1)社区管理体制的形成

社区建设是社会服务在新形势下的必然延伸。自从20世纪80年代后期社区服务在中国兴起以来,加强社区建设和社区发展的呼声越来越高。随着经济社会发展和改革的不断深化,原有计划经济体制下的"政社合一"、"政企合一"的社会组织结构已经转化,单位制逐步被打破,"单位人"逐渐转向"社会人"、"社区人",社会服务、社会管理等职能大量地从企业和政府部门中剥离出来,中国的社会组织功能发生了巨大的结构性变化。"街道组织"作为唯一的管理主体,依靠单一的行政手段、行政资源已经不能对社区事务实施全面、有效的管理,计划经济体制下"街道"作为行政组织履行行政管理的方式已经不能适应社区多元的功能需求,改革城市社区管理体制势在必行。

20世纪90年代初,中国提出了"社区建设"的思路,并在全国若干个城市进行了社区建设的试点。2000年12月,中共中央办公厅、国务院办公厅转发了《民政部关于在全国推进城市社区建设的意见》,将社区定义为"聚居在一定地域范围内的人们所组成的社会生活共同体",并指出:"目前城市社区的范围,一般是指经过社区体制改革后作了规模调整的居民委员会辖区。"《民政部关于在全国推进城市社区建设的意见》标志着城市社区建设已经进入在全国全面推进阶段。

2002年以后,中国城市社区建设进入一个不断完善和深化的阶段。中共十六届六中全会通过的《中共中央关于构建社会主义和谐社会若干重大问题的决定》和中共"十七大"报告明确提出,把"社区建设成为管理有序、服务完善、文明祥和的社会生活共同体",这是对中国特色社区建设总体目标的高度概括。其中,管理有序主要是指社区各类管理组织健全,职责明确,体制合理;社区党组织核心领导作用得到发挥,社区民主协商机制和各项民主制度健全规范,居民群众在基层社会、经济、政治、文化和其他公共事务中切实能够当家作主,形成党领导下的充满活力的居民自治机制;社区安全防范体系完善,群防群治网络和社会矛盾纠纷调处机制健全,政府行政管理和社区自我管理有效衔接,政府依法行政和居民依法自治良性互动,社区秩序井然,居民群众安居乐业。服务完善主要是指服务设施、服务项目、服务手段齐全,能够为社区成员多样化、个性化的需要提供满意的服务。文明祥和主要是指居民群众崇尚科学、崇尚学习,群众性精神文明建设活动普及深入,学习型家庭、学习型组织普遍建立,居民自觉遵纪守法,家庭、邻里团结和睦、文明礼貌,科学健康文明的生活方式得以普遍形成,居民群众具有较强的公德意识、环保意识,人人养成了节约、环保、卫生的良好习惯,社区环境优美。

(2)中国城市社区管理体制的基本架构

中共中央办公厅、国务院办公厅《关于转发〈民政部关于在全国推进城市社区建设的意见〉的通知》中要求,各级政府要形成"党委和政府领导,民政部门牵头,有关部门配合,社区居委会主办,社会力量支持,群众广泛参与"的推进社区建设的整体框架。按照这一精神,中国现行的社区管理体制为党委政府领导、民政部门主导、有关部门负责、社区居委会主办、社会力量广泛参与。

①党委政府领导

为了加强对社区建设工作的领导,全国各省、市的各级政府机关及其派出机构(街道办事处)都成立了社区建设领导协调机构,负责对辖区内社区建设的日常工作。

②民政部门主管

民政部是推动社区建设工作的主管职能部门,由其"基层政权和管理司"统一负责组织推动社区建设的开展,其主要职责为调查研究、建章立制、指导协调和检查监督。

③有关部门负责

社区管理是一个系统工程,需要相关部门的配合。以区一级政府的做法为例。一般的做法是,在区委区政府层面成立社区建设指导委员会,由区委、区政府、区人大和区政协的"一把手"分别担任主任、副主任,区委组织部、宣传部和区政府民政局、财政局、城市管理局等20多个部门的主要领导作为成员,既是集体决策机构,又是集体授权机构。社区建设指导委员会的下属机构社区建设办公室设在民政局,由民政局代表社区建设指导委员会监督各政府部门职责落实情况,协调各部门之间的关系。通过这种制度设计,形成各部门之间的互动机制(参见图6-1)。

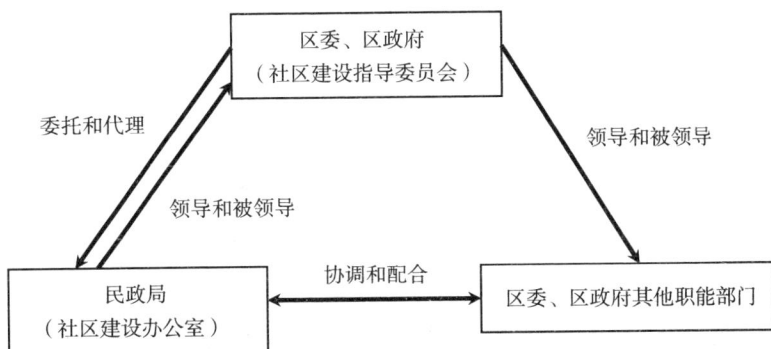

图 6-1　政府部门在社区管理中的互动关系

资料来源:丁茂战:《我国城市社区管理体制改革研究》,中国经济出版社2009年版,第52页。

④社区居委会主办

社区居委会在国家宪法、法律和政府的法令、行政法规范围内,在社区党组织的领导下,在区、街及各业务主管部门的指导下,按照《中华人民共和国城市居民委员会组织法》规定的权利、义务对社区事务行使议事、协调、服务、监督和管理的权利,开展社区民主自治工作。

⑤社会力量广泛参与

社区建设是系统工程,有赖于政府和非政府组织的介入,更有赖于社区居民和社会单位的广泛参与。《民政部关于在全国推进城市社区建设的意见》中提出,"资源共享、共驻共建、充分调动社区内机关、团体、部队、企业事业组织等一切力量广泛参与社区建设,最大限度地实现社区资源的共有、共享。营造共驻社区、共建社区的良好氛围。"

（3）走向社区治理体制——社区管理体制改革的方向

中国经济社会的快速发展对社区管理体制的完善提出了更高的要求。1991年,民政部提出社区建设的思路以来,中国的社区管理体制不断得到发展和完善,城市社区功能不断拓宽,社区已经逐步成为多种社会群体的聚焦点、多种利益关系的交汇点、多种社会组织的落脚点和党在社会执政的支撑点,在满足人民群众需求、整合各种利益关系、化解社会矛盾、维护社会稳定方面发挥着越来越重要的作用。但是,随着改革开放进程的不断推进和社会主义市场经济的不断发展,中国的经济体制、社会结构、利益格局和人民的思想观念也在发生深刻的变化,社会管理的难度不断加大。因此,通过社区管理体制改革来加强城市的管理能力、维护社会稳定、促进社会和谐势在必行。

社区管理体制改革就是在现有的体制基础上,通过整合社区资源,吸收社会力量参与,构筑与社会主义市场经济相适应的社区治理新模式,形成政府调控机制与社会调控机制互联、政府行政功能与社会自治功能互补、政府管理力量与社会协同力量互动的社区治理体制和运行机制,对社区进行有效覆盖和全面管理,最终形成以社区党组织为核心、以社区自治组织为基础、以社区服务站为依托、以社区社会组织为补充、驻社区单位密切配合、社区居民广泛参与的现代社区治理结构,为构建社会主义和谐社会打下基础①。

（二）中国城市社区服务

中国的社区服务,是根据中国国情,以社会保障为基础,融福利服务和社会服务为一体的具有中国特色的社区服务。中国的社区服务最初是在政府和民政部门的积极倡导下逐步发展起来的。中共十六大首次将"发展社区服务,方便群众生活"写进了党的政治报告。2006 年 4 月,国务院《关于加强和改进社区服务工作的意见》出台,提出要逐步建立与社会主义市场经济体制相适应,覆盖社区全体成员、服务主体多元、服务功能完善、服务质量和管理水平较高的社区服务体系,努力实现社区居民困有所助、难有所帮、需有所应。这是中国社区服务历史上第一次以国务院的名义下发的文件,充分体现了中国政府对居民群众民生权利的高度重视。

1. 中国社区服务的特点

中国的社区服务是指在党和政府的主导和扶持下,依托民间组织、政府相关部门及其派出机构、群众自治组织等多元主体,动员社区力量,利用社区资源,直接为各类社区成员(包括社区居民和社区内单位等)提供福利性、公益性服务和便民利民的生活服务,以不断满足社区成员日益增长的物质文化需要的过程。也就是说,中国的社区服务既包括无偿、低偿的社区福利性、公益性服务,又包括低偿、有偿的社区便民利民服务。

在计划经济时期,中国的社区服务是政府包办式的自上而下的供给模式,政府是社区服务的唯一主体。随着社会转型和经济转轨,中国的社区服务逐步转向政府、社会、市场的合作互动,呈现出一些新的特点。第一,服务主体多元化。政府虽然仍是社区服务的主体,但不是唯

① 丁茂战:《我国城市社区管理体制改革研究》,中国经济出版社 2009 年版,第213 页。

一的主体,一些民间组织、群众自治组织和私人企业开始加入到社区服务的行列中来,参与社区服务产品的生产和供给。第二,服务对象多元化。社区居民、社区特殊群体、弱势群体以及社区内单位等都是社区服务的对象。第三,服务性质多元化。既有公益性、福利性的社会救助、社会福利和优抚保障服务,也有面向群众的有偿的便民利民服务。第四,服务形式的多样化。政府的行政性服务、社会的互助性服务、市场的经营性服务并存。

2. 中国社区服务的发展现状

20 世纪 80 年代中期以来,在政府行政力量的推动下,中国的社区服务发展迅速,覆盖的领域越来越广,覆盖的内容越来越多,为促进经济发展、维护社会稳定、提高人民生活质量发挥了重要作用。

一是社区服务设施建设取得初步进展。截至 2010 年年底,全国共有 84689 个城市社区,共建成综合性的社区服务站 30021 个、街道社区服务中心 3515 个、便民利民服务网点 69.3 万个。还建有社区卫生服务中心(站)、社区文化中心(室)等专项社区服务设施。

二是社区服务内容不断拓展。劳动就业、社会保障、生活救助、文化娱乐、社会治安等政府公共服务事项逐步向社区覆盖,广泛推行社区志愿者注册登记制度,社区志愿互助服务蓬勃开展。超市、菜场、早餐等生活保障性商业网点得到重点配套,家政服务、物业管理、养老托幼、食品配送、修理服务、废旧物品回收等便民利民服务项目逐步进入社区,极大地方便了社区居民生活,提高了生活质量。

三是社区服务队伍不断壮大。不仅有依法选举产生的居委会成员,也有面向社会公开招聘的专职社区工作人员。一大批素质高、能力强、作风正、愿意为群众服务的城乡居民走上社区工作岗位。此外,越来越多的社区居民成为社区志愿者,活跃在社区服务各领域,成为推动社区建设和社区服务的重要力量。

四是社区服务方式不断改善。不少地方依托街道社区服务中心、社区服务站,实行"一站式"服务;不少地方利用现代信息技术,推动社区信息化建设,方便快捷地满足了居民多样化需求。有的地方通过政府购买服务、设立项目资金、开展项目补贴等方式,引导社会组织、企事业单位和居民参与社区管理和服务活动,增强了社区服务的活力和社会组织的服务能力。

五是社区服务制度环境初步形成。国家围绕老年人、未成年人、残疾人权益保护工作出台了法律,围绕社区卫生、社会救助、劳动就业、文化教育、社区服务设施等内容出台了相关政策,各地也相继出台了积极推进社区服务的政策措施,社区服务的政策法规逐步完善,各级党委政府对社区服务的重视程度越来越高,社区居民对社区服务的认同感越来越强。

尽管中国的社区服务体系建设已经取得了长足的进展,但是仍然存在许多困难和问题。随着中国经济发展和城镇化进程的加快,社区已成为中国各类社会群体聚集点和各种社会矛盾交汇点。目前,城市社区服务存在的突出问题有:社区服务设施短缺,有些街道、社区仍然缺乏服务场所;社区服务内容亟待丰富,需求和供给有脱节现象,供给方式较为单一;社区服务人才短缺、素质偏低,结构有待优化;社区服务体制机制不顺畅,缺乏统一规划,投入不足、各自为政、重复建设的问题较为突出,资源整合不够,社会参与机制有待完善。尽快形成解决这些问题的体制机制,已成为中国社区服务发展的关键。

3. 城市社区服务的发展方向:转变政府职能和发展民间组织

(1)把转变政府职能作为城市社区服务发展的前提条件

中国的历史发展和行政特点决定了政府在社区服务中扮演着十分重要的角色,政府化的社区服务实践类型是我国社区服务发展进程中必要而又必然的形式,政府对中国社区服务的开端与发展起了重要的推动作用,如果没有政府的干预和推动,中国的社区服务不可能在较短时间内取得长足的进步。但是,随着中国经济转轨与社会转型,政府在社区中的越位与缺位问题不断暴露出来,已经影响到了社区服务的健康发展。政府能力的有限性一方面造成了社区服务机构低效运作,另一方面使居民的多样化、专业化需求不能及时得到满足,使政府不得不直接面对社区服务中的各种矛盾,因此,迫切需要政府转变职能,使政府职能与政府能力有效协调。通过转变政府职能,使政府从"无限政府"转变为"有限政府",使有限的职能在社区服务中得到最有效的运用。同时,积极培育和发展多元化的社区服务主体,有效承接政府转移出的职能。

(2)把扶持民间组织作为政府职能转变的结构性承接载体

中国政府积极推动民间组织成为社区服务最主要的供给主体。2006年4月,国务院在《关于加强和改进社区服务工作的意见》(以简称《意见》)中特别要求在把社区服务的各项工作落到实处时,要积极培育发展社区服务民间组织,重点培育发展为社区老年人、未成年人和残疾人服务的组织和公益慈善、群众性文体活动组织。要积极为社区民间服务组织开展活动创造条件。有条件的地方可以把部分社区服务公共设施交由民间组织使用,或提供必要的活动场地和办公设备。可以通过竞聘等方式,为民间组织配备少量工作人员,加强服务组织协调。要加强社区志愿服务的规范化建设,建立社区志愿者激励机制,支持和鼓励工、青、妇、残、老等群团组织志愿者进入社区开展活动。《意见》中要求充分发挥社区民间组织的服务作用,积极支持民间组织开展社区服务活动,支持和鼓励社区居民成立形式多样的慈善组织、群众性文体组织、科普组织和为老年人、残疾人和困难群众提供生活服务的组织。《意见》表明,政府越来越重视民间组织在社区服务中的地位和作用,并积极倡导和支持民间组织成为社区服务的供给主体。

(3)把培育发展与监督管理并重作为管理社区民间组织的基本原则

培育发展意味着鼓励支持对社会进步能起到良好作用的民间组织不断获得发展,促使其作用进一步得到发挥;加强对民间组织的管理和监督,就是要对非法民间组织和民间组织的违法行为坚决打击,依法查处,只有把培育发展与管理监督有效地结合起来,才能真正促进民间组织的健康发展。以上海为例。上海结合本地实际,探索出一种社区民间组织的枢纽型管理模式。所谓枢纽式管理,就是在政府部门和社区民间组织之间设立一个管理载体——社区民间组织服务中心,由该中心从党的建设、业务工作和保障工作三个方面对社区内的民间组织开展服务和管理。其具体运行方式是在街道(镇)、区两个层面成立民间组织服务中心,分别对辖区内各依法登记的民间组织履行以下职能:建立辖区内民间组织的党员情况档案库,开展党建工作,实现社区民间组织党建工作全覆盖;整合辖区内民间组织人才资源,加强动态管理;代办民间组织工作人员养老、医疗、失业保险等;对辖区内新成立的民间组织进行前置评估调查并出具意见;开展与民间组织相关的业务培训和咨询服务,提供信息、举办理论研讨会、专题报告会等;提供各类有偿中介服务;对非法民间组织活动进行预警并协助查处等。服务中心所需人员坚持社会招聘与内部调剂相结合、以专职人员为主、兼职人员为辅的原则,做到结构配置合理。经费保障以政府购买服务的方式实行财政补助、从党费中给予适量补充,预算合理、使用规范。中心办公场地主要由街道提供支持。通过枢纽式管理,主要在社区这个层面实现了对民间组织的有效管理与全面服务,具体落实了培育发展和管理监督的责任,为推进政府职能转变、改进社会管理方式,加强党的执政基础、增强民间组织自我发展能力提供了社会化管理的运作平台。

专栏 6-1　北京市朝阳区构建"一刻钟社区服务圈",不断提升居民的幸福感和满意率

北京市朝阳区以"一刻钟社区服务圈"建设为载体,加强社区服务,满足群众需求,动员社会参与,不断提升和谐社区建设水平。

2011 年年初,朝阳区共建成 119 个"一刻钟社区服务圈"。"服务圈"的建设充分发挥了政府职能部门、社区服务站、志愿者组织、驻社区单位、企业及个人的作用,扎实做好社区公共服务、公益服务、便民服务和虚拟服务,为"一刻钟社区服务圈"建设提供有力支撑。

1. 制定朝阳区社区公共服务指导目录,做好社区公共服务的支撑。指导目录是社区居民享受政府基本公共服务的"基本菜单"。朝阳区制定社区公共服务指导目录,将 97 项公共服务项目落实到了基层。

2. 推进志愿服务工作,做好社区公益服务的支撑。朝阳区成立了全市首家志愿者"公益储蓄中心",在街道设立分中心,在社区、商务楼宇设立服务站,依托"公益储蓄中心"网站,整合部门资源,建立志愿者实名数据库,并通过时间储蓄、精神激励等方式,倡导"有时间做志愿者、有困难找志愿者",搭建了志愿服务供需信息对接平台、形象展示平台。

3. 整合地区服务资源,做好社区便民服务的支撑。社会化是社区服务工作的重要原则。朝阳区坚持以社会效益为目的,以经济效益为手段,积极统筹社区社会单位的资源,不断丰富社区服务内容。加大学校、部队等社会单位的公共服务设施对居民开放的力度,区内 83 所学校的体育设施向社会开放,160 余个单位的食堂、会议室、运动场和体育设施有组织地对居民开放,较好地解决了居民文体活动设施少、场所小的问题。各街道还积极整合辖区银行、邮局、医院、物业等社会单位资源,为居民提供服务。

4. 运用信息技术手段,做好社区虚拟服务的支撑。朝阳区积极运用现代信息技术,提高社区服务的信息化水平。在区级层面,整合区政府所有热线电话资源,进一步完善 96105 热线电话、社区服务网、短信、彩信平台功能,提高咨询、服务、举报投诉、社区服务及民生监测等工作的系统化水平。各街道、社区也积极构建"虚拟社区",满足居民个性化需求。

5. 培育社会组织,增强服务专业性。社区社会组织是社区服务的重要组织者。朝阳区在 23 个街道全部成立社会建设协调委员会,在社区积极成立居民事务协调委员会,搭建第三方社会建设协调机构,为社会各界有序表达诉求、参与社会建设提供平台。联合专业机构、大专院校,成立社会工作事务所,并通过购买服务、项目运作等方式参与社区服务。

（三）中国城市社区自治

社区建设的长远目标是实行社区居民的自治,这个自治正如2000年11月由中共中央办公厅和国务院办公厅转发的民政部《关于在全国推进社区建设的意见》中所表述的,社区居民自治是在党和政府领导下的自治,也就是说,这种自治是在自我管理、自我服务、自我选举和自我监督层面上的自治,所要达到的是民主选举、民主决策、民主监督和民主管理。

1. 城市社区居民自治的由来

中国的城市社区居民自治既不是全意义上的联邦主义的自主自治和集体自治,更不能等同于完全的地方自治。中国的社区自治组织是指社区的主体组织,即社区居民委员会。社区居民委员会的成员经民主选举产生,负责社区日常事务的管理。社区居民委员会的根本性质是党领导下的社区居民实行自我管理、自我教育、自我服务、自我监督的群众性自治组织。

根据1954年宪法精神,国家制定并通过了《城市居民委员会组织条例》,第一次以法律形式宣布居民委员会是"群众自治性的居民组织"。于是,居民委员会建设在全国展开。1958年之后,尤其是"文化大革命"期间,以居民委员会为代表的基层群众自治制度受到严重破坏,中国的基层民主也因此陷入全面危机。改革开放后,中国基层民主重新获得发展。1980年1月19日,国家重新颁布了1954年通过的《城市居民委员会组织条例》,从而使城市基层群众自治制度开始得以恢复和发展。1989年,在原来的《城市居民委员会组织条例》基础上形成的《中华人民共和国城市居民委员会组织法》也在全国人大常委会获得通过。至此,城市基层群众自治制度有了成熟的法律基础。

2.城市社区居民自治体制的基本框架

（1）核心是党的领导

在目前中国的社区中,全部建立了社区党组织,有的是设立社区党委,有的是设立社区党总支,下设党支部。党支部设在居委会上是中国基层民主与西方社会基层民主的最大区别,因为只有这样,才可能在实现居民自我管理、自我教育和自我服务的同时而不至于偏离社会主义发展的大方向。从社区居委会的角度讲,把党组织建立在居民区,能更好地贯彻党的群众路线,使居委会能够在党的领导下更好地实现居民自治。

（2）关键是居委会建设

《城市居民委员会组织法》规定,城市居委会是居民自我管理、自我教育、自我服务的基层群众性自治组织。社区居民自治体制的框架是:社区党支部——领导核心;社区居民代表大会——议事决策核心;社区居民委员会——既是执行者又是社区居民代表会议闭会期间的决策者。社区居民自治的体制构架并没有改变居民委员会的性质——基层性、群众性和自治性,也没有改变社区居民委员会在居民自治中的主体地位——它仍然是居民自治的主要组织载体。

从体制上讲,社区居民自治的体制构架突出了社区居民委员会的主要组织载体地位。在制度建设上,建立、健全了居民代表会议、居民会议等各种会议制度,建立了必要的财务、审计制度。例如,在北京东华门街道的韶九社区,大大小小的社区制度就有 70 多项。同时,社区在居民委员会的主导下设立了居民小组、志愿者队伍等组织。在运行机制上,首先,着重于完善居委会的选举机制。例如,北京在 2003 年居委会的换届选举中,几乎每个街道都有一个社区居委会直接选举的试点,居民委员会由居民会议、居民代表会议选举产生并受其监督。在北京市东城区九道湾居委会选举改革试点的过程中,从选举方式的抉择到初步候选人的产生,从正式候选人的确定到最终选举居民委员会,都充分尊重居民的意愿,体现了居民委员会产生过程中的群众性、自治性。其次,转变传统的考核机制,取消一些行政性的以居委会为单位的考核内容和考核指标,使居民成为考核主体,以居民的满意度作为考核居委会工作实绩的标准。

(3)重点是服务居民

从功能上讲,居民自治的体制构架在加强居委会的传统功能的同时还衍生出新的功能,主要体现在以下五个方面:一是宏观规划。全国大多数社区都结合本社区的实际情况,以关注居民的需求为出发点,对社区发展进行统一规划,确定社区的长期、中期、近期发展目标和任务。二是议事决策。定期召开居民代表会议和居民会议,商讨本社区全体居民的重大事项和公益事业,并作出相关决定。三是组织管理。由于居民委员会直接面对的是广大居民,事情繁杂多样,这些事情若全部让居民委员会来完成是不可能的,这就需要组织居民开展自我管理、自我教育和自我服务的活动,就日常的居民自治事务进行管理。四是协调沟通。居民委员会对内在本社区创造了和睦宁静的社区环境,对外代表居民与政府以及物业公司等进行谈判协调,维护居民的利益。五是监督社区。定期听取社会工作者的工作汇报,检查工作落实情况,就其工作进行评议并提出工作建议。总之,社区居民委员会的功能就是服从和服务城市居民的意志和利益需求,集中精力为社区居民服务。

3. 社区居民自治的案例——上海市浦东新区潍坊街道的基层居民自治创新

浦东新区潍坊街道经过十多年的不断探索,走出了一条居民民主自治的新路子,其创新特点主要体现为"四自":

①居委会居民自选。"小区居委会,民主来选举"。早在 1999 年,潍坊街道源竹居委会试点"直选"取得成功,2000 年推广到 14 个居委会。到 2006 年,潍坊街道 27 个居委会全部采用"海选"方式选举,是上海最先实行百分之百"海选"街道。通过"海选",使热心社区事业、具备社会动员能力和实践工作能力的人士走到前台,使居委会成为居民

更加信赖,能够代表、维护和实现群众利益的自治组织,更好地体现了基层人民群众当家作主的权利。

②重大问题居民自治。"小区是我家,居民共当家"。居委会作为传递民意的通道,利益汇聚的桥梁,涉及居民区公共生活的一些重大问题,通过居委会牵头进行协商,实行自治。以潍坊街道"宜居家园"建设为例。当时,基层政府主动投入巨资为老百姓改善居住环境,结果却是众口难调。有车的家庭强烈要求拓宽小区道路,无车的家庭则坚决反对;窗前绿化,楼层低受影响的家庭要求调整,不受影响的则不同意调整。面对这一难题,潍坊街道广泛征求意见,拟定多个方案,让大家来决策后再实施,居民都很满意。

③群众团队居民自组。"小区有舞台,大家来参与"。潍坊街道现有居民自组的文体团队 200 多个,街道还每年定期举办体育健身节、文化艺术节、教育读书节和科学普及节,这些主题鲜明、丰富多彩的活动,吸引了居民的广泛参与,有效促进了社区的文明程度和居民素质的提高。

④家园管理居民自理。"小区是个家、管理靠大家"。小区居民自愿担任志愿者,积极参与小区管理,进行家园自治已蔚然成风,出现了"双增双多"现象,即社区归属感增强了,热爱小区的居民多了;参与自治的意识增强了,愿为小区服务的居民多了。截至 2011 年,潍坊街道共有小区志愿者服务站 27 个,参加社区志愿者活动的文明单位 37 个,各种志愿者服务队近百个,志愿者 1 万余人。

思考题

1. 不同的经济体制对城市社区管理有什么影响?

2. 从社区管理模式走向社区治理模式,您认为中国应加强哪些方面的工作?

3. 在中国的城市社区居民自治体制中,如何做到在加强党对居民自治的领导的同时又能促进居民自治的健康发展?

参考文献

陈宪等：《社区经济与社区服务》，上海：上海大学出版社，2001 年。

程玉申：《中国城市社区发展研究》，上海：华东师范大学出版社，2002 年。

林尚立等：《社区组织与居委会建设》，上海：上海大学出版社，2001 年。

卢汉龙：《社区服务的组织建设》，《上海社会科学院季刊》2002 年第 2 期。

马西恒、刘中起：《都市社区治理：以上海建设国际化城市为背景》，上海：学林出版社，2011 年。

彭勃：《当代中国城市社区变革》，北京：中国社会出版社，2007 年。

（一）中国城市文化遗产保护历程

文化遗产,广义地说,包括有形物质文化遗产,也包括无形的非物质形态的文化遗产,如戏剧、音乐、民俗、节日活动等。在有形的物质文化遗产中,又包括可移动文物,如古玩、字画、典籍等,不可移动文物如古遗址、古建筑、古窟寺等。在《文物保护法》中"不可移动文物"的章节下,包括"文物保护单位"、"历史文化街区"、"历史文化名城",这里的"文物"概念实际上是广义的文物,与国际上"文化遗产"(heritage)的概念相近。在中国的城市规划界,经常将"文物保护单位"、"历史文化街区"、"历史文化名城"统称为"历史文化遗产",不包括无形文物和可移动文物,可被视为"文化遗产"的狭义概念。本章中使用的"文物"、"历史文化遗产"两词均取其狭义的含义。

1. 改革开放前的城市文化遗产保护

中国是个具有 5000 年文明史、拥有 56 个民族的文明古国,文化遗产相当丰厚。但是,由于历史的原因,中国对历史文化遗产的保护比欧洲晚得多。19 世纪后期、20 世纪初期,随着帝国主义入侵中国,一些欧美国家的传教士及学者来到中国,其中有很多人是为了掠夺中国的文物和财富。中国现代意义上的文物保护开始于 20 世纪 20 年代的考古科学研究,北京大学于 1922 年设立考古学研究所,后又设立了考古学会,这是中国历史上最早的文物保护学术研究机构。当时的政府在 1930 年 6 月颁布了《文物保护法》,以后又公布了《古物保护法细则》,于 1932 年设立了中央文物保管委员会,也做过一些有益的工作,但由于政局动荡和战乱,各地大量文物疏于管理,法规形同虚设。

1949 年以后,中国政府针对战争造成的大量文物破坏及文物流失现象,颁布了一系列有关法令,设置了中央和地方管理机构,成立考古研究所,推行了一系列保护文物的举措,至 20 世纪 60 年代中期已初步形成了中国文物的保护制度。这个时期的重要特点表现为保护的是单个的古建筑的文物,也包括建筑物和历史遗迹、风景名胜景点。1961 年 3 月,国务院颁布《文物保护管理暂行条例》,同时公布了 180 个第一批全国重点文物保护单位,实施了以命名“文物保护单位”来保护文物古迹的制度。

1966 年开始的“文化大革命”使国家的法规制度受到严重破坏,文物保护事业蒙受巨大损失。

2. 改革开放之后的城市文化遗产保护

1978 年以后,文物保护和城市规划管理工作逐步得到恢复。1982 年国务院公布了第二批全国重点文物保护单位,1982 年 2 月公布首批 24 个国家级历史文化名城,标志着历史古城保护制度的创立。1982 年 11 月颁布了《文物保护法》。1984 年 1 月,国务院颁布《城市规划条例》,规定城市规划应当切实保护文物古迹,保护和发扬民族风格和地方特点。1986年,国务院公布了第二批38个国家级历史文化名城,并在文件中规定了保护有价值的历史街区、建筑群、小镇、村落等历史地段,各省还可以公布本地的省级名城。至此,中国历史文化遗产保护的概念由"点"的保护,扩展到"面"的保护,即以文物建筑、建筑群为中心的保护扩展到城市中某个地区或整个城区,建立了历史文化名城保护以及风景名胜区的保护制度,形成了中国历史文化遗产的分级保护体系(参见专栏7-1)。

专栏7-1 中国历史文化遗产的分级保护体系

与国外不同,按照中国现行的法律政策,可以把历史文化遗产保护分为三个层次,即保护文物保护单位、保护历史文化街区、保护历史文化名城。对文物保护单位,遵循不改变原状的原则,可称为"原物"保护;对历史文化街区,保护街区整体风貌,建筑只求保存外观、允许改造内部,可称为"原貌"保护;对历史文化名城中既非文物保护单位、又非历史文化保护区的其他地区,可进行新的建设,只要求在建设中保护和延续古城的格局和风貌特色,可称为"风貌"保护。这种分层次的有差别的保护方法符合中国历史文化遗产保护现状的实际情况,能有效解决保护与建设之间的矛盾。

1990年以后,由于城市经济的迅速发展和房地产业的兴起,许多历史城市中有价值的历史街区和地段遭到破坏,致使历史环境的保护面临新的问题。因此,1994年3月由建设部和国家文物局联合聘任组建了"全国历史文化名城保护专家委员会",以加强对名城的保护监督和技术咨询,以及协助各地政府对名城的保护和管理工作。此外,国家文物局于2002年颁布了修订后的《文物保护法》;建设部于2005年发布国家标准《历史文化名城保护规划规范》;国务院于2008年发布《历史文化名城名镇名村保护条例》,以完善中国的历史文化遗产保护事业,使其逐步走向法制化轨道。

（二）中国城市文物古迹保护

1. 中国城市文物古迹的保护方式和保护原则

文物古迹包括古文化遗址、古墓葬、古建筑、古窟寺、石刻、壁画、近现代重要史迹和代表性建筑等。根据《文物保护法》的规定，中国政府按照历史、科学、艺术价值对各类重要的遗址、遗迹等不可移动文物，以定为各级文物保护单位的方式加以保护。全国共有县级重点文物保护单位6万处，省级重点文物保护单位近7000处，国家级重点文物保护单位1268处。

《文物保护法》是国家文物古迹保护的法律基础，该法确定了文物保护的方针，即"保护为主，抢救第一，合理利用，加强管理"。保护的目的是真实全面地保护并延续其"历史信息"和全部价值。所有的保护措施都应该遵守不改变文物现状的原则。

2. 建筑类文化遗产保护的法律规定

在《文物保护法》中，对建筑类文化遗产的保护是文化遗产保护重点之一。《中华人民共和国文物保护法》第十七条规定，在"文物保护单位的保护范围内不得进行其他建设工程或者爆破、钻探、挖掘等作业"。特殊情况者必须保证文物保护单位的安全，在征得上级人民政府文物行政部门同意的情况下，经当地人民政府批准方可实施。在全国重点文物保护单位的保护范围内进行大型施工，必须征得国务院文物行政部门的同意和当地人民政府的批准。

各级文物保护单位除需划定保护范围外，还需在文物保护单位的周围"划出一定的建设控制地带"，以保证历史建筑与周边环境的和谐统一。"在文物保护单位的建设控制地带内进行建设工程，不得破坏文物保护单位的历史风貌"，"不得建设污染文物保护单位及其环境的设施，不得进行可能影响文物保护单位安全及其环境的活动。对已有的污染文物保护单位及其环境的设施，应当限期治理"。"建设工程选址，应当尽可能避开不可移动文物；因特殊情况不能避开的，对文物保护单位应当尽可能实施原址保护。""无法实施原址保护,必须迁移异地保护或者拆除的,应当报省、自治区、直辖市人民政府批准;迁移或者拆除省级文物保护单位的,批准前须征得国务院文物行政部门同意。全国重点文物保护单位不得拆除;需要迁移的,须由省、自治区、直辖市人民政府报国务院批准。"

此外,《中华人民共和国文物保护法》第二十一条还对历史建筑保护的责权问题做了具体规定:"国有不可移动文物由使用人负责修缮、保养;非国有不可移动文物由所有人负责修缮、保养。非国有不可移动文物有损毁危险,所有人不具备修缮能力的,当地人民政府应当给予帮助;所有人具备修缮能力而拒不依法履行修缮义务的,县级以上人民政府可以给予抢救修缮,所需费用由所有人负担。"同时对"不可移动文物进行修缮、保养、迁移,必须遵守不改变文物原状的原则"。《中华人民共和国文物保护法》第二十二条规定:"不可移动文物已经全部毁坏的,应当实施遗址保护,不得在原址重建。"因特殊原因需要在原址重建的,需要向上级主管部门报批。

3. 文物建筑保护中"不改变文物原状"的原则

1982年,中国将"不改变文物原状"原则写入《文物保护法》,明确要求"对不可移动文物进行修缮、保养、迁移,必须遵守不改变文物原状的原则"。按照这一原则,对文物建筑的修缮应坚持"四个保存",即保存原来的建筑形制、保存原来的建筑结构、保存原来的建筑材料和保存原来的工艺技术。这一原则有利于保护文物建筑的真实性和完整性。文化建筑是历史的物证,不改变其原状,是谨慎保存历史空间和文化记忆的良方,便于人们借此追踪文脉,感受历史。

"不改变文物原状"原则要求在文物建筑保护中具备一系列保障措施。第一,要有坚持尊重历史的理念。要尊重各时代为文物建筑所做的正当贡献,对于去除后代修缮痕迹、恢复到一定历史时期状态的做法,进行充分鉴别和谨慎论证。第二,要以保护原物为主。坚持以保存原物加固为主,以修复原物消除隐患为主。第三,保护历史古貌。尽可能多地留存文物建筑的原汁原味,减少现代人干预的痕迹。第四,评估与研究。对文物建筑进行价值和现状评估,制定文物建筑保护修缮的具体措施,延长文物建筑的寿命。第五,加强科技创新。在科学研究和充分试验的基础上,采用新技术、新材料对原材料进行加固补强,确保文物安全。第六,保护非物质遗产。在文物建筑保护维修过程中,坚持使用传统工艺、技术、材料,以保存凝聚古代技术精华的工艺的真实性并使之得以传承。

专栏7-2 西藏拉萨布达拉宫的保护

拉萨布达拉宫是世界上现存规模最大、保存最完整的宫堡建筑群之一。2002年对布达拉宫开展了第二次全面保护维修工程。

依照遵循原设计的原则,维修人员首先对布达拉宫的各部分建筑进行了详细的测绘和研究。由于布达拉宫建筑的群体可以分成若干单元,各单元的建造年代、功能及建造方法并不完全一致,因而需要逐个单元进行测绘和分析,再制定维修保护方案。同时,维修人员还对西藏特有的建筑材料和传统工艺进行认真研究,注重传统工艺与现代科技的结合,采用新技术、新材料对原材料进行加固补强,弥补传统工艺、材料的不足,实现文物保护技术的传承、完善和发展(图7-1)。

图7-1 布达拉宫雪景(新华社记者普布扎西摄)

（三）中国城市历史文化街区保护

1. 中国历史文化街区保护的定义和保护原则

1982 年颁布的《文物保护法》规定，"保存文物特别丰富，具有重大历史价值和革命意义的街区（村、镇）定为历史文化街区（村、镇）"。在建设部和国家文物局起草的《历史文化名城保护条例（送审稿）》中"历史文化街区"的定义是："城市中保留遗存较为丰富，能够比较完整真实地反映一定历史时期传统风貌或民族地方特色，存有较多文物古迹、近现代史迹和历史建筑，并具有一定规模的地区。"这个定义突出了"传统风貌"和"一定的规模"这两个关键点，体现了它与"文物保护单位"在层次上的差别。

历史文化街区的保护原则有三个。第一，是保护真实历史遗存，这和文物古迹保护类似；第二，是保护外观整体风貌，这与文物古迹保护有差别，它意味着内部可以改造更新，也意味着保护的重点不只是建筑物，还包括环境风貌等多重内容；第三，是维护并发扬原有的使用功能，保护的不仅是物质躯壳，还包括它们承载的社会、文化活动，以保持活力，延续生活。

2. 历史文化街区保护规划的要点

第一，划定保护范围和建筑控制地带的界限。历史街区的范围应同时满足历史街区的三个核定标准，即历史真实性、生活真实性和风貌完整性，根据街区的具体情况来划定。所谓历史真实性标准是指历史街区内应保存有一定数量和比例的记载历史信息的真实的物质实体，如历史性建、构筑物等，它们是街区整体氛围的主导因素。历史真实性的定量标准主要从历史街区内建筑的年代来分析。一般情况下，中国历史街区中能体现传统建筑风貌年代的历史建筑的数量或建筑面积占街区建筑总量的比例应达到 50% 左右。所谓生活真实性标准是指历史街区不仅是过去人们生活和居住的场所，而且现在仍然并将继续发挥它的功能，是社会生活中自然而有机的组成部分。生活真实性有两个评判标准：一是原有居民的保有率,这个标准是可以量化的;二是原有生活方式的保存度,即历史街区应该是该城市或地区传统文化和生活方式保存最为完整、最有特色的地区,其原有的传统生活方式的保存度应该是该地区最高的,这是一个定性的指标。目前中国历史街区的人口保有率应在60%左右,这样基本可以保证历史街区的社会生活结构和方式不被破坏,同时原有居民的保有率又可以满足现行国家居住标准和现代生活标准。所谓风貌完整性标准包含有两层含义:一是该区域内视野所及范围风貌基本一致,有较完整和可整治的视觉环境;二是历史街区要有合适规模,规模的确定应兼顾两个方面的要求:历史街区是建筑行为受到限制即风貌整治的实施地区,所以范围划定不宜过大;同时又要求有相对的风貌完整性,能具有相对完整的社会生活结构体系,因此范围划定不宜太小。因此,历史街区内风貌好和较好的建筑比例应达到50%左右,最低不应低于30%;风貌差的障碍建筑比例一般应控制在20%左右,不应高于30%。另外,历史街区总体应该有一个规模控制,核心保护区的面积建议在15—30公顷,而历史街区的总面积建议在30—55公顷左右。

第二,确定区内建筑物保护和整治的做法,可分为四种情况。已定为"文物保护单位"和规划认为应该定为"文物保护单位"的,按"文物保护单位"办法做;较好地保存着历史风貌的"历史建筑",外观依原貌维修整饰,室内可以按现代生活的要求进行改建,增加必要的设施。内部的结构已遭较大损坏的,可以更换结构,但其外观还应维持历史的面貌;外观与历史风貌相协调的新建筑,可以保留不动;地区内与历史风貌相冲突的新建筑,如高大的现代建筑等,应该进行改造,或在立面上加以处理,或砍掉几层,或者将来拆除。

第三,确定地区环境要素的保护整治要求,包括要按照历史风貌维修路面、维修驳岸、保护古树等。

第四,改造、建设地区的市政设施,解决排雨水、排污、供电、电讯、消防等问题。

为了更严格地制止破坏历史文化街区的行为,2003年11月建设部公布了《城市紫线管理办法》(以下简称《办法》),对国家历史文化名城中的"历史文化街区"、省级人政府公布的"历史文化街区",以及"历史文化街区"以外经县以上人民政府公布的"历史建筑"划出保护界限,称为"紫线"。《办法》规定了紫线要包括保护的核心地段和外围建设控制区,紫线范围内确定的保护建筑不得拆除,建筑物的新建和改建不得影响该区的传统格局和风貌,不得破坏规划保留的园林绿地、河湖水系、道路和古树名木等。

3. 中国近年来历史街区保护和整治的成功实例

自从确立了历史街区保护制度,中国的历史街区保护工作取得了长足的进展,开展了很多历史街区的保护和整治工作。下面介绍几个中国历史街区保护比较成功的实例。

(1)平遥南大街

在山西省晋中市平遥县,有一座具有 2700 多年历史的平遥古城,是第二批国家历史文化名城。位于平遥古城中心区的南大街于 1997 年进行了整治,将原来架在空中的电缆和电信线缆埋入地下,把沥青路面恢复为条石铺砌,并鼓励沿街居民开店铺和办民俗展览。经过修整,该街区很好地保存了原有的历史风貌,同时又繁荣了经济,发展了旅游(图 7-2)。

图 7-2　平遥南大街整治后街景(新华社记者范敏达摄)

（2）丽江

丽江古城位于云南省丽江市，是第二批被批准的国家历史文化名城。该古城利用第一批国家历史街区保护资助对街区的排水工程和照明工程进行改造，恢复了历史风貌，促进了古城的保护和经济的发展（图7-3）。目前，丽江古城和山西平遥古城一起成为中国仅有的以整座古城申报世界文化遗产获得成功的两座古县城，也是中国著名的旅游胜地。

图7-3 丽江古城街景（新华社记者蔺以光摄）

（3）黄山市屯溪老街

屯溪老街位于安徽省黄山市屯溪区，于1995年被确定为当时的建设部试点保护的历史街区。该历史街区的改造采取政府投资改善基础设施，居民自己出资整饰店面的方式共同完成。经过改造的屯溪老街的旅游业发展良好,成为黄山旅游者的必游之处(图7-4)。

图7-4　黄山市屯溪老街(新华社记者王雷摄)

(4)桐乡市乌镇古街

　　位于浙江省桐乡市的乌镇是一座风貌保存比较完整的江南古镇。1999年起桐乡市组织成立了专门机构,制定一系列政策文件①,有步骤地对历史街区进行了环境和建筑整治,完整地保护性恢复了原来的历史风貌和景观。乌镇用旧料来更换修补老屋、老街、老桥的办法,重现古镇原貌,供电、通信、有线电视等线路从以往架在空中的方式改为全部埋入地下的方式,沿街每户设抽水马桶,旅游事业得到快速发展(图7-5)。

---

① 桐乡市组织了乌镇保护与开发的专门机构——乌镇古镇保护与旅游开发管理委员会,制定的政策文件主要有《乌镇保护与旅游开发拆迁办法》、《乌镇古镇保护与开发管理办法》、《加快乌镇古镇保护与旅游开发的若干政策意见》等。

图7-5　桐乡市乌镇古街(新华社记者谭进摄)

（四）中国历史文化名城保护

1.历史文化名城保护的定义和选定标准

（1）历史文化名城的定义

1982年公布的《文物保护法》第二章第8条规定："保护文物特别丰富,具有重大历史价值和革命价值的城市,由国家文化行政管理部门会同城乡建设环境部门报国务院核定公布为历史文化名城"。历史文化名城是中国特有的概念,它并非保护城市全部,它的保护内容和范围是通过城市规划来确定的,这和国外的情况不太一样①。

（2）历史文化名城的选定标准

中国选定历史文化名城主要有三条标准:第一,城市历史悠久,仍

---

① 王景慧:《历史文化遗产保护中城市规划的作用——论城市规划与文物保护的互动》,《中国文物科学研究》2006年第1期。

保存有较为丰富、完好的文物古迹,具有重大的历史、科学、艺术价值;第二,城市的现状格局和风貌仍保留着历史特色,并具有一定数量的代表城市传统风貌的街区;第三,文物古迹主要分布在城市市区和郊区,保护和合理使用这些历史文化遗产对该城市的性质、布局、建设方针有重要影响。

2. 中国历史文化名城的特点

中国的历史文化名城主要有以下两个特点。

第一,数量相对较多。中国现有国家级历史文化名城 101 座,分别是国务院于 1982 年公布的第一批共 24 个,1986 年公布的第二批共 38 个,1994 年公布的第三批共 37 个,2001 年分两次公布的 2 个。就数量而言,中国的历史文化名城堪称世界之最。例如,英国确定的国家名城只有 4 座,但是,与中国的情况不同的是,该国将更多的保护重点集中在保护区与文物古迹方面,仅英格兰就有登录建筑① 50 万处,保护区 8000 多处。

第二,类型复杂。根据形成历史、自然和人文地理以及城市物质要素和功能结构等方面的特征,可以将 101 座历史文化名城划分为七种类型。一是古都型,以都城时代的历史遗存物、古都的风貌为特点的城市。二是传统风貌型,保留了某一时期及几个历史时期积淀下来的完整的建筑群体的城市。三是风景名胜型,自然环境对这类城市的特色形成起着决定性的作用,由于建筑与山水环境的有机结合而显示出其鲜明的个性特征。四是地方及民族特色型,位于民族地区的城镇由于地域差异、文化环境、历史变迁的影响,显示出不同的地方特色或独有的个性特征,民族风情、地方文化、地域特色构成城市风貌的主体。五是近现代史迹型,以反映历史的某一事件或某个阶段的建筑物或建筑物群为其显著特色的城市。六是特殊职能型,城市中的某种职能在历史上有极突出的地位,并且在某种程度上成为这些城市的特征。七是一般史迹型,以分散在全城各处的文物古迹作为历史传统特色体现的主要方式。

① 文物登录制度是西方发达国家广泛采用的历史保护制度。

3. 历史文化名城的保护原则和保护内容

（1）保护原则

历史文化名城的保护原则是既要使城市的文化遗产得以保护，又要促进城市经济社会的发展，不断改善居民的工作生活环境。城市是有生命的有机体，有成千上万的人在那里生活和工作。城市经济要发展，设施要改善，人民的生活水平要提高，要实现现代化，因而保护历史文化名城还要积极利用丰富的历史文化资源，充分发挥其在城市经济、社会、文化等多方面的促进作用。

（2）保护内容

中国历史文化名城主要保护三方面的内容：一是保护文物古迹和历史地区，这可以划出具体的保护范围界限；二是保护和延续古城格局和风貌特色，这是对古城的全面要求，要通过城市规划提出一系列的保护控制要求及管理措施来实现；三是继承和发扬优秀历史文化传统，这不只是文物和城市规划部门的事，还需要全社会来共同关注。

专栏 7-3 苏州古城整体保护

中国江苏省苏州市的苏州古城，面积 14.2 平方公里，历经 2500 多年，城址未变为世所罕见。苏州古城是中国首个实行整体保护规划和实践的城市，多年来苏州城极好地保护了古城的旧貌，和苏州 20 世纪 80 年代的照片相比，目前苏州古城的天际线未有显著改变。2003 年，苏州市对城市总体规划进行新一轮修编，划定了 29 个历史地段；还研究制定了《城市规划若干强制性内容的暂行规定》，对古城的建筑高度、色彩、形式、体量进行了规定，以此来保护古城整体风貌。在全国率先实施了城市紫线管理，把古城保护、文物保护纳入城市规划强制性内容之中。2012 年 10 月 26 日，苏州在古城保护方面又推出一个重大举措——挂牌成立苏州国家历史文化名城保护区。苏州古城整体保护的持续推行为全国古城的整体保护提供了很多可资借鉴的宝贵经验。

在保护历史文化名城中,从城市整体角度采取综合性保护措施是历史文化名城保护的特点和要旨。只有从全局角度寻求正确处理保护与发展关系的途径,才可以既满足城市发展建设的要求,又为保护文物古迹、历史街区创造条件。这些措施包括确定适合于保护历史古城的社会经济发展战略;确定合理的城市布局和发展方向,保护古城,开发新区;改善古城功能,保护古城空间形态,保护重要景观间的视廊,给文物古迹以突出的展现。在历史文化名城的非历史传统地区,即城市新区,新的建设本不必受到诸多限制,但作为一个城市整体,还应该创造自己的城市特色,避免千城一面。对有深厚历史文化传统的历史文化名城来说,应该尊重历史传统,延续历史传统,建设与历史相联系的美好城市特色。

专栏7-4　杭州"保老城建新城"双赢发展策略

浙江省杭州市是中国七大古都之一,中国首批历史文化名城,以西湖等名胜古迹享誉海内外。改革开放以来,杭州市始终把建立历史文化名城,保护历史文化遗产作为第一生产力,在城市化进程中很好地协调了"保老城"与"建新城"的关系,在保护名城与城市化推进之间找到了最佳平衡点。杭州按照"保老城、建新城"的理念,把保护的重点放在老城区,"保老城"中"城"的保护,就是重点保护好西湖,保护好杭州老城区"腰鼓城"的布局结构和"三面云山一面城"城市空间轮廓线。"建新城"就是把建设、发展的重点、产业集聚的重点、人口集聚的重点全部转移到新城区,通过建设钱江新城,推动杭州城市发展由"西湖时代"迈向"钱塘江时代",推进城市又好又快地发展。经过短短十多年时间,沿钱塘江两岸整个城市的布局框架已经拉开,新城的规模已经形成,大量的人口和产业在新城集聚,大大减轻了老城区的压力和负担,不仅使历史文化名城得到了更好保护,而且有力地推动了杭州城市沿江跨江发展,实现了保护与发展的"共赢"①。

---

① 王国平:《城市怎么办》,人民出版社2010年版。

思 考 题

1. 中国城市文化遗产保护理念的转变是什么?

2. 中国城市文化遗产保护的实现路径有哪些?

3. 中国城市文化遗产保护利用有哪些新的经验模式?

参考文献

阮仪三、王景慧、王林:《历史文化名城保护理论与规划》,上海:同济大学出版社,1998 年。

单霁翔:《留住城市文化的"根"与"魂"——中国文化遗产保护的探索与实践》,北京:科学出版社,2010 年。

王林、王骏:《历史街区保护规划编制方法研究》,《城市规划》1998 年第 3 期。

王景慧:《历史地段保护的概念和作法》,《城市规划》1998 年第 3 期。

Robert Riddell, *Sustainable Urban Planning*, Blackwell Publishing Ltd, London, 2004.

Stephen M. Wheeler, *Planning for Sustainability*, Routledge, London, 2004.

Preface

What is the state system of China? How has the Communist Party of China (CPC) managed to exercize long-term governance and to lead the Chinese people from one victory to another? What are the 'secrets' of the CPC's governance? What is China's development road? What significant strategies have been adopted in China? What is the next step in China's development? Why has China been able to achieve such rapid economic development? These are just some of the many questions frequently asked by the international community, especially foreign political parties and statesmen on their visits to China. For the purpose of providing answers to these questions and enabling readers to be informed about the real China and the CPC, we arranged for the *Understanding Modern China* Series (hereinafter referred to as the Series) to be written, to serve as elementary documents introducing the CPC, as well as China's development road, development theories and development experience.

The *Series* is inspired by the new philosophies, new ideas and new strategies for the country's governance put forward by General Secretary Xi Jinping since the 18th National Congress of the CPC, aimed at the following aspects: strenuously reflecting the development vision of 'the Chinese Dream' and the development prospects of the 'Two Centenary Goals'; strenuously reflecting the coordinated promotion of the overall situation of a five-pronged approach to building socialism with Chinese characteristics (to build up socialist economy, socialist democracy, socialist advanced culture, socialist harmonious society, and socialist ecological civilization), and the 'Four-Pronged Comprehensive Strategy' (comprehensively completing the building of a Moderately Prosperous Society, comprehensively deepening reform, comprehensively advancing the rule of law, comprehensively exercising strict party goverance); strenuously reflect the 'new normal' facilitating and leading China's economic development and the implementation of the 'five major development concepts' (to promote innovative, coordinated, green, open, and shared development); strenuously reflecting the three major economic development strategies of the 'Belt and Road', the coordinated development of Beijing, Tianjin and Hebei province, and the Yangtze river economic belt. On the basis of a great number of fresh cases and experiences, the Series tells China's story, transmits China's voice, analyzes China's problems, and offers China solutions.

The Series has been written on the basis of telling China's story and transmitting China's voice, oriented around the following four aspects: the first is to illustrate the new measures taken to deepen reform since the 18th National Congress of the CPC, the new ideas on economic development and the new philosophy on foreign affairs, on the basis of an all-round introduction to the achievements since the reform and opening up; the second is to analyze the reason for the achievements, the underlying operating law, and the process of evolution, while presenting the development achievements of China's economy and society; the third is to keep to problem orientation and demand orientation, rather than attempt to be all-embracing and systematic, so as to clear up targeted doubts and confusion on the basis of the demands of foreign readers; the fourth is to introduce China not only in terms of 'where it is coming from', but also in terms of 'where it is going', for the purpose of enabling readers to know about China's historical development process on the one hand, and on the other hand, exemplifying and clarifying how China assures the organic unification of its past, present and future, the organic combination of inheritance and innovation, and how China is planning its future development.

Under the guidance of the International Department of the CPC Central Committee, the writing of the Series has been organized by China Executive Leadership Academy Pudong (CELAP).

The International Department of the CPC Central Committee is the functional department of the CPC in charge of foreign affairs. So far, the CPC has established connections of various types with more than 600 political parties and organizations in over 160 countries and regions, which include left-wing and right-wing parties; both ruling parties and opposition parties. Foreign affairs work is of paramount importance to the CPC, and an indispensable component of national diplomacy as a whole, whose target is to promote state-to-state and people-to-people communication and understanding.

CELAP is a national leadership institution in China, and as a platformon which international cooperative training and exchange are carried out, CELAP has held fast to its characteristics of internationality and openness since March 2005 when it was founded. CELAP spares no effort in implementing international cooperative training, with target participants being foreign political parties and statesmen, high-ranking business executives and senior professionals. By the end of 2015, CELAP had offered training programs to more than 6,000 participants from over 130 countries, and thus has won wide recognition and received a favorable reception from the countries, regions and participants that are involved.

To cater for the needs of foreign participants, CELAP initiated the writing of the Series at the beginning of 2012, and after four years of modifications and improvements, the finalized manuscripts were completed at the end of 2015. The first batch of 10 books to be published in this Series are: *China's New Strategies for Governing the Country; The Communist Party of China: the Past, Present and Future of Party Building; China's Reform, Opening Up and Construction of Development Zones; An Insider's Guide to the Inner Workings and Structure of the Chinese Government and Public Services; New Analysis of Urbanization in China; China's Agriculture and Rural Development in the Post-Reform Era; The Evolution of China's Diplomacy in the Modern Era; The Selection and Appointment of Officials in China; Leadership Education and Training in China; and Shanghai – the 'Pacesetter' of China's Reform and Opening Up.*

The authors of the Series are mainly professionals in CELAP, and functionaries and specialists in the Development Research Center of the Shanghai Municipal People's Government, Shanghai Institute for International Studies and Hangzhou Research Center for Urban Studies.

The Series is published in Chinese and English, with the English translation done mainly by senior professors at Shanghai International Studies University, to whom thanks are due. Gratitude also goes to the People's Publishing House for its great support and positive suggestions in the process of writing and translating.

Writing such a series of textbooks for mature foreign students is a first in China. Constructive criticism is welcome, for the Series as a new endeavor can hardly be free from mistakes.

Editorial Committee of the *Understanding Modern China* Series
January 2016
(Translator: Wang Xin)

Alain Charles Asia (ACA) Publishing Ltd is delighted to be associated with the People's Publishing House to bring this series of 10 *Understanding Modern China* books to an English-speaking readership.

ACA, formerly known as ACP (Alain Charles Publishing) Ltd Beijing, was founded in October 1989 and was the first foreign-owned publishing company to be allowed to open an office in China.

In 2007, ACP Beijing was renamed ACA Publishing Ltd to better reflect its focus on China and the Asia-Pacific region. The company specialises in publishing books about China for international readers and has offices in Beijing and London.

ACA Publishing Ltd,
April 2016

Contents

Introduction

Urbanization, an inexorable trend of economic and social development, can act as a benchmark to gauge the economic and societal progress of a country or region. Over the past six decades or so since the founding of the People's Republic of China (PRC), and especially since the reform and opening-up process was launched, we have witnessed a marked upward spike in China's urbanization. With a population of 1.3 billion, China's urbanization will have a major impact on the development of the world as well as on the country itself. Joseph Eugene Stiglitz, the acclaimed American economist, notes that there will be two major events affecting the development of human society in the 21st century: one is the next round of the US-led new technological revolution, and the other is China's urbanization. The treasured efforts and practices of China, therefore, will make a significant contribution to global urbanization in the years to come.

1. Objectives

With time and space respectively as the vertical and horizontal axes, the authors of this book study urbanization in China to dynamically explore the evolution of the economy, society, ecology and culture associated with urbanization, to display the overall distinctive properties of urbanization in present-day China and to reveal the idea, the way and the experience of the country that is already well on its way to being urbanized. The ultimate objective is to acquaint readers with China's development strategy and philosophical outlook adopted in urbanization so that they may, in the long run, apply what they learn to their own local administration.

2. Framework

This book consists of seven chapters in total. Chapter One describes the past and the present of urbanization in China and comes up with some policies and measures for addressing current problems so as to ensure the sound development of China's urbanization.

The second chapter looks at the history of China's urban-rural planning since its inception, sums up the lessons and experience in its historical development, and then outlines the executive and operative systems, so that readers will have a global perspective of China's urban-rural planning.

Chapter Three reviews the evolution of the industrial layout and distribution in cities in China during its transition from a planned economy to a socialist market economy. It includes a detailed introduction to the establishment of development zones and construction of new towns or newly developed urban districts that function as the primary spatial carriers for the development of urban industries in China.

Chapter Four is devoted to elaborating on the impressive achievements, serviceable practices, overarching problems and workable countermeasures in China's urban infrastructure construction.

Chapter Five depicts the basic framework worked out since the implementation of reform and opening up for the paid use of urban land, with the focus on a detailed presentation of the property system, the management of utilization and the market regulation of urban land in China that gives an overall insight into China's urban land system.

Chapter Six reconsiders the evolution of the urban community management system in China, examines its background and the striking features that distinguish the system, and introduces the subject of urban community services and the self-management of urban communities in China.

By means of case analysis, the last chapter sums up China's practices in its effort to work out a graded or assorted protection of its historical and cultural heritage.

3. Highlights and Challenges

This book has a number of distinguishing features: by looking back to the recorded history of urbanization in China, the authors have dwelt on the perceived changes taking place in towns and cities since the start of reform and opening up and in the meantime expounded how the Chinese government has been working to set up and bring into force an institutional framework to guarantee that urbanization develops in a sustained way, so that readers will be well versed in China's realities and relevant background information that will help them further explore the development of urbanization in China.

The most challenging task for the authors is to address foreign readers' demands and interests, analyze the general features and requirements of cross-cultural communication, describe the national realities in plain but vivid language, narrate the history of China's urbanization by means of lively examples, and provide overseas students with teaching materials that are enjoyable, readable and pragmatic.

4. Directions

This book combines flexibility and openness in terms of its table of contents and teaching requirements as well as in the presentation and arrangement of chapters. Instructors, therefore, are encouraged to adopt an open and flexible teaching principle so that they can make the best use of it. The book is expected to have lasting relevance since the content of each chapter reflects the most basic and fundamental structure of knowledge; a coursebook compiled with a passive mentality would not be able to capture the latest state of affairs in China's urbanization. This being the case, all teachers are advised to energetically seek fresh information, keep on learning and acquire new skills so that they can stimulate interest in class. As for students, they should work to integrate or incorporate what they learn from this book with social realities so that they will have a deeper insight into the social and economic development in China.

Occasional slips are inevitable in a book and all suggestions will be highly appreciated. This book has been a joint effort: chapters one, two, three and five were written by Chu Tianjiao, while chapter four was jointly written by Chu Tianjiao and Zhu Yuan; chapter six was composed by Chen Zheng, while the concluding chapter was a joint effort between Li Mingchao and Shao Ying.

CHAPTER 1
Ongoing Urbanization in China

I. Development and Current Situation

Urbanization means a shift or transition of people who were dependent on agriculture to non-agricultural sectors, along with a growing intensification of production and pattern of life.[①] Urbanization in China, which accounts for a quarter of the population of all developing countries, will make a significant contribution to global urbanization in the 21st century. From 1975 to 2000, the urban population of the world increased by 1.317 billion, with an average annual growth of 52.68 million; out of this total, 1.164 billion were from developing countries, giving an average annual increase of 46.52 million. From 1978 to 2003, China's urban population increased by only 352 million, with an average annual growth of 14.05 million. This gave a growth rate that was just a quarter of the world average and approximately one third of that of developing countries during the same period. In years to come, the robust development of urbanization in China will help address many important issues and it will be regarded as one of the most positive aspects of human development in the 21st century.

1. Development and Current State

Since the founding of the PRC in 1949, urbanization in the country can be broken down into two periods consisting of separate phases.

During the early years of the PRC, China adopted a strategy in which

---

① Zhou Ganzhi. *A Probe into Urbanization with Chinese Characteristics* [J]. *Urban Planning International*. 2009 (S1)

heavy industry was given top priority. Naturally, the implementation of the strategy made it necessary and even compulsory for many rural labor forces to move to state-owned enterprises (SOEs). This being the case, industrial cities, particularly those in inland China, were the first to enjoy preferential development. Consequently, the growth rate of China's urban population rapidly outstripped the growth rate of its total population. From 1952-1965, the urban population increased from 71.63 million to 130.45 million, with a growth rate of 82.1%. During this period, the overall population grew from 574.82 million to 725.38 million, with a growth rate of 26.2%. The percentage of the urban population increased to 18% in 1965, up from 12.5% in 1952 and 16.3% in 1958.

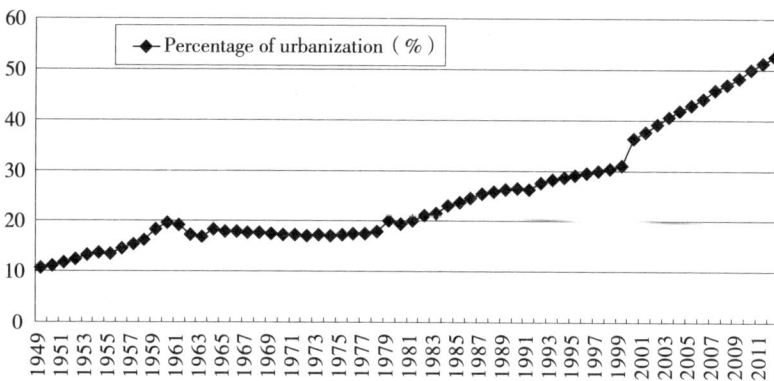

Figure 1-1 Percentage of urbanization in China (1949-2012)

A. Period of planned economy

i). 1952-1965: heavy industry prevails

During the early years of the PRC, China adopted a strategy in which heavy industry was given top priority. Naturally, the implementation of the strategy made it necessary and even compulsory for many rural labor forces to move to state-owned enterprises (SOEs). This being the case, industrial cities, particularly those in inland China, were the first to enjoy preferential development. Consequently, the growth rate of China's urban population rapidly outstripped the growth rate of its total population. From 1952-1965, the urban population increased from 71.63 million to 130.45 million, with a growth rate of 82.1%. During this period, the overall population grew from 574.82 million to 725.38 million, with a growth rate of 26.2%. The percentage of the urban population increased to 18% in 1965, up from 12.5% in 1952 and 16.3% in 1958.

When the First Five-year Plan was launched in 1953, China began to deploy a sizeable number of farmers for large-scale industrial construction. Industrialization spurred on urbanization and the urban population started to grow in a planned manner. The level of urbanization increased markedly to 16.25% in 1958 from 10.60% in 1949, with an annual growth rate of 0.63%. Under the system of the planned economy, those living in rural areas began to migrate steadily to cities via a recruitment drive, the urbanization rate standing at 15.4% in 1957 when the urban population multiplied to 100 million.

From 1958-1965, the number of residents living in urban areas changed radically. Between 1958 and the first half of 1960, the Chinese government, in an attempt to tap into its huge workforce, embarked on a massive investment drive and launched a campaign of socialist construction that sparked the 'Great Leap Forward' in industry and agriculture. In its empty pursuit of illusory economic advancement, the government embarked on the large-scale recruitment of workers in rural areas, which resulted in 30 million farmers moving into towns and cities. Those years represented the fastest growth in urbanization in the history of China, when the urbanization rate climbed by 1.45% annually. From 1963 to 1965, when food supplies failed to keep up with demand in cities because of a nationwide reduction in grain yield, 26 million people who had just entered cities had to be relocated to the countryside; during these two years, China experienced its most rapid decline in urbanization, when the annual rate fell to 1.0%.

ii). 1966-1978: the 'Cultural Revolution' is launched

The Cultural Revolution started in 1966, and the turmoil it inflicted did not come to an end until 1977. During these chaotic years, urbanization in China got bogged down and even regressed. On the one hand, the government appealed to more than 10 million urban youths to settle down in rural areas so as to alleviate unemployment and in the meantime the urban population fell by another 5 million when a huge number of government officials and intellectuals were mobilized to transfer to the countryside; on the other hand, the government injected a large amount of capital into the industrialization of inland areas where a great many military and heavy industrial enterprises that were formerly situated along coastal areas were relocated. Industrial construction went into operation on the basis of 'large distribution with small concentration', while plants and factories were built in locations that had to be 'close to mountains, scattered and sheltered'. Investment in urban construction was negligible at the time and, for that reason, there were few newly-built cities. From 1965-1975, the growth rate of China's overall population was higher than that of urban residents, with the percentage of the urban population being generally constant and staying much the same or even shrinking: 18% in 1965, 17.4% in 1970, 17.3% in 1975 and 17.9% in 1978.

B. Period of market economy

i). 1978-1996: urbanization rises after the start of reform and opening up

Beginning in 1978, China embarked on reform and opening up along with the adoption of a socialist market economy, and at the same time enacted policies that encouraged and promoted urbanization. Many counties were upgraded to cities and their number increased from 191 in 1978 to 666 in 1996. Meanwhile, the proportion of the urban population increased from 17.9% to 29.4%, China's urbanization level having soared by 11.8% in 18 years.

ii). After 1996: urbanization gathers pace with the deepening of reform and opening up

After 1996, urbanization in China started to develop at an ever quickening speed. The implementation of reform and opening up over the previous two decades facilitated economic progress, financial accumulation and income growth. It also promoted China's urbanization as a result of an upsurge in the construction of development zones, new urban districts and international metropolises. During the two decades, market demand for urbanization grew stronger than ever before when economic globalization helped open the economy wider to the outside world as the country sped up its marketization by means of economic restructuring. In the meantime, institutional innovation carried out by the government not only reduced transaction costs for urbanization, but also helped boost the expected rate of return with marked reduction of risks. These government and market factors made it possible for China's urbanization to enter a period of accelerating development, so much so that the urbanization rate snowballed from 29.4% in 1996 to 52.6% in 2012, the total urban population having increased from 359 million to 710 million.

2. Current Features

(1) Urbanization rate increasing at top speed for over three decades, a rare global phenomenon

Since the reform and opening up was implemented in 1978, the pace of urbanization in China has quickened, with small towns and cities emerging in large numbers. During this period, urbanization has expanded at around twice the world average speed. The progress of urbanization has varied among individual countries across the globe (see Figure 1-2); for example, the growth in urbanization level from 20% to 40% took 120 years to achieve in the UK, one century in France, eight decades in Germany, four decades in the US, three decades in the former Soviet Union and Japan, and 22 years in China. Even so, the urbanization level in China is still lower than the world average as well as the average in similarly industrialized countries.

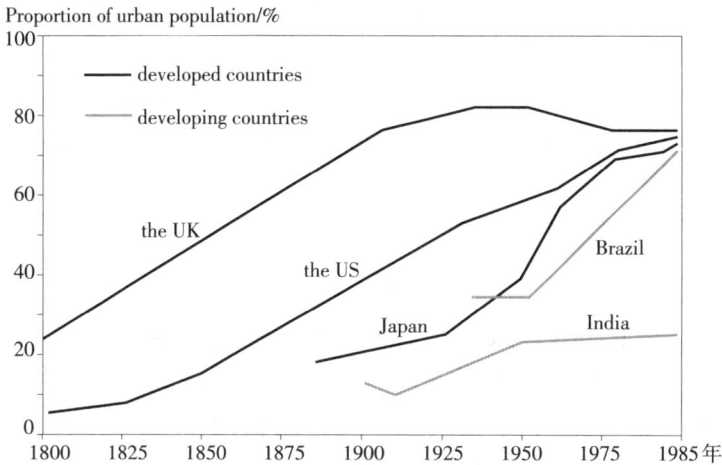

Figure 1-2 Evolution of urbanization rate in some countries

(2) Proliferation in urban residents primarily resulted from migration of rural people to urban areas, aside from natural growth; migrants and settled population to coexist for a long period

As China's household registration system became more flexible after reform and opening up, plenty of rural people moved into cities and better developed coastal areas. Large in number, extensive in range and far-reaching in influence, this labor force constituted the largest floating population ever seen in China's history. Floating peasant-workers started to become apparent in 1984. By the end of the 1980s, there were only 30 million migrant peasant-laborers, but after a number of ups and downs, the total reached 226 million by 2012. Since it was relatively difficult to move to urban areas, and particularly large cities, and because peasant-workers still had their own land and property back in their home towns and villages, of those who left home for cities, only

17% settled down to become urban residents; the remaining 83% were like migratory birds. This phenomenon contrasts with what happened in some European countries, where urbanization was initially the result of bankrupt farmers. Though a floating population can benefit both the migrants' old and new destinations, it is definitely a hindrance to the growth of industrial technology and upgrading of urbanization. It is only natural that some peasant-workers will not be accepted as permanent urban residents, and so the floating population will not evaporate in the immediate future.

(3) China's urbanization is burgeoning, driven by both secondary and tertiary industries, of which the latter will ultimately prevail

China's urbanization is now at an intermediate stage. As is shown in the history of world urbanization, a country will enter the stage of rapid development when the rate of urbanization reaches 30%; its progress will slow down when the rate stands at 70%. In 1978, the percentage of China's urban population was 17.92%. By 1996, however, the rate rose to as high as 30.48%. We may well say that China's urbanization gathered pace from then on and the share of the urban population climbed to 43.9% by 2006.[1] That is to say, the proportion of urban residents rose during the decade at an annual growth of 1.34%, which was nearly twice the rate recorded between 1978 and 1996 when the annual increase was only 0.7%. By the end of 2012, the proportion of the urban population rose to 52.6% and China's urbanization was growing at an annual rate of 1.54% during the five years from 2007 to 2012. In this light, urbanization in China is now developing at an accelerating speed, the essential feature of it being the quick but steady expansion of the urban population (see Figure 1-3).

Primary industry has been a mainstay of China's overall industrial development and a major source of urban employment, though the tertiary industry will feature more prominently in the process of urbanization in years to come. In 2012, the share of primary, secondary and tertiary industries was respectively 10.1%, 45.3% and 44.6% in China's industrial structure. According to the *Development Report on China's Floating Population* (2013), data collected by the National Health and Family Planning Commission of the PRC in 2013 showed that the proportion of manufacturing employees among China's floating population was 33.3%, which was 4.1% lower than

---

[1] See *China Statistical Yearbook* (2007), page 105

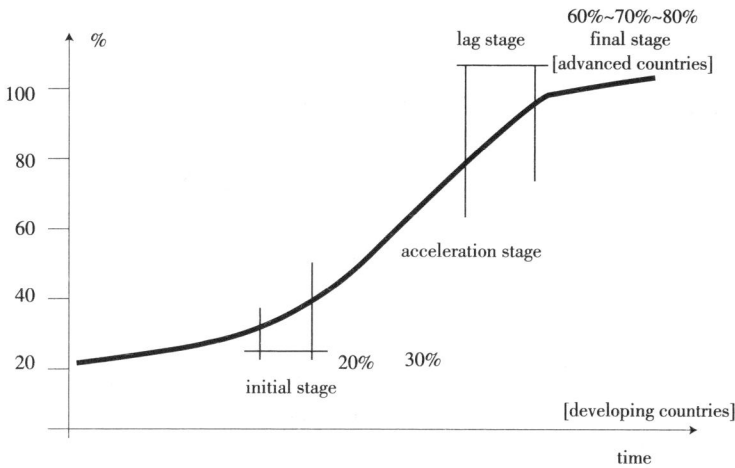

Figure 1-3 Developmental stages of urbanization

that in 2011. In the same year, however, employee numbers in the tertiary sector multiplied, with the percentages of those employed in wholesale and retail and catering industries being 20.1% and 11.3% respectively, which were 2% and 1.4% higher than those in 2011. This being the case, secondary and tertiary industries born out of urbanization will become the primary driving forces in China's urbanization in years to come.

(4) Twin effect of government dominance and market forces in urbanization

China began to exercise the policy of reform and opening up in 1978. On the one hand, the government offered to facilitate the country's urbanization, believing that this was one of the central solutions to issues pertaining to agriculture, rural development and farmers. In its 10th Five-year Plan, the government advanced the strategy that urbanization must be accelerated and that some of the policies previously stipulated to deter rural residents from entering cities must be revised. In the 11th Five-year Plan, the government further proposed that urbanization must proceed in a sound way. On the other hand, urbanization clearly gathered pace after the market mechanism was applied to the relocation and employment of the labor force, the development of real estate and construction of urban infrastructure. At a work conference on urbanization held by the CPC Central Committee in December 2013, the government made it clear that urbanization must be people-centered so as to improve the caliber of urban residents and the quality of their lives; and besides, the regular 'citizenization' of the resident population who have the capacity to be employed and earn a decent living in cities must be given top priority. It further underscored the fact that urbanization entailed both the decisive role of the market in resource allocation and the indispensable functions of government in creating an institutional environment, working out development plans, constructing infrastructure, providing public services and reinforcing social governance. In the final analysis, the Party Central Committee was responsible for the stipulation of fundamental policies and determination of the overall planning and strategic layout of urbanization, while local governments should be realistic in carrying out general planning, working out relevant programs and handling operation and management in a creative way.

(5) Huge regional disparities in urbanization

Due to disparities in natural environments, social situations and economic circumstances, differences and discrepancies are striking in the urbanization of individual places. In 2012, the percentages in China's eastern, western and central regions were 56.4%, 53.4% and 44.9% respectively (see Figure 1-4). In eastern coastal regions, convenient transportation and favorable locations

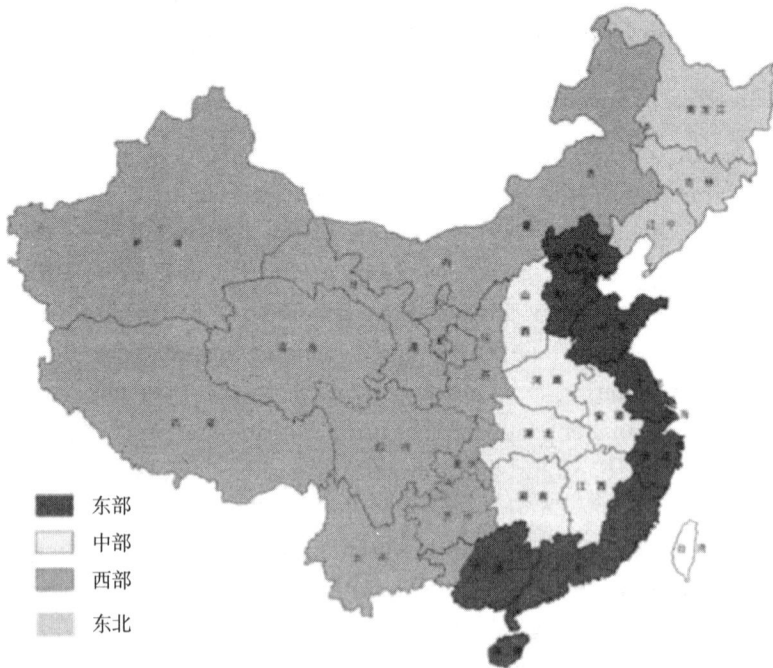

东部
中部
西部
东北

Figure 1-4 Regional divisions in China: eastern, western and central regions

made it possible for them to have rapidly constructed clusters of urbanized districts marked by interlocked and agglomerated cities. For central regions, urbanized districts took shape along railway lines and expressways, though they lagged behind the eastern regions due to the negative effect of resource-oriented development. For western regions, however, plagued by backward economic and social development and coupled with a fragile eco-system, urbanization was much slower outside a few key cities that urbanized at a relatively fast rate. Moreover, confined by the previous size of cities, regional disparities in urbanization were all the more significant.

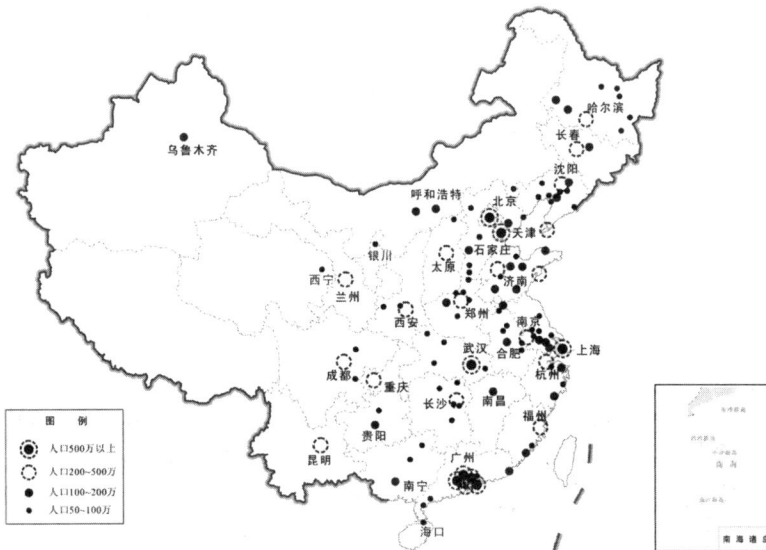

Figure 1-5 Distribution of megalopolises in China

(6) Clashes arising from urbanization: industrialization, informatization, marketization and economic globalization

In developed countries, urbanization that came along with industrialization happened hundreds of years ago. By contrast, China has been lagging behind for about 150 years. Therefore, China will definitely be confronted with intertwined conflicts and contradictions in its effort to complete the task of urbanization within decades, while the same process took almost two centuries in developed countries. China not only has to simultaneously work on urbanization and industrialization, but is faced with challenges from informatization, marketization and economic globalization. We may well say, therefore, that China's urbanization is proceeding as if within a pressure cooker of time and space. As luck would have it, urbanization in China has come about in a peaceful and stable environment, secured by a superior socialist system. Due to compressed time and space, however, many predictable and unpredictable risks, conflicts and contradictions will confront us because we shall have to address all the problems simultaneously that other countries encountered over a period of time.

II. Challenges and Problems

1. Challenges

(1) Challenges from resources and ecological environment
A. Challenges from resources

A scarcity and waste of resources, which have been impacting on the sustained progress of urbanization in China, is a hurdle that must be cleared.

These resources include water, land and energy sources, without which the process of urbanization will come to a halt. Take water, for example. Barring other negative factors such as maldistribution, China has only 2,290 cubic meters of fresh water per person. With a dramatic proliferation of the urbanized population, water supply for both homes and industry has increased significantly. To make things worse, severe pollution of both surface and underground water has widened the discrepancies between the spatial layout of urban areas and the capacity of water resources. At present, around 400 of the country's 655 cities suffer from water deficiency, and about 200 of them have been plagued by acute water shortage. The daily water deficit in urban areas across the country has hit 16 million cubic meters, with an annual shortage of about 6 billion cubic meters. The result is that water supply has to be restricted in some cities in the north.

As for land resources, conflict between the huge demand for land for urban construction and the amount available is increasingly intense, given the extreme scarcity of land resources. With the acceleration of China's urbanization, the deficiency of land resources, notably arable or cultivated land, has become stark. The preliminary result of the Second National Land Census that ran from 2001 to 2009 noted that China had only 2.026 billion mu (521,000 square miles) of arable land. This was little more than the 1.8 billion mu of cultivated land that China had been warned was necessary to sustain the bottom line of its food security or decent food supply.

Things are now looking particularly grim regarding the utilization of land in China. On the one hand, a shortage of land for urban construction is becoming the biggest problem standing in the way of a city's future development. On the other hand, the waste of land that prevails in urban construction has gravely impeded the promotion of the overall quality and normal performance of cities, brought down their load-bearing capacity at large and ultimately hampered the sound development of urbanization.

As far as energy is concerned, the challenges confronting China's urbanization arise from an energy shortfall and inefficient utilization, of which the former primarily features lack of supply to meet urban demand for energy, particularly petroleum and electricity. As urbanization proceeds, the development of heavy chemical industries, a boom in the urban population and improvements in living quality all increase demand for energy. Since 2003, acute power shortages have been experienced across the country and more than 20 provinces (or municipalities) have been forced to restrict electricity consumption. In 2009, China imported 204 million tons of oil, an increase of 13.9% on the previous year. That same year also witnessed a consumption of 2.74 billion tons of coal, an increase of 3% compared with the year before. Along with the rapid rise in energy consumption in urban areas, inefficiency has emerged as another problem. At present, the overall rate of energy utilization in China is approximately 33%, which is 10% lower than that in developed countries.

B. Challenges from the ecological environment

In the early days, China largely depended on industrialization to promote urbanization. During this time, there was an inadequate supply of sewage treatment facilities, which led to severe industrial pollution and discharge of urban pollutants. Meanwhile, the quick expansion of urbanization inflicted enormous problems in terms of solid waste pollution, water pollution, air pollution as well as traffic jams. In most cities, the huge amount of waste produced in confined industrial and residential areas outweighed the self-purification capability of the urban environment. It is only natural, therefore, that the increasingly grave pollution would precipitate a huge ecosystem predicament.

In 2008, China generated 1.901 billion tons of industrial solid wastes, an increase of nearly 1.1 billion tons compared with the amount produced in

2000. In the meantime, the output of household refuse also went up, reaching 154 million tons at a time when the treatment rate of urban household waste was only 66.8% on average. Water pollution in urban areas is closely related to industrial wastewater and domestic sewage, the latter of which has grown to become the leading cause of urban water pollution. As a result, drinking water sources are below acceptable levels in nearly half of the towns and cities across the country. Though air quality in urban areas is generally better than it was years ago, the problem is still acute. Of the 519 cities monitored in 2008, only 21 (accounting for 4% of the total) attained the primary standard, with 378 (72.8%) reaching the secondary standard, 113 (21.8%) meeting the third grade and seven (1.4%) failing to satisfy the third standard. Of the cities at prefecture level and above, 71.6% were up to par, and of the cities at county level, 85.6% reached the standard. Air pollution is particularly bad in the north and among large and super-large cities across the country as well as cities in coal-producing areas. Traffic jams are exacerbating the problem in big cities; the number of vehicles per road mile has been rising year by year, while average driving speeds have been falling.

(2) Challenges from the expansion of domestic demand

Compared with previous plans, the 12th Five-year Plan is notable for its focus on demand. The keynote of the 11th Five-year Plan was about how to promote growth, push forward technological progress and develop emerging industries, driven by a desire to improve competitiveness and productivity. The paramount idea of the 12th Five-year Plan was to stimulate domestic demand, in which urbanization played a crucial role. Urban construction, construction of infrastructural facilities and generation of urban agglomerations have created immense demand for materials. Then comes the phenomenon of migrant farmers, who represent the foundation of urbanization. In the long-run, farmers will rise to become members of the middle classes by seeking new, better-paid jobs. In this regard, urbanization sustains the expansion of the middle class. When more and more farmers settle down in cities, demand will grow, which will help develop both industry and the service sector. Urbanization, therefore, plays a central role in promoting domestic demand.

(3) Challenges from mediation of social conflicts

The second key element of the 12th Five-year Plan echoed a feature of the previous plan, namely the maintenance of social stability. The main difference between the two was that the former leant much more weight to mediating social conflicts. It was proposed in the 12th Five-year Plan that residents' incomes should grow in line with economic development, with an unstated ambition to bridge income gaps. Centering on China's urbanization, the government will work to expand the coverage of social security and, by boosting employment, adjusting public policies and helping farmers become urban residents, narrow income gaps while also bridging disparities in the supply of public goods. Urbanization should bring about an increase in employment and income of farmer-workers on the one hand, and narrow the gulf in the supply of public goods on the other. That is one of the most important aspects in addressing China's social problems.

2. Problems

(1) Inferior global competitiveness of key urban agglomerations

Viewed from a global context, key urban clusters in China have a relatively large proportion of manufacturing, though they are short of world-class manufacturing enterprises. Central cities are suffering both insufficient high-end capability and inferior development quality. Urban manufacturing industries and service sectors are, on the whole, at the low end of the international industrial chain due to their inferior development. In Beijing and Shanghai, the share of tertiary industry is now over 50%, but sectors such as international finance and cultural media are clearly underdeveloped. In terms of accounting, advertising and other consulting services, there are equally big gaps between them and the cities in developed countries. The infrastructure at an international level is inadequate and fails to satisfy the residential and entrepreneurial requirements of a high-end population.

(2) Inferior quality of human settlement

Housing conditions have yet to improve for urban residents on low incomes and migrant workers, who cannot afford to live in decent homes. Retrofits of urban squatter settlements, state-owned farms and forestry centers, as well as industrial and mining areas, are severely deficient. In general, reconstruction is arduous, ancillary facilities are insufficient and infrastructure is over-used.

Residents commonly face arduous commutes. Traffic jams are outrageous in big cities and seem to be getting worse. In super-large cities, the all-day saturation of main roads exceeds 70%. The average vehicle speed in downtown areas during rush hour is below 20 kilometers per hour. In the urban center of Shanghai, for instance, the saturation of half of all lanes is as high as 95% during rush hour and the average vehicle speed is only 10 kilometers per hour. In 2006, the average commuting time for Beijing residents was 43 minutes. In addition, the construction of integrated urban traffic networks has been slow and hub layouts are often irrational, leading to inefficiency in traffic flows because the means of transportation have been impeded. Third, the development of regional rail links is still at a primary stage, meaning that commuting between cities, industrial districts, seaports and airports is largely borne by expressways. Coordination between construction planning of highways and the development of urban agglomerations is inadequate, with the flow of the finished transport links differing considerably. Due to the rapid expansion of cities along routes built in earlier days, they have almost become inner-urban highways. Metro lines in big cities have yet to form effective networks that connect with bus routes and regional traffic, thereby impeding the operation of traffic management and organization.

Public service facilities fail to meet demand. Though educational and medical resources are rich in Beijing and other cities, services in surrounding areas are strikingly inadequate. Community-level hospitals, cultural centers, libraries, sports facilities, centers for youths and the elderly and other facilities closely bound up with the life of urban residents are scarce and suffer from a lack of routine maintenance and management funds. Service levels at social facilities are low and do not meet people's growing material and cultural needs. In the outskirts of cities and rural-urban fringe zones, social service establishments are inadequate and have failed to keep pace with demand.

Security and pollution problems are also apparent in urban areas; more than half of the cities across the country face water shortages, ageing waterworks and similar issues; the accumulated volume of urban household waste has reached 6 billion tons and will continue to grow in future at an annual rate of 4.8%, leading to the creation of towering garbage mountains around cities; air pollution is widely reported and more than half of urban residents live in foul atmospheric environments; most cities lack the capacity to resist natural disasters and urban malfunctioning is frequent thanks to climatic or human-generated causes.

(3) Small towns of low load-bearing capacities

In urban agglomerations, small towns are faced with insufficient momentum of development, indistinctive economies with local characteristics, lower levels of population aggregation and lack of scale. The number of residents in an average county town is about 80,000. Apart from the county towns, barely 400 designated townships have a population of more than 50,000, accounting for less than 3% of the total number. Planning and construction here is of an inferior quality, and the same applies to infrastructure and public services. A majority of minor towns will find it hard to bring about integrated infrastructure of urban water supply and sewage disposal as well as decent social services in commerce, science and technology, and education. This in turn makes it hard to attract population and industries, not to mention their ability to offer services to neighboring rural areas.

(4) Lack of substantial progress in overall urban-rural planning

Urban agglomerations have witnessed a clash of interest between cities and rural areas. With the expansion of urbanization, farmers who have lost land have been forced to go to cities. Much to their frustration, however, they generally find it hard to adapt to urban society. Rural-urban fringe zones are places where surplus workforces from the countryside aggregate. Migrant workers living in those places are still confronted with difficulties in areas such as housing, employment, children's education and social security.

Due to China's traditional preference for cities over the countryside, rural areas have long been overlooked in terms of overall consideration, and appropriate support and nurturing. In rural regions, there has been an under-investment in construction of infrastructure, while public service networks are not well established and social security systems have yet to be set up. When enormous surplus workforces flock to cities from the countryside, many elderly people are left to stay at home and, as a consequence, the rural population is now experiencing a downward trend in the number of working-age people. Grass-roots organizations are weakened in rural areas, which also suffer from a lack of vitality and development in agricultural activities. Much research associated with the building of a new countryside has involved discussions on village construction but little work has been done on promoting social and economic development in rural areas. Some researchers are blind to local practices and realities when they mindlessly propose the large-scale relocation of villages and residential centers.

(5) Pending changes in development theory

Although the construction of urban clusters in China has boomed in recent years, it has often been carried out blindly and in haste. In some areas, despite the fact that social and economic development has lagged, the connections between cities is not sufficiently close and the ecological environment is fragile; two or three cities, if they are relatively adjacent or are situated near water, will be rushed in an attempt to forge an urban agglomeration.

In other places, luxury and extravagance is pursued in urban development and construction. Some cities spend large amounts on iconic or landmark projects that are huge profile, large in scale and highly energy-consuming. Aside from being out of tune with the overall style of the cities, the projects are expensive to maintain and operate and are typically under-utilized Many other cities take a keen interest in building man-made water views or landscapes and some have gone so far as to construct vast artificial lakes in the northwest of the country where water resources are scarce. Some mountainous cities, with no regard to the peculiar topographical features of the location, decide to roll out extensive rectangular or chessboard-styled urban layouts while the establishment of public services and amenities closely bound with the life of urban-rural residents are under-invested. According to a survey conducted by Renmin University of China, despite the extra investment in urban construction and the substantial results achieved by local governments, residents' satisfaction with cities is strikingly deteriorating.

Uncalled-for expansion is widely found in industrial development zones when some cities exploit the land for industrial purposes. More often than not, an industrial development zone would occupy an area of 100 square kilometers and more. In some places, industrial parks are so disproportionate in number as to have triggered vicious competition, with the consequence that the cost for development has been forced down and excess production capacity has resulted.

III. New Urbanization Strategies and Solutions

It was noted for the first time in a report to the 18th National Congress of the CPC that new urbanization is both a vehicle for building an affluent society in an all-round way and a focus for changing the growth mode of the economy. The characteristics of new urbanization in a Chinese context are that it is intensive, intelligent, green and low-carbon. It is based on the idea of a scientific outlook on development and adheres to the principles of being people-centric and preserving the culture and environment, while simultaneously pushing forward industrialization, informatization, urbanization and modernization of agriculture in order to promote the quality and level of urbanization, urban-rural integration and coordinated development between regions.

1. Regular Migration of Rural Population to Urban Areas

The migration of rural residents to towns and cities is not entirely a market process. Government policies are needed to provide guidance and intervention in order to effect a well-organized transfer. Besides, the tools for implementing the policies are equally necessary. The policies for an orderly shift of rural people to urban areas should be worked out as follows.

First, those who enter cities could be grouped into types. For floaters or floating peasant-workers, a two-way flow policy is suggested, which means that they can retain their dual status or identities as both workers and peasants. This means their legal interests such as pay, working hours, official holidays and safety protection are secured by law. For those who have stable jobs and residences in cities, conditions should be created for them to become urban residents, after which they will be entitled to the same rights and obligations as local residents. For rural folk whose contracted land has been requisitioned by the government due to urbanization, they will have to be transformed into or acknowledged as urban residents for whom the municipal government should offer employment assistance, technical training, unemployment insurance and subsistence allowances. Rural residents should be encouraged to come to settle down in small towns and small and medium-sized cities. Super-large cities should center on industrial restructuring to gradually bring into being a mechanism by which they can harness excessive population growth by means of economic measures.[1]

Second, studies on predicting occupational demand and laws of population mobility should be underpinned. Information systems of occupational demand and population migration should be established

---

[1] See *The 11th Five-year Plan for National Economic and Social Development of the People's Republic China*. Beijing: People's Publishing House, 2006

by both the state and local governments so that information about occupational demand will be monitored and provided in line with the needs of industrialization, economic development, urbanization and the construction of national defense.

Third, policies for managing census registers should be reformed and a unified system for managing urban-rural household registers should be progressively worked out.

Fourth, population transfer and industrial restructuring should be integrated as a whole so as to optimize demographic structures, reshape the pattern of population distribution and ultimately create coordination and balance between population, employment, resources, the ecological environment and other parameters.

2. Well-organized Spatial Patterns for Urbanization

Most important of all, big cities should be allowed to develop fully so that their leading role can be deployed in driving development. As is widely accepted, it has been one of the laws in urbanization for big cities to take the lead in development. At the initial and intermediate stages of urbanization, free expansion and full development of big cities play a major role in upgrading the level and quality of urbanization and it is arguably the primary prerequisite for the completion of urbanization and formation of a relatively perfect urban system. Without free and full development of big cities, the idea to first bring about the extensive development of small and medium-sized cities is but a fantasy conceived of by those who seek in vain to go beyond the development stage.

Second, urban clusters should play leading roles in pushing forward urbanization so that they will help create metropolitan regions or megalopolises and urban clusters before boosting their further development. On this basis, China will gradually establish a sustainable and highly coordinated spatial framework of urbanization with the coastal regions and Beijing-Guangzhou-Harbin Railway as the longitudinal axis, the Yangtze River and Longhai Railway as the horizontal axis, and a significant number of urban clusters as the main body surrounding which other cities and towns are distributed in a scattered pattern that are regularly interspersed with permanent arable land and ecological zones. Megalopolises that emerged up to two decades ago have long been taken as advanced forms in the development of cities. They have acted as 'dynamos' that spearhead economic growth in the modern market economy, often occupying a central position in innovation and the accumulation of wealth. A megalopolis centers on one or several big cities around which are aggregated many small or small and medium-sized towns, covering an area that can be as vast as tens of thousands of square kilometers. In 1976, Jean Gottmann, the well-known French geographer, observed that six world-level megalopolises had by then taken shape across the globe, the Yangtze River Delta being among them. Things have moved on since then. At present, the GDP generated by the three megalopolises in the US and Japan account for 65% and 69% respectively of their national totals. It is predicted that 12 megalopolises will exist in China by 2020. Today, it already has three megalopolises – the Beijing-Tianjin-Hebei, Yangtze River Delta and Pearl River Delta megalopolises – and their combined GDP now accounts for 38% of the national total. For the time being, the three megalopolises should continue to play leading roles in coordinating responsibilities and complementing each other's advantages between cities within the metropolitan regions so that their collective competitiveness will be enhanced. As for the regions that are basically qualified for developing into urban clusters, they should work to intensify coordinated planning with large and super-large cities as locomotives and give full play to central cities so as to bring into being some new urban clusters that occupy less land, offer more employment opportunities, are capable of pooling more factors and have a more rational distribution of population.

Finally, towns and small and medium-sized cities should be guided to develop intensively in cultivating special industries according to their own characteristics so that their comparative advantages will become apparent. In regions where no urban agglomeration can occur due to their thinly-scattered populations and deficient resources, they should be encouraged to develop around existing cities, county towns and well-qualified designate townships to build them into centers that aggregate economy, population and public services. As striking as big cities are, most urban populations across the globe have been living in towns and small and medium-sized cities. In this light, substantial measures should be taken for expanding the scale of small towns to facilitate the aggregation process.

3. Efficient and Economic Use of Resources for Eco-protection

First, the government should strengthen its policy guidance for, and studies on, energy-saving technologies connected with construction, transportation and other key sources of energy consumption. Measures should be worked out for standard systems, supervision and implementation that aim to promote environmental protection and reduce the consumption of energy, land, water and raw materials. Energy and land-saving construction projects should be factored into the index framework and system of land for urban-rural construction. Research should be conducted into the index system of designing residential communities and isolated buildings in cities as well as the control index system for residential construction planning in rural areas, both systems having to be strictly implemented. The thermal insulation system of structures currently in use should be improved and the application of solar and other renewable energies in construction should be accelerated. Computation systems for the life-cycle cost of buildings should be established and strengthened, and effective reward mechanisms must be formulated for energy saving, water conservation and waste reclamation. Investigation of urban water-supply networks and household water instruments should be underpinned in order to reduce leakage. Studies on fuel-efficient vehicles should be reinforced and the application of clean and renewable energies should be promoted. In single-center cities, public transport should be given top priority and carpooling should be encouraged. Rapid, convenient and comfortable public transport systems, including exclusive bus lanes, should be set up. In super-large cities, congestion charging could be adopted. Supporting policies should be stipulated, cooperation agreements should be made in industrial sectors, and demand-side management ought to be implemented with legal, power pricing and funding support. Security mechanisms should be established for the market of renewable energy generation in order to stimulate investment in renewable energies and promote technological progress in developing and utilizing renewable energies with the guarantee of stable and sustainable measures.

Second, construction of eco-cities should be advocated. Urban areas should be taken as compound ecosystems composed of society, the economy and environment in planning, construction and management. Ecological cost or natural capital should be included in economic analysis and policy making of governments at all levels. The protection of urban ecosystems and promotion of urban environmental quality as well residents' living conditions should be listed among the key indicators for evaluating urban construction and performances of local governments.

Third, modes of production and consumption should be changed.

Urban areas consume and discharge huge quantities of materials every day. Take Zhuhai in Guangdong province, for example. In 2000, the city had an average daily demand for 5,820 tons of coal, 1,595 tons of fuel, 600,000 tons of water and 1,127 tons of food. Each day it discharges 602 tons of industrial solid waste, 300,000 tons of waste water and 1,000 tons of garbage. Unless the modes of production and consumption in cities are changed, it will not be possible to adequately address the problems of wasting resources and environmental pollution simply by means of advanced technologies and infrastructure construction. In this light, we must work out policies for product recycling and reclamation, encourage energy- and resource-saving products, promote public transport, propagate and appeal to saving energy, change lifestyles and entertainment, and work to integrate protection of the environment and sanitation with economic planning and policies. With the assistance of the market mechanism and economic measures, we will be able to establish clean and ecological cities.

Fourth, land-use planning and policies adapted to the market economy should be formulated. For example, maximum and minimum plot rates should be nailed down for industrial land. For residential land, additional charges should be imposed on those developing land at low volumes and those holding multiple homes in order to avert the wasting of land and excessive use of land. In line with the goals of urban economic and social development during a given period and by means of investigation and developing prediction, directions and guidelines for developing underground space should be proposed according to the planning for ground or surface construction for the purpose of determining the goal, function, scale and layout of urban underground space as well as the overall arrangement of all underground facilities. Super-large cities should take the lead in working out planning for utilizing underground space.

Fifth, pilot tests should be conducted with the help of foreign practices to economize and recover investment in energy-saving by means of internal contracts. This policy, which aims to address problems relevant to the mechanism generated in the start-up of capital and effective recovery of capital, is exercisable inside a mega unit. If the economic analysis and recommendations about energy saving wins the stamp of approval by superior departments, then the mega unit will be entitled to set up the project and enter into a contract with its subordinate executing entities. After that, the capital will start to go into the energy-saving project. Upon completion of the project, energy costs will be reduced and these savings will be returned to the unit. Such projects may include heating-supply control, ventilation, daylighting, wall and roof insulation, protection of football fields, street lamps, automatic temperature control, water saving and cogeneration. Easy to implement, these projects can address problems related to varied channels of expenditure on and investment in energy, but also significantly reduce users' costs.

4. Reinforcing Management of Urban Planning

First, planning for the size and layout of cities should be adapted not only to the local land and water resources, environmental capability, geological structure and other natural bearing capacities, but also to local economic development, employment space, infrastructure and public service capabilities.

Second, urban planning and construction should be improved as a whole. Protection of urban water sources must be reinforced and water supply facilities should be adequately established. Cities short of water should moderately rationalize the scale of construction and must be deterred from developing water-intensive industries and artificial water landscapes. Cities suffering from overuse of groundwater should resist further exploitation to avoid land subsidence. Segmentation between sectors and regions should be subjugated in constructing urban roads, waterworks and drainage systems, telecom and cable TV, as well as in energy and environmental protection. Coordinated construction should be executed based on unified planning so as to reduce mindless removal and reconstruction. A city's disaster-prevention and mitigation capacities should be reinforced, as should emergency response and recovery capabilities. The legal interests of relocated households must be guaranteed in the regular renovation of dilapidated houses and 'urban villages'. The planning, designing and building of urban areas must be carried out in a way that is sensitive to history and traditional culture, highlighting distinctive features, protecting national characteristics, and preserving cultural relics and scenic resources. The implementation of urban planning must be supervised and the integrated administration of cities should be pushed forward so that the overall urban management will be enhanced.

Third, division or segregation between sectors in planning should change. The relationships between regional planning, land-use planning, urban planning and other primary categories of spatial planning are in urgent need of adjustment and clarification Urban and land-use planning work should be incorporated within the territory of cities and, in the meantime, integrated with the planning of social and economic development. The government should straighten out structural relationships between relevant functional departments, reinforce the legal framework and bring into being a national planning system that is unified and strong in controlling and regulation.

Fourth, the mechanism of urban-rural planning, in accordance with the *Urban and Rural Planning Law*, should be brought into full play by promoting the planning of the main functional regions or development priority zones so that strategic planning for cross-regional spatial development will be followed.

Fifth, village populations have fallen as many households have relocated and massive homesteads have been discarded after farmers have left their hometowns for cities. Therefore, the government should reintegrate the establishments in rural areas, rationalize the layout of rural settlements and facilitate the transfer of homesteads left behind by farmers in towns according to law so that the land will be protected for fairer use.

5. Developing Industry-financed Agriculture and Urban-sustained Rural Areas

Concerted and coordinated urban-rural development is central to the accomplishment of sustainable urbanization. At present, the Chinese government has publicized its new thinking on social and economic development: to have industry nurture agriculture and cities support the countryside so as to achieve the concerted and coordinated development of them all. The government, in an effort to establish a stable and gradual growth mechanism of agricultural input, has resolved to restructure the pattern of national income distribution and is determined to carry out a substantial preferential policy for agriculture, the countryside and farmers in its financial expenditure and investment in fixed assets based on current agricultural inputs. That means that the government is determined to bring to an end its trajectory of development at the initial stage of industrialization when agriculture was relied on as the viable source of government revenue to supply accumulated capital for industry; from now on, agriculture and the rural sector will be eligible for government support. To this end, the Chinese government will strive to accomplish the following things:

First, it will further reinforce investment in rural infrastructure, bring small and medium-scale rural infrastructure construction into the scope of government investment in its capital construction of all levels, and increase its investment in irrigation and water conservation as well as country roads and other small-scale rural infrastructure.

Second, it will improve the security mechanism for rural compulsory educational expenditure financed in large part by the government, further increase its investment in the rural public health system, upgrade the assistance system for rural vulnerable groups, enhance the coverage of social security in rural areas, strengthen investment in agricultural research, intensify scientific and technological innovation in agriculture, and establish an agricultural technical promotion system, so as to promote the development of science and technology, education, culture and medical services in rural areas on the one hand, and improve employment opportunities for farmers on the other.

Third, it will conduct studies and work out a new land-use pattern for both construction and agriculture during the process of urbanization and in the meantime formulate supporting policies designed to increase charges for the paid use of newly-added construction land. While tightening up the collection, management, use and supervision of land-leasing fees, it will adjust the distribution structure of land revenue and permit peasants whose land is expropriated to have a share in projects as shareholders or leaseholders of the estates of contracted land so that they can enjoy the value-added payoff of land. Based on the returned 15% of land-leasing fees invested in rural infrastructure and social projects, the return rate of land-leasing fees will be increased step by step and further invested in rural infrastructure and social projects.

Fourth, the government will improve urban employment policies in an effort to create more job opportunities for peasants in cities. It will carry out reemployment training programs for peasant-workers with the government and enterprises sharing the costs and gradually establish a unified urban-rural labor market. It will spare no efforts in finding solutions to the problems relating to the schooling of migrant workers' children, public health, cultural life, social security and other issues so as to establish an institutional environment that is accessible to farmers. In the final analysis, the government will ultimately change the urban-rural dual structure.

CHAPTER 2

Development of Urban-rural Planning in China

I. Urban-rural Planning in China since 1949

After the founding of the PRC in 1949, modern urban planning has witnessed many ups and downs, as indeed has Chinese society. In general, we can split this period in two, with 1978 as the dividing point. This chapter aims to look back on this time and summarize the evolution of China's urban planning before and after the reform and opening-up process.

1. Urban-rural Planning Prior to Reform and Opening Up

(1) Initial stage of urban planning (1949-1952)

Before 1949, cities in China typically had the characteristics of a semi-colonial and semi-feudal society. Most inland cities and towns had a poorly developed industrial sector and appalling living conditions; at the time, there was a lack of both modern industries and modern municipal works or public facilities. By contrast, the big colonial cities along the coast were more commercially developed and often had quite advanced municipal facilities, although divisions and conflicts between social groups were alarming, with slums and western-style houses standing in stark contrast. Take Shanghai, for example. In the 1930s, the 'Paris of the Orient' was widely known as the world's fifth largest city and a prosperous international metropolis, where the Bund, crowded with people and vehicles, displayed the grandest western architecture (see Figure 2-1). In contrast to the prosperity and modernity of the foreign concessions, however, were the dwellings of the poor. Along the Zhaojiabang River, for example, was a well-known shanty settlement (see Figure 2-2) that was jam-packed with a mosaic of ramshackle shacks, tiny gambling houses known as 'crawling dragons', bamboo scaffolding projecting over the water, shabby boats on the river and dilapidated sheds under bridges that were occupied by tens of thousands of paupers.

Figure 2-1 The Bund in Shanghai (1930s)

Figure 2-2 Shanty settlement in Zhaojiabang, Shanghai (1930s)

During the economic recovery following the ravages of war, the priority was to quickly restore devastated factories and enterprises and in the meantime construct more plants and businesses. One such company was Anshan Integrated Iron and Steel Works in Liaoning province. With regards to urban construction, the government, due to its limited economic capability, was only in a position to focus on the renovation of some shanty settlements in certain big cities so that the housing and living conditions at grassroots level would be improved; a relatively well-known example involved the reconstruction of Longxu Ditch in Beijing. As was the case with the Zhaojiabang shanty settlement in Shanghai, the region along the ditch was then known as the most poverty-stricken place in Beijing. Moreover, the water channel was heavily polluted and foul smelling all the year round. After the founding of the New China, the reconstruction project conducted in this area was completed within only three months.

With the recovery and focus on city construction, urban planning also got under way. Beginning in 1950, research institutions related to urban planning and construction management offices were established one after another in big cities.[①] In September 1952, the central government convened the National Urban Construction Symposium, at which it formally proposed that city planning must be highlighted. After that, it set up urban construction institutions and reinforced its leadership in city construction.

After three years' adaptation, recovery and development, China's urban planning and construction sectors started to embark on a new stage, its target being the development of industrial cities.

(2) Import and development of 'Soviet-mode' urban planning (1953-1957)

This phase witnessed the formulation and implementation of China's First Five-year Plan for the national economy. During the period, 'Soviet-mode' planning was imported at a time when China was in pressing need for a city planning system as it carried out large-scale industrial construction centered on 156 priority projects with help from the former Soviet Union, and to properly address their relationships with existing cities.

The 'Soviet model' conceived of urban planning as the materialization

---

① Leon Hoa. *Reconstruction of China: Urban Planning within Three Decades* [M]. translated by Li Ying. Beijing: SDX Joint Publishing Company, 2006, page 28

and extension of national economic planning. In fact, the architects of the former Soviet Union's urban planning simply held that the features of socialist cities could simply boil down to productivity or productiveness, believing that cities must undertake industrial production and that the main advantages of socialist cities and their planning involved planned production and the nationalization of land.

In the early years of the PRC, the formulators of China's urban planning adopted the entire catalogue of procedures and methods laid down by the former Soviet Union. In 1956, preparation and modification of the *Provisional Regulations for Formulation of Urban Planning*, the first technical law on city planning in China, was completed with the participation of Kravchuk, leader of the expert group from the former Soviet Union, counselor of China's Construction Commission and expert on urban planning. The Provisional Regulations have had a long-lasting influence on China's urban planning and construction, even to the present day.

Having drawn so much on the practices of the former Soviet Union, including the whole category of urban planning theories and methods aligned with the system of planning, China's city planning and construction at the time featured a rigid planned economy and a touch of 'classical formalism' that highlighted plane composition, stereoscopic dimension, symmetry of axes, radiating roads, facing views, and double-curbside blocks and street views (see Figure 2-3). In addition, there was a time when economic efficiency was ignored due to its over-pursuit of scale, area, novelty, speed and standard in urban construction.

(3) Urban planning turmoil and disruption phase (1958-1977)

This period lasted for as long as two decades. However, because of the considerable fluctuation in politics and the economy, city planning and construction was thrown into turmoil and even disrupted. This was particularly the case after the start of the Cultural Revolution in 1966, when urban planning was severely impacted. Normal operations were suspended, institutions closed down, professional teams disbanded, urban planning education at colleges and universities was canceled, and literature damaged; the professional contingent were left in an even more fragile and unstable condition. The outcome was that urban development ground to a standstill, urban planning became virtually stagnant, city construction and management were thrown into semi-anarchy, places of interest and

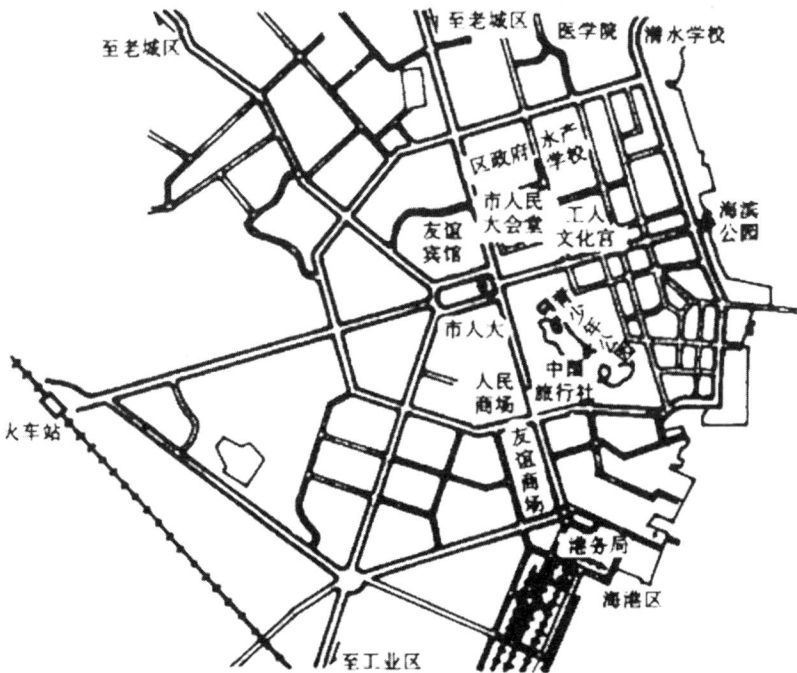

Figure 2-3 Structure of the ring-shaped new urban area in Xiashan, Zhanjiang (quoted in Urban History of China by Dong Jianhong, China Architecture & Building Press, 2004, page 390)

green landscapes were usurped or vandalized, and unauthorized buildings sprouted everywhere; the chaotic urban layout caused irreparable damage and left behind a mass of intractable legacies.

2. Urban-rural Planning after 1978

When the Cultural Revolution came to a stop at the end of 1976, China started to embark on a new historical period of development. The convening of the Third Plenary Session of the 11th Central Committee of the CPC, more than anything else, brought about an even more profound change for China's economy and society; urban planning and construction entered a new stage of development. This period could be further subdivided into four stages as follows.

(1) Restoration of urban planning (1978-1980)

The Third Conference on Urban Development held in 1978 reviewed the practices and lessons in urban planning over the previous three decades and proposed that city planning should be restored and strengthened. In October 1980, the National Construction Committee held the National Work Conference on Urban Planning, where delegates joined in a discussion about how city planning should adapt to the goals of the four modernizations in terms of: economic and social development; the overall position and functions of urban planning in national construction; and the responsibilities of mayors in the planning, construction and management of their cities, discussed and passed the legislation on urban planning. The conference formulated the guideline that the size and scale of big cities should be controlled, that medium-sized cities should be developed moderately, and that the development of small cities should be given priority. It was urged that both the general and detailed urban programs of all cities must be worked out by the end of 1982. Having helped straighten out the ideas on city planning, the conference was a landmark event in the historical development of urban planning in modern China.

(2) Legalization of urban planning (1980s)

During the 1980s, master urban planning work was carried out across the country for the benefit of urban construction. By 1986, 96% of planned cities and 85% of counties and townships nationwide had completed their general planning for construction, of which 80% had passed approval. The drawing up and approval of the second wave of urban planning underlined that China had entered a period of urban construction and development in line with the planning scientifically worked out.[1]

On December 26, 1989, the Standing Committee of the Seventh National People's Congress passed the *Urban Planning Law of the PRC*. This identified by means of legislation the position and role of urban planning in national construction, teased out the various relations in the compiling and management of urban planning, defined its contents and methods, and highlighted the procedure and jurisdiction of its management, so that the authority and status of urban planning were secured, with the formulation and implementation of it being guaranteed by law. That truly constituted a milestone in the establishment and management of China's urban planning, signifying that the country had embarked on the

---

[1] Dong Jianhong. *Urban History of China* (third edition) [M]. Beijing: China Architecture & Building Press, 2004, page 400

trajectory of urban governance according to law in its city planning and construction.

Special Column 2-1 The first legislation on urban planning

On December 26, 1989, the National People's Congress passed the *Urban Planning Law of the PRC*, the country's first state law on modern city planning. The law is composed of 46 articles in six chapters and its contents are as follows: (1) general provisions: limitations, relevant definitions and stipulations on institutions; (2) formulation of the plan for a city: organizations and principles for the compiling of city planning, stages, requirements, approval and modification; (3) development of new urban areas and redevelopment of existing urban areas: principles for the planning of new and old districts, and the layout of some important facilities; (4) implementation of city planning: promulgation of city planning, 'one proposal and two permits' (see Section 4 of this chapter for contents) and relevant development control; (5) legal liability; (6) supplementary provisions.

— Excerpted from *Urban History of China* by Dong Jianhong, Beijing: China Architecture & Building Press, July 2004, pages 400-401

(3) Reform of urban planning (1990s-2007)

In the 1990s, particularly after Deng Xiaoping delivered his Southern Tour speeches and the decision to establish a socialist market economic system was made at the 14th National Congress of the CPC, city construction started a stage of faster development. In the meantime, however, with an undue emphasis on things large and foreign, huge projects, squares and European-style projects proliferated across the country. Several cities boasted implausibly that they would build an international metropolis, 'villa areas' and 'development zones' of all descriptions were everywhere, as the Urban Planning Law was flouted and the abuse and unauthorized acquisition of land went on unchecked, along with ecological damage and a waste of capital. In May 1996, the State Council, in order to quell the chaos and disorder in city planning, promulgated the *Notice on Strengthening City Planning*. The Notice stipulated that the 80 large cities whose non-agricultural population totaled more than 500,000 must submit their comprehensive planning to the State Council for examination and approval. In line with this, the Ministry of Construction laid out regulations on the new wave of comprehensive urban planning, demanding that the size of cities must be brought under strict control, that the goal of development for modernized cities must be well studied and established, that the optimization of industrial structure must be highlighted, that the setup of cities must be readjusted and that macroeconomic regulation must be strengthened.

By the end of the 1990s, the third round of comprehensive planning for planned cities had largely been compiled. In modifying urban planning, market economic theories and laws were widely applied. At the same time, people began to explore in practice compiling methods for urban planning adapted to the requirements of the development of the market economy in their stress on the guidance of regulatory detailed planning in developing land. In Shenzhen and other cities, with the establishment of a statutory planning system,① technical documents of urban planning were turned into local regulations after being approved legally and urban planning therefore became a public policy. In the meantime, computers, networks, remote sensing and other new technologies were widely applied in the making and management of city planning. During this period, the role of urban planning was elevated within the context of the socialist market economy, while administration according to the law was held in higher regard.

(4) Integrated urban-rural planning (after 2008)

Since the start of reform and opening up, the construction of a legal system in China's urban-rural planning had lagged behind the rapid progress in urbanization. Prior to 2008, the legal system as a whole in urban-rural planning could be generalized as 'one law with one regulation'. 'One law' refers to the Urban Planning Law, while 'one regulation' is the *Management Regulation on Planning and Construction of Villages and Towns* issued by

---

① The statutory plan was drawn up annually by sectors responsible for urban planning in line with both global and zoning urban plans. It laid down for districts within the zone detailed stipulations and regulations on the nature of land use, intensity of development, auxiliary facilities, traffic networks, urban designing and others. In making its zoning program and detailed planning, Shenzhen included the preparation of a statutory plan with the principal aim of further clarifying the plan for the nature of land use, intensity of development and auxiliary facilities within each district. The statutory plan took legal effect with the approval of the Municipal Planning Committee and no-one was entitled to make an unauthorized change. With regard to the making of its statutory plan, Shenzhen used to consult with the public; the transparency of its urban planning was increased when opinions from the public were adopted in modifying the statutory plan by the municipal planning sector. The statutory plan helped strengthen the spirit of legality in making urban planning, as well as increase public understanding of and participation in urban planning

the State Council in June 1993. The detachment between cities and the countryside in the making and implementation of planning that has resulted in a lack of coherence and coordination in urban-rural planning was out of step with the boom in China's economy and society. As urbanization progressed, many villages and small towns became designated towns in which planning and management are hard to coordinate because they involve two legal systems. Even in the economically developed coastal region, many areas are untouched by the coverage of urban-rural planning. The development of urbanization has stimulated a need to perfect the existing legal system for urban-rural planning.

On October 28, 2007, based on the practices of the Urban Planning Law, the *Management Regulation on Planning and Construction of Villages and Towns*, and the management of China's urban-rural planning after reform and opening up, the *Urban and Rural Planning Law of the PRC* was promulgated at the 30th meeting of the Standing Committee of the 10th National People Congress. It took effect on January 1, 2008. In this law, the formulation, implementation, modification, supervision and liability of planning, particularly the making and carrying out of the planning of townships and villages, were stipulated at length.

Special Column 2-2 Improvements in the Urban and Rural Planning Law compared with the Urban Planning Law

Qiu Baoxing, vice minster of China's Ministry of Housing and Urban-rural Construction, notes that improvements in the Urban and Rural Planning Law, compared with the Urban Planning Law, can be summarized in seven aspects.[①]

First, in the Urban and Rural Planning Law, the dual urban-rural legal system previously formulated has been integrated.

Second, with respect to the guidelines on which they are based, the Urban Planning Law draws attention to 'guiding construction', while the Urban and Rural Planning Law highlights resource conservation. From compilation to implementation, the Urban and Rural Planning Law stresses the preservation and protection of farmland, natural resources, cultural heritage and places of interest,

---

① This part of the discussion largely referred to *Urban and Rural Planning Law in the Eyes of Qiu Baoxing* by Liu Hua, China Construction, 2008 (2), page 14

and works to exercise various protection measures of all resources with planning areas.

Third, with regard to methods and approaches, the Urban Planning Law attaches importance to planning and approval while the Urban and Rural Planning Law lays stress on execution and supervision of planning. To reinforce supervision, the Urban and Rural Planning Law specifically included an extra chapter on supervision and examination that emphasizes superintendence by the National People's Congress, the public and superior departments.

Fourth, the subjects of liability shall not be penalized in case of breaching planning in the Urban Planning Law, while accountability is clearly specified and self-discipline of departments in charge of urban-rural planning is reinforced in the Urban and Rural Planning Law. For instance, relevant administrative liabilities have been well defined for those directly in charge of and responsible for the commission or approval of commission of an illegal act, and in cases of an abuse of power, malpractice or favoritism that constitutes a crime, criminal responsibility shall be affixed.

Fifth, the Urban Planning Law underlines the role and function of planning departments while the Urban and Rural Planning Law gives priority to public participation and social supervision. For example, in line with the Urban and Rural Planning Law, a notice shall be announced for at least 30 days prior to the approval of urban-rural planning. The departments responsible for working out urban-rural planning shall take full account of expert and public opinions and have the reasons for the adoption of opinions attached to the materials to be submitted for approval. Before submitting for approval, village planning shall be decided after adequate discussion at villagers' meetings. The approved urban-rural planning shall be made known to society in a timely manner, apart from those matters that should not be made public according to laws and administrative regulations.

Sixth, the Urban and Rural Planning Law has further improved the handling mechanism for unauthorized construction and set down, according to law, administrative penalties and coercive measures for them to be ordered to stop building, to be rectified within the deadline, to have a penalty imposed on them, to be dismantled within the time limit, and for the property to be confiscated. In the meantime, it is stipulated that the local people's government shall oblige the departments concerned to seal the construction sites and conduct compulsory demolition if the relevant parties fail to stop building or dismantling within the time limit.

Seventh, with the acceleration of urbanization, no planning will be able to accommodate the rapid change of urbanization without adequate resilience. To this end, the Urban and Rural Planning Law accentuates the modification of planning and has specifically included an extra chapter in which the essentials and procedures for modification are clarified.

II. Designers and Executives of Urban-rural Planning in China

The administrative system of urban-rural planning is associated with the establishment of planning administrations at all levels as well as the right and obligation in mapping out and implementing urban-rural planning.

In accordance with China's Urban and Rural Planning Law, the Ministry of Housing and Urban-rural Construction, the urban-rural planning administrative agency under the State Council, is in full charge of the country's urban-rural planning. The urban-rural administrative departments of local governments above county level are responsible for urban-rural planning within their administrative regions. The urban-rural planning administrations of all levels play the overarching role in developing (inclusive of compiling and approving) and implementing the planning.

1. Administration and Establishment of Urban-rural Planning

(1) Formulation

A. The competent department in charge of urban-rural planning under the State Council shall, together with other departments under the State Council, organize the establishment of the national urban system planning.

B. The people's government of a province or autonomous region shall organize the establishment of its provincial urban system planning.

C. The people's government of a city shall organize the establishment of its overall planning.

D. The county people's government shall organize the establishment of overall planning of the town where the county people's government is located. The overall planning of any other town shall be established by the people's government of that town.

E. The formulation of regulatory detailed planning of a city shall be organized by the competent sector under the city people's government in conformity with the requirements of its city planning.

F. The regulatory detailed planning of a town shall be established by the people's government of the town in accordance with the requirements of the town's master planning; the regulatory detailed planning of the town where the county people's government is located shall be established by the competent urban-rural planning department under the government of the same level in conformity with the requirements of the comprehensive planning.

G. The site detailed planning of a key district shall be drawn up by the competent urban-rural planning department under the city or county people's government jointly with the people's government of the town.

H. The planning of the township or administrative village shall be established by the people's government of the townships or the administrative village.

(2) Examination and approval

A. The national urban system planning shall be filed by the competent department of urban and rural planning under the State Council, with the State Council exercising examination and approval.

B. The provincial urban system planning shall be filed by the people's government of a province or autonomous region, with the State Council exercising examination and approval.

C. The overall planning of a municipality directly under the central government shall be filed by the people's government of the municipality with the State Council for examination and approval. The overall planning of a city where the provincial or autonomous region people's government is located, or which is specified by the State Council, shall be filed with the State Council for examination and approval after it is examined and approved by the provincial or autonomous region people's government. The overall planning of any other city shall be filed by the people's government of the city, with the provincial or autonomous region people's government exercising examination and approval.

D. The overall planning of a town where the county people's government is located shall be filed by the county people's government with the people's government at the next higher level exercising examination and approval. The overall planning of any other town shall be filed by the people's government of that town, with the people's government at the next higher level exercising examination and approval.

E. The people's government of a town shall, in accordance with the requirements of the overall planning of that town, organize the establishment of a regulatory detailed planning and file the planning with the people's government at the next higher level for examination and approval. The regulatory detailed planning of the town where the county people's government is located shall be established by the competent department of urban and rural planning under the county people's government in accordance with the overall planning of the town, and be filed with the standing committee of the people's congress at the same level and the people's government at the next higher level for archival purpose upon the approval of the county people's government.

F. The planning of a township or administrative village shall be submitted by the people's government of the township or town to the people's government of the next higher level for approval. The planning of a natural village shall be discussed and agreed upon at the villagers' meeting or villagers' representative meeting prior to submission for examination and approval.

G. The provincial urban system planning established by the people's government of a province or an autonomous region or the overall planning established by the people's government of a municipality or county shall, before it is submitted to the people's government at the next higher level for examination and approval, be deliberated on by the standing committee of the people's congress at the same level, and the deliberation opinions of the members of the standing committee shall be submitted to the people's government at the same level for consideration.

The overall planning of a town established by the people's government of the town shall, before it is submitted to the people's government at the next higher level for examination and approval, be first deliberated on by the people's congress of the town, and the deliberation opinions of the deputies shall be submitted to the people's government at the same level for consideration.

When filing a provincial urban system planning, a city overall planning or a town overall planning for examination and approval, the organ establishing the planning shall file the deliberation opinions of the members of the standing committee of the people's congress at the same level or the deputies to the people's congress of the town as well as the changes in the planning made in accordance with the opinions.

H. Before filing an urban or rural planning for examination and approval, the organ establishing it shall announce the draft of the planning and collect opinions from experts and the general public by way of argumentation, hearing or other ways. The draft shall be announced for at least 30 days.

2. Administration and Implementation of Urban-rural Planning

During the implementation phase, the competent administrative department responsible for urban planning is supposed to carry out the following duties: to approve land use and construction projects, to supervise, inspect and finally accept completed projects, to impose penalties, and to conduct an administrative review or reconsideration.

The Urban and Rural Planning Law authorizes all competent local urban-rural planning departments to examine and approve land use and construction projects within the planning areas. All competent local administrative departments in charge of urban-rural planning are supposed to enter into the checking and final acceptance of the completed key construction projects within the planning areas and are entitled to supervise and inspect construction projects within the planning areas to confirm their conformity to the requirements of the planning.

All competent local administrative departments responsible for planning have the right to impose penalties on illegal construction. If the disputing party remains unconvinced with the administrative penalty, it is allowed to ask the administrative department at a higher level in charge of planning for an administrative review within the time limit or immediately sue at the People's Court.

The implementation of planning, therefore, largely rests with local competent administrative departments in charge of urban-rural planning and the administrative sector or sectors of a higher level are only responsible for administrative reviews or reconsiderations.

Special Column 2-3 Supervision and inspection in complementing urban-rural planning

As a centerpiece of the management of urban-rural planning and a major means to guarantee that it is worked out scientifically and seriously, supervision and inspection runs throughout the whole process of formulation and implementation of urban-rural planning. To reinforce surveillance on urban-rural planning so as to ensure it is taken seriously, an extra chapter on supervision and inspection is included in the Urban and Rural Planning Law to strengthen supervisory and inspection measures as well as supervision by the people's congress, the general public and executive sectors on urban-rural planning so that the mechanism of supervision and management of urban-rural planning will be legislatively underpinned and the guidance and regulation of urban-rural planning in urban-rural construction will be further boosted.

1. Administrative supervision in urban-rural planning

The stipulations of the Urban and Rural Planning Law on urban-rural planning with regard to administrative supervision are as follows:

(1) Supervision and inspection of people's governments above county level and their competent urban-rural planning departments on lower-level governments and their competent urban-rural planning departments in their execution of the formulation, approval, implementation and modification of urban-rural planning. For instance, the urban-rural planning mechanism of supervisors established jointly by the Ministry of Construction, Sichuan, Guizhou and other provinces (or cities) effectively involves supervisors being sent by the people's government of a higher level and its competent urban-rural planning department

to lower-level people's governments and their competent urban-rural planning departments to have an overall supervision on the formulation, approval, implementation and management of urban-rural planning.

(2) Supervision and inspection on the implementation of urban-rural planning by competent urban-rural planning departments under local people's governments above county level, namely the relative person of management commonly referred to.

2. Supervision of people's congress on urban-rural planning

Article 52 of the Urban and Rural Planning Law stipulates that a local people's government shall report the implementation situation of urban-rural planning to the standing committee of the people's congress at the same level or the people's congress of the township or town, and shall be subject to the latter's supervision.

3. Supervision of the public on urban-rural planning

It is stipulated in the Urban and Rural Planning Law that supervision, inspection and disposal of urban-rural planning shall be disclosed to the general public pursuant to the law for people to consult and supervise.

Source of data: Office of Economic Law of the Commission of Legislative Affairs of the NPC Standing Committee, Law Department of Agro-Environmental Protection of the Legislative Affairs Office of the State Council, Urban and Rural Planning Department of the Ministry of Housing and Urban-rural Development, *Interpretation on the Urban and Rural Planning Law of the People's Republic of China*, edited by the Policy and Law Department and published by Intellectual Property Press (2008)

III. Drafting, Modification and Implementation of Urban-rural Planning

The operating system of urban-rural planning consists of the compilation, modification and implementation of planning (often referred to as development planning and development controlling in many other countries).

1. Drafting

Despite variations in the formulating mechanism used in different countries, two parameters are universally recognized: urban-rural development planning and controlling. Urban-rural development planning, which constitutes the medium- and long-term objective in planning urban development as well as the countermeasure for land use, traffic control, allocation of facilities and environmental protection, aims to provide a guiding framework for the planning of development control of all areas in cities. As the legal basis on which the planning formulated is implemented, the planning of development control shall be compiled in accordance with relevant planning laws in terms of both contents and procedures, which is why it is otherwise referred to as statutory planning.

In China, urban-rural development planning is comparable to comprehensive urban planning (including district planning of large and medium-sized cities) and comprehensive planning of towns, townships and villages; and planning of development control is tantamount to regulatory planning. The regional urban system planning of all levels provides the basis for comprehensive urban planning, while site detailed planning only serves as the foundation for development control in given cases (e.g., the key areas whose construction plan has been put into practice).

2. Modification

To guarantee that urban-rural planning is carried out scientifically and seriously and to bring it under full supervision in order to improve the sustainable development of urban-rural construction, the Urban and Rural Planning Law includes an extra chapter on the modification of urban-rural planning so that a strictly-controlled mechanism for averting any attempt to change statutory planning will be legislatively defined and established.

(1) Modification of provincial urban system planning, overall city planning and overall town planning

Article 47 of the Urban and Rural Planning Law stipulates that only the authority responsible for the formulation of urban-rural planning shall be entitled to modify provincial urban system planning, overall city planning and overall town planning within its power limits and in accordance with prescribed procedures in any of the following cases:

A. Changes in urban-rural planning established by the people's government at a higher level require modification of the planning;

B. Adjustment of administrative divisions requires modification of the planning;

C. A significant construction project approved by the State Council requires modification of the planning;

D. Modification is necessary upon evaluation. Article 46 says that the organ establishing a provincial urban system planning, overall city planning or overall town planning shall organize related departments and experts to evaluate the implementation of the planning on a regular basis and collect public opinion by argumentation, hearing or other ways. The organ shall submit an evaluation report attached with the collected opinions to the standing committee of the people's congress at the same level, the people's congress of the town and the organ examining and approving the planning;

E. Other circumstances under which modification is necessary as deemed by the organ examining and approving urban-rural planning.

Before modifying the provincial urban planning system and the overall planning of cities and towns, the organ establishing it shall summarize the implementation of the planning and report the situation to the organ responsible for examining and approving the planning. If the modification involves the mandatory content of the city or town overall planning, the organ establishing it shall submit a special report to the organ that examines and approves the planning, and shall gear up for the modification plan after obtaining the consent of the organ examining and approving the planning. The modified provincial urban system planning, overall city planning or overall town planning shall be filed for approval in accordance with the examining and approving procedures.

(2) Modification of immediate construction planning

Regulatory detailed planning constitutes not only the immediate legal basis for a city or town to exercise planning administration, but also the legal precondition for the leasing of the right to use state-owned land as well as the development and construction relevant to it (see Chapter 5 for more about land used for construction in China). In this light, it directly determines the market value of land as well as the immediate interests of stakeholders. No unit or person, therefore, shall be entitled to any unauthorized modification of the regulatory planning.

Modification of regulatory detailed planning must be conducted in strict conformity with legal procedure. According to Article 48 of the Urban and Rural Planning Law, to modify regulatory planning, the organ establishing it shall register the necessity of the modification, take counsel with interested persons within the planning area, submit a special report to the organ examining and approving it, and stand ready for the modification plan after obtaining the consent of the organ examining and approving the planning. The modified regulatory detailed planning shall be filed for approval in accordance with the examining and approving procedures as prescribed in Articles 19 and 20 of this law. If the modification involves the mandatory content of the city or overall town planning, the overall planning shall be modified first.

3. Implementation

The Urban and Rural Planning Law stipulates that the system of 'one proposal and two permits' (a written proposal of location, a construction land-use permit and a planning permit on construction project) shall be adopted in China's urban planning administration and that the system of planning permission for rural construction shall be exercised in China's rural planning administration. The legally stipulated written proposal of location, the construction land use permit, the planning permit on the construction project and the planning permit for rural construction have combined to constitute the primary means and modes in the implementation and administration of China's urban-rural planning, of which the issuing of the written proposal of location pertains to administrative examination and approval while the construction land-use permit, the planning permit on construction project and the planning permit for rural construction belongs to administrative licensing.

(1) Administration of location planning for construction projects

The administration of location planning for construction projects guarantees the competent administrative department responsible for urban-rural planning to first determine or select the locations of construction projects in compliance with the urban-rural planning and related laws and regulations so that all construction shall be arranged in agreement with the urban-rural planning and then issue the written proposals of locations after checking and verification.

The Urban and Rural Planning Law clearly defines the applicable range of the written proposals of location. Article 36 of the law stipulates: "As for a construction project that is subject to the approval or verification of the related department as required by state provisions, if the right to use state-owned land is appropriated, the construction entity shall, before filing the project with the related department for approval, apply to the competent department of urban and rural planning to issue a written proposal of location."

(2) Administration of construction land-use planning

The administration of planning for construction land enables the competent administrative department responsible for urban-rural planning, in conformity with the legal norms of urban-rural planning and the planning established according to law, to determine the site, location and range of the land for construction, examine and verify the gross areas of the construction projects, furnish design conditions for land use and issue construction land-use permits.

As for now, the construction entities in China have two main ways to acquire the right to use state-owned land: appropriation and leasing (see Special Column 2-4). The land for construction acquired through different means involves different planning management.

Special Column 2-4 Acquisition of the right to use land for construction[①]

At present, construction entities in China have two main ways to acquire the right to use state-owned land: appropriation and leasing.

Appropriating the right to use state-owned land means that land users shall be consigned with the land after they have paid compensation, resettlement allowance and other expenses with the approval of the people's government at or above county level. Appropriated land falls into four general categories: land used by state organs and the army, land for common facilities and public welfare establishments, land for energy development, transportation, hydraulic engineering and other infrastructure supported by the

---

① See Chapter 5 for more about China's land system

state, and land for other uses stipulated by laws and administrative regulations.

Leasing of the right to use state-owned land means that the state consigns the right to use state-owned land within a term of years to the land users who pay to the state leasing fees for the right to use the land. Leasing of the right to the use of state-owned land may be materialized by means of tender invitation, auction, quotation or agreement. In conformity with current laws and regulations, land for commerce, tourism, entertainment industries, commercial housing and all kinds of uses of land for business purposes shall have to be obtained through tender invitation, auction or price-listing.

A. Application for construction land-use permit in case of appropriation

If the right to the use of state-owned land for a construction project within a city or town planning area is appropriated, upon the approval or verification of the related department, or archiving of the project, the construction entity shall apply to the competent department of urban and rural planning under the people's government of the city or town for permitting land use for construction. The department shall issue a construction land-use permit after checking and verifying the location and area of the land used for construction as well as the scope of areas where construction is permitted in accordance with detailed regulatory planning.

The construction entity may only apply to the competent department of land under the local people's government at or above county level for land use after obtaining the land-use permit. The competent department of land may appropriate land to it upon the approval of the people's government at or above county level.

B. Application for planning permit on construction project in case of assignment

If the right to use state-owned land within a city or town planning area is leased, the competent department of urban and rural planning under the people's government of the city or county shall, before leasing, raise planning requirements such as the location of the land to be leased, the nature of its use and development intensity as a component of the leasing contract for the right to use state-owned land on the basis of detailed regulatory planning.

If the right to use state-owned land for a construction project is obtained through leasing, the construction entity shall, after concluding the leasing contract for the right to use state-owned land, obtain the land-use permit from the competent department of urban and rural planning of the people's government of the city or county upon the strength of the approval, or verification or archive-filing documents of the project as well as the leasing contract for the right to use state-owned land.

(3) Management of construction engineering planning

The management of construction engineering planning authorizes the competent administrative department responsible for urban-rural planning to organize, regulate, guide and coordinate all kinds of construction projects so as to have them included in the system of urban-rural planning before issuing planning permits for rural construction in accordance with the urban-rural planning legally established as well as related legal and technical norms.

To build any structure, fixture, road, pipeline or other engineering project within a city or town planning area, the construction entity or individual shall apply to the competent department of urban and rural planning under the people's government of the city or county or the town people's government specified by the people's government of the province, autonomous region or municipality directly under the central government for a construction project planning permit.

(4) Management of rural construction planning

To build facilities needed by township and village enterprises, village public utilities or public welfare establishments within a township or village planning area, the construction entity or individual shall file an application with the people's government of the township or town, which shall submit the application to the competent department of urban and rural planning of the people's government of the city or county for issuing a planning permit for rural construction.

When building premises needed by township and village enterprises, rural common facilities or public welfare establishments within a township or village planning area, no farm land may be used. Where it is really necessary to use farm land, the competent department of urban and rural planning under the people's government of the city or county may issue a planning permit for rural construction after the construction entity or individual reckons with the examining and approving formalities for changing the purpose of farm land in accordance with the relevant provisions of the Land Administration Law of the PRC.

The construction entity or individual may not handle the examining and approving formalities for land use until they obtain the planning permit for rural construction.

CHAPTER 3

Industrial Distribution in Cities

I. Dominant Functions of Cities and their Industrial Layout

The function of cities refers to the part they play in national or regional economic development.[1] With the growth of cities from small towns with a single function into metropolises with multi-faceted roles, their dominant functions have been undergoing dynamic change. The industrial layout of cities is the spatial manifestation of their functions[2] and the evolution of the leading functions of cities in China constitutes the root cause for the adjustment of urban industrial layout.

1. Changes in the Dominant Function of Cities

(1) Production as the dominant function of cities prior to reform and opening up

China has enjoyed thousands of years' agricultural civilization. At the founding of the PRC, the country was still in the preindustrial era when its cities with an indistinctive function of production were in large part exchange centers for commodities that offered fragmentary services such as political leadership, administrative jurisdiction by military means, with their consumer attributes far outweighing their production properties. In 1952, the nation's total industrial output accounted for only 17.6% of gross domestic product (GDP). Cities relied on rural areas for farm products, while they were incapable of providing adequate and decent manufactured

---

[1] Yu Hongjun & Ning Yuemin. *Outline of Urban Geography* [M]. Hefei: Anhui Science and Technology Press, 1983

[2] Chu Tianjiao. *Revelations from the Evolution of the CBD in Urban Transformation in Singapore* [J]. *Modern Urban Research*, 2011,(10)

goods for both themselves and the countryside. Therefore, the promotion of production and the transformation of consumer cities into cities also featuring production became a pressing need for consolidating the newly-established people's regime, improving the living standard of the public and enabling China to survive and then prosper among world nations in the long run. When the first Five-year Plan was under way, therefore, China started to set about developing urbanization with a focus on the construction of key projects empowered with industrialization.

From the 1950s to the 1970s, under the guidance of the urban development strategy to slow down the expansion of big cities and boost the growth of small and medium-sized cities, urbanization in China progressed in a gradual and fluctuating way. With the driving of key projects, a number of new cities were constructed while old cities were developed into regional industrial production centers. The capital of the country and all provincial capitals prospered into production centers with degrees of comprehensiveness and specialization, but the majority of county towns also fared well and began to develop the so-called 'five types of small industries'.[1] As a result, production-based urban systems of different levels took shape across the country. The share of secondary industrial output in GDP rose steadily to 48.5% by 1980. However, due to an excessive emphasis on the manufacturing function of cities, coupled with an exorbitant stress on the roles of cities as industrial bases, the development of heavy industry was over-emphasized while light industry and the service sector trailed behind

---

[1] 'Five types of small industries' is the general reference to small local or regional factories and mines. During the 1960s, it referred to small workshops, small coal mines, small power stations, small fertilizer plants and small machinery works. Later on, small cement plants and other small enterprises were further included. In 1970 when the fourth Five-year Plan was carried out, the central government appealed to all provinces and autonomous regions to speed up the development of five types of small industries and decided that eight billion yuan would be appropriated from the state revenue as a special fund for the development of five types of small local industries. The growth of small industries that helped change the structure of China's industrial economy increased the proportion of small and medium-sized industrial entities in industrial enterprises and made it possible for small and medium-sized enterprises to rationally undertake responsibilities in line with the principle of specialization and cooperation. Small and medium-sized enterprises could complement or supplement large enterprises and, what is more, they could make better use of local resources. In summary, the development of small enterprises significantly enhanced the strength of the local economy and greatly improved the economic situation of individual counties that would change their previous practices from sole reliance on agriculture to an adequate amount of industry with agricultural production as the focus, and in the meantime moderately increase the income of non-agricultural employers. On the other hand, however, the booming development of five types of small industries had its flaws and would bring about negative consequences

with the result that urban infrastructure, service facilities and housing supply became extremely deficient.[1] During this period, the growth in agricultural labor productivity and the ability to supply agricultural products clearly lagged behind the pace of industrial development in cities. Moreover, the household registration system and other measures that imposed restrictions on the transfer of surplus labor forces in rural areas to non-agricultural sectors in cities made urbanization fall behind industrialization. This period, therefore, is also referred to as an era of 'industrialization without urbanization'. From 1949-1980, the number of cities in China increased from 136 to only 193, with an average annual growth rate of 1.84, while the proportion of the non-agricultural population to the total population in urban areas grew respectively from 9.1% and 10.6% to 13.7% and 19.4%.[2]

(2) Focus on coordination between production and service after reform and opening up

Beginning from the mid-1980s, China started to focus on the driving role of big cities in developing regional economies. It also lent support to the development of enterprises under all forms of ownership, small and medium-sized enterprises and township enterprises in rural areas along with its efforts to develop small cities and towns so as to promote the interaction between cities and regional economies from the bottom up. The vigorous expansion of small cities and towns made it possible for the massive surplus rural workforces to easily transfer to non-agricultural sectors and thus helped alleviate the pressures on the migration of population in medium- and large-sized cities.

The service industry plays a remarkable role in guaranteeing the driving role of medium- and large-sized cities in the growth of a regional economy. Since the 1980s, considerable progress has been made in China's infrastructure construction and service industry, the urban economic structure having thus been adjusted and the economic strength intensified. The rapid development of economies under all forms of ownership and township enterprises helped promote the rapid expansion of moderate-sized cities and small towns, which not only touched off the climax of urban construction between the end of the 1980s and the beginning of the 1990s, but also brought into being a number of agglomerated urban areas in eastern China. The number

---

① Chu Tianjiao. *General Mechanism of Regional Expansion in Urbanization* [J]. *Economic Geography*, 1998, (6)
② Zhou Yixing. *Urban Geography* [M]. Beijing: Commercial Press, 1997

of cities increased from 193 in 1980 to 668 in 1998, with an average annual growth of 26.39 cities and the ratio of the non-agricultural population to the total population rising, respectively, from 13.7% and 19.4% to 23.97% and 30.4%. The function of the tertiary industry in economic development received greater attention and its development was subsidized, the proportion of its contribution to GDP having increased from 21.4% in 1980 to 32.9% in 1998. During this period, the percentage of secondary industry only increased from 48.5% to 48.7%, while the proportion of industrial output shrank from 44.2% to 42.1%. Industrial output, however, still outweighed that of tertiary industry and the number of non-agricultural employees did not surpass those living and working in rural areas until 1997, which indicates that China at the time was still at the stage of development with industrialization as the driving force.[1]

As it came to the 1990s, the function of cities in China started to shift from a focus on production to the services sector.[2] Generally, if the number of employees in the tertiary industry is more than half of total employment, it is an indicator that the country has entered a post-industrial society where manufacturing industry has given way to the service-oriented economy. Pilot projects were under way in the late 1980s in China. Starting from the 1990s, paid transfer or assignment of land and the reform of state-owned enterprises (SOEs) and the housing system in cities were launched in a comprehensive way, which triggered the relocation of urban industries,[3] the vast stretches of industrial land in downtown areas having thus been transformed into land for tertiary industry. The rapid progress of real estate, finance, insurance, transportation, post and telecommunications and other sectors demonstrated a gradual strengthening of the leading role of tertiary industry. With the adjustment of industrial and land-use structures as well as rising public demand for promoting the quality of their life, city governments set about intensifying environmental renovation, upgrading infrastructure and service facilities, constructing green space and improving living conditions in downtown areas, thereby starting to transform production-centered cities

---

[1] Xu Xueqiang. *Urbanization in China: Theory and Practices* [M]. Beijing: Science Press, 2012

[2] Research group of 'Development Trend of Urban Planning in China' from China Academy of Urban Planning and Design. Development Trend of Urban Planning in China, 1997-1998 [J]. *Urban Planning Forum.* 1998, (4). pages 3-11

[3] Chu Tianjiao. *Dynamic Mechanism of Regional Industrial Division and Cooperation within the Context of Economic Globalization* [J]. Academic Journal of Zhongzhou, 2010, (2)

into service-oriented and lifestyle-based metropolises such as in Beijing, Shanghai, Guangzhou and Shenzhen. In these cities, the functions of both traditional shopping centers and modern business districts became more prominent[1] and well-appointed and environment-friendly residential and recreational centers were built in the outskirts of downtown areas to cater for residents of different income levels.

2. Dominant Function and Adjustment of Industrial Layout, with Shanghai as an Example

The industrial distribution in Shanghai before the 1980s was heavily skewed towards the city center. The layout was a legacy of the city's historical development and was a result of the single function of cities that prevailed in the planned economy. As industry in Shanghai took shape during the semi-colonial era before the PRC was founded, a large number of plants and factories were concentrated within the concessions downtown. After the New China was established, Shanghai worked out its guideline of urban construction to build itself into a production-centered city (see Figure 3-1).

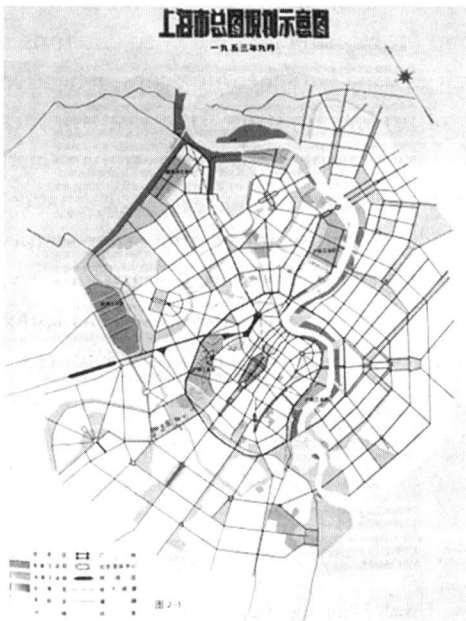

Figure 3-1 Sketch map of the General Planning of Shanghai worked out in September 1953 with the guidance of A. S. Mukhin, an expert from the former Soviet Union

① Chu Tianjiao. *Life Insurance Companies in China: Distribution and Selection of Locations* [J]. World Economic Geography, 2010, (1)

It is only natural, therefore, that an over-reliance on the established industrial base would result in single function of the city and in the meantime the rational distribution of industry would be overlooked.

In the 1950s, Shanghai finished building eight industrial parks in Pengpu, Beixinjing and other suburban areas, along with seven industrial satellite towns beyond the city suburbs, such as Minhang, Wujing and Anting (see Figure 3-2). As the inner city was constantly expanding, however, the problem with the industrial concentration in the downtown area had still not been thoroughly addressed by the 1980s. According to statistics, the number of industrial enterprises, the employed population and gross industrial output within the inner city and covering an area of 216 square kilometers accounted for, respectively, 47%, 60% and 66% of the city's entire industry by the end of 1987. Industrial density was even higher in the 10 administrative districts in the downtown area, with their numbers making up 43.8% of the city's total by 1990. The high industrial density in downtown areas gave rise to a shortage of land for industrial enterprises, aggravated urban traffic pressure, caused heavy pollution and

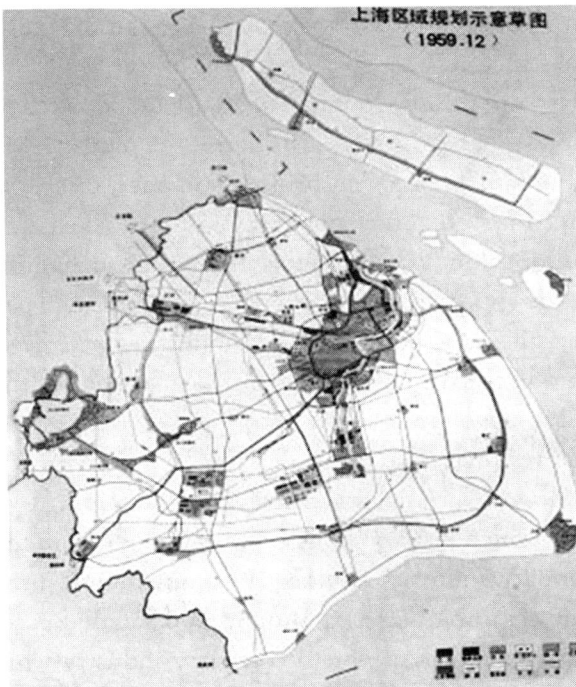

Figure 3-2 Draft of the regional planning of Shanghai
worked out in 1959

confronted urban development with a growing 'spatial crisis'. As a heavy user of urban land, industry's booming progress held up the development of the tertiary industry and impacted the performance of the city's comprehensive role.

In the reorientation of its function after the 1990s, Shanghai defined its strategic development goals to establish the city as an international economic, financial, commercial and shipping center and to restructure its industry. Conforming to the goal of urban development, Shanghai followed a policy of 'simultaneous promotion of secondary and tertiary industries' in industrial development throughout the 1990s with priority given to tertiary industry, while adjusting secondary industry and developing primary industry, thereby bringing about a pattern of economic development that was largely driven by secondary industry joining forces with tertiary industry. The exercise of industrial restructuring throughout the period helped increase the share of tertiary industry in GDP from 31.9% in 1990 to 50.6% in 2000; the proportion of secondary industry in GDP dropped from 61.7% to 47.5% over the same period, while the percentage of primary industry fell from 3.8% to 1.8%.

As the distribution of industry was manifested in the spatial projection of its industrial structure, Shanghai's industrial layout, which had previously been oriented toward the development of an urban industrial structure, had to be reshaped so that its spatial distribution of industry came into line with its global urban development planning: finance, trade, commerce and other service sectors were given supremacy in the city center, while a large number of traditional industrial enterprises that were densely distributed in the downtown area were readjusted and relocated. Industrial parks and bases mainly built on pillar and new technology industries were developed in the suburbs and modern ecological and protected urban agriculture businesses were promoted in the outskirts of the city.

By way of restructuring the industrial layout in the 1990s, there emerged a framework of industrial distribution pertaining to a metropolis like Shanghai in which tertiary industry was highlighted in the downtown area and secondary industry assumed a dominant role in the suburbs. Specifically, the central urban area (around 600 square kilometers within the outer ring) was mainly devoted to tertiary industry while secondary and primary industries were developed in the suburbs (approximately 5,700 square kilometers beyond the outer ring). Industrial distribution assumed a pattern in which the tertiary industry, along with some textiles and other light industries, formed the downtown industrial circle while the suburban industrial circle took shape in the outskirts where machinery, electronics, automotive, textiles, emerging heavy chemical industries and allied businesses were prioritized; the basic raw materials industry was developed in the urban fringes and urban agriculture featuring ecology, recreation and breeding was well promoted. Through industrial restructuring, Pudong and other suburban districts or counties turned into important supporting and sustaining areas for Shanghai's industrial development by 2000. By this time, the number of industrial enterprises, employed population and gross industrial output in this area all exceeded 70% of the city's total.

II. Construction of Development Zones: a New Industrial Space

Development zones are important spatial carriers of China's urbanization drive, and key regions that motivate the spatial restructuring of urban industry in China. To have an insight into the evolution of China's urban industrial layout, we have to be well acquainted with the construction of its development zones. As is well known, China's urban population began to burgeon after 1978. And it was the construction of development zones that provided the spatial vehicle and industrial conditions for the expansion of the urban population; if we had simply relied on the natural growth of urban areas, there would not have been adequate room to accommodate an annual increase of around 10 million urban residents. During the renovation of many large and super-large cities and the refurbishment of a great many old urban industrial bases, the policy goal of the 'retreat of secondary industry and advance of tertiary industry' was made possible because the construction of development zones offered maneuvering space for industrial restructuring and emerging industries.

1. History of Development Zones

The genesis of development zones is known to be city-based. They are particular places where preferential policies and special management systems are exercised by the Chinese government as one of the strategic choices in the face of economic globalization and the global revolution in economic technologies. Since the implementation of reform and opening up, China has been exploring its own development path that leads to modern industrialization with Chinese characteristics. It has endeavored to construct development zones that focus on establishing parks of various descriptions, whereupon those parks have become regions of most agglomerated modernized industries that enjoy the fastest economic development, largest foreign investment and the most advanced technologies. The agglomerated modern industrial parks armed with the most advanced technologies function as important platforms and they are flag bearers for China's industrialization, urbanization and internationalization. They have long been the leading growth poles in regional economic development and they have won the stamp of approval of the Party Central Committee and the State Council and commanded the attention of countries worldwide, especially developing ones. By the end of 2006, China had a total of 11,568 state- and province-level development zones with a planning area of 7,629 square kilometers. They were largely distributed in coastal regions or along rivers (the Yangtze in particular), railways (notably the Longhai Railway) and borders or in inland capitals of provinces, autonomous regions, prefectures as well as in central cities (see Figure 3-3). The construction of development zones in China occurred in three stages, as follows.

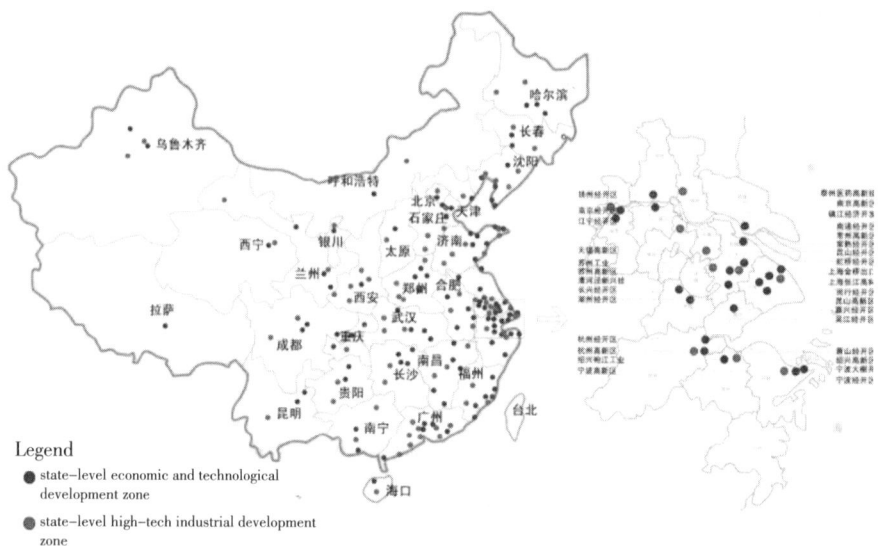

Figure 3-3 Distribution of state-level economic and technological development zones and high-tech industrial development zones

(1) Exploratory stage (1984-1991)

China's reform and opening up started with the construction of development zones. This stage witnessed the inauguration of state-level economic and technological development zones (ETDZs) and high-tech industrial development zones.[①]

A. Construction of state-level ETDZs

In 1984, the party and the government made a decision to open Dalian, Tianjin, Guangzhou and 11 other port cities to the outside world. It also approved the construction of 11 ETDZs in Dalian, Qinhuangdao, Ningbo, Qingdao, Yantai, Zhanjiang, Guangzhou, Tianjin, Nantong, Lianyungang and Fuzhou so that China could bring in advanced and much-needed technologies from abroad, establish Sino-foreign joint or cooperative ventures, exclusively foreign-owned enterprises and Sino-foreign cooperative research institutes, develop joint production and cooperative research design projects, develop new techniques and high-end products, increase export earnings, supply interior regions with new materials and key components, and disseminate new technologies and techniques along with scientific managerial expertise and practices.[②] In 1986, the State Council approved the construction of two more ETDZs at Hongqiao and Minhang in Shanghai. All these zones have since become the most dynamic and attractive regions to investors and have played pivotal roles in driving China's industrialization, urbanization and construction of a well-off society in a comprehensive way.

B. Construction of state-level high-tech industrial development zones

In 1988, the government, in order to boost technological innovation and commercialization of research findings, approved the establishment of state-level high-tech industrial development zones, the first one being Zhongguancun Science and Technology Park in Beijing. That same year, Caohejing Hi-Tech Park was constructed, based on the Instrumentation and Electronics Industrial Zone, Microelectronics Industrial Zone and

---

① Gu Chaolin & Wang Hesheng. *Construction and Growth of Development Zones in China* [A]. edited by Niu Fengrui, Pan Jiahua & Liu Zhiyan. *Development of Cities in China within Three Decades* [C]. Beijing: Social Sciences Academic Press, 2009

② *Circular of the State Council on Forwarding the Summary of the Forum of Some Coastal Cities.* May 4, 1984

Bioengineering Base located in Shanghai.

(2) Stage of booming development (1992-1996)

After two years' improvement and rectification from 1989 to 1990,[1] China's economy moved into a phase of revival and rapid progress in 1991 when the construction of development zones started to gather pace while various development areas advanced rapidly and bonded areas, tourist resorts and other new types of development zone were established.

During this period, development zone construction began to push westward along the great rivers and a nationwide 'development zone spree' was under way when all provinces and cities across the country spared no effort in constructing their own development zones. By the end of 1994, a total of some 700 state-, province- and city-level development zones had been established, including 32 state-level economic and technological zones, 52 national high-tech industrial parks, 13 national bonded areas, 11 national tourist resorts and the Suzhou-Singapore Industrial Park. Among these development zones, the bonded areas and 91.7% of national tourist resorts were located in eastern coastal regions, while the locations of other types and levels of development zones were quite widely dispersed.

Construction of development zones at this stage had three main features. First, the scale and quality of foreign investments were upgraded. Multinational corporations replaced small and medium-sized enterprises to become major investors. They invested in projects with a reasonably high technical content and funded a number of research and development centers,[2] foreign investment in China having then grown substantially in scale. Motorola, for instance, invested 1.1 billion US dollars in Tianjin Development Zone in 1992 to become the leading foreign-owned enterprise in China at the time. Second, the zones made high profile achievements in terms of economic strength, value of industrial output, tax revenue and economic benefit. In 1996, the industrial output of

---

[1] With the rapid progress in reforming the economic system from 1985 to 1988, the overheated development of China's economy persisted while inflation worsened. From 1989 to 1990, China positively adjusted its economic structure by cutting down the total demand of society and tightening control over expenditure and credit and in the long run managed to bring inflation under control, its industrial restructuring having thus been launched

[2] Chu Tianjiao & Song Tao. *Spatial Patterns and Contributing Factors for R&D Investments of Multinational Corporations in Developing Countries* [J]. Economic Geography, 2006, (1)

the 14 economic and technological development zones in the coastal regions increased by 858% compared with that in 1991. Third, the share of economic output of development zones in the cities in which they were located increased. In 1996, the industrial output of Guangzhou Development Zone accounted for 11.2% of the city's total, while that of Tianjin Development Area took up 18% of the city's total, which indicates that development zones had already become sizable growth poles in the urban economy.[1]

(3) Stage of sustained progression (1997-date)

The outbreak of the Asian financial crisis in 1997 gave rise to a sharp downturn in foreign investment in China's development zones. The crisis highlighted the huge risks involved in developing an export-oriented economy and triggered a phase of adjustment, transformation and upgrading in the construction of development zones. In this period, the guideline for the construction of development zones was shifted from a dependence on attracting foreign capital to one that stressed the need to introduce both domestic and overseas capital, cultivating embeddedness of industries and promoting the transformation and upgrading of industrial structure. In the meantime, differences between development zones were exposed in terms of economic performance and waste of land resources. In 2004, the government reorganized all development zones and optimized their structure by canceling or merging many zones that were inferior in economic performance. By 2007, 1,568 state- and province-level development zones had passed national approval after rectification and reorganization, of which 223 were state level (see Table 3-1). Those zones that passed approval were of great importance to the nation's economy in attracting investment, generating imports and exports, and overall industrial development (see Table 3-2). To date, national high-tech industrial development zones have evolved into important bases of China's modern manufacturing industry and high-tech industrialization.

[1] Wang Fengyu & Zhu Xiaojuan. *China Development Zones Development Review and Strategic Thinking* [J]. Yunnan Geographic Environment Research, 2006, (4). page 96

Table 3-1 Types and numbers of development zones in China (2007)

Levels	Types	Number	Remarks
State-level development zones	Total	223	
	ETDZs	54	Including Suzhou Industrial Park, Jinqiao Export Processing Zone (Shanghai), Ningbo ETDZ, Haichang Taiwanese Investment Zone (Xiamen) and Yangpu Economic Development Zone (Hainan) that enjoy preferential policies for state-level ETDZs
	High-tech industrial development zones	54	
	Export processing zones	57	
	Bonded areas	16	
	Bonded logistic parks	6	
	Taiwanese investment zones	4	
	Cross-Strait sci-tech industrial parks	2	
	Border economic cooperation zones	14	
	Border trade districts	2	
	National resort districts	12	
	Cross-border industrial zones	1	Zhuhai-Macau Cross-border Industrial District is China's only state-level development zone across two administrative regions
	Finance and trade zones	1	Lujiazui Finance and Trade Zone in Pudong, Shanghai, is the country's only state-level development zone, mainly engaged in finance and trade
Province-level Development Zones	Total	1,345	
	Economic development zones	810	
	Industrial parks	535	Includes 64 high-tech industrial parks
Total		1,568	

Source: National Development and Reform Commission (NDRC)

Table 3-2 Major economic indicators for state-level development zones for the
economic and technological industry (2006)

Indexes	GDP (billion RMB)	Industrial added value (billion RMB)	Tax revenue (billion RMB)	Total export-import volume (billion USD)	Total export volume (billion USD)	Total import volume (billion USD)	Actual foreign investment (billion USD)
Development zones	1,013.690	741.424	157.002	283.096	149.233	133.863	14.712
National total	20,940.7	9,035.1	3,763.6	1,760.7	969.1	791.6	63.0
Percentage of development zones in national total	4.84%	8.21%	4.17%	16.08%	15.40%	16.91%	23.35%

Source: Ministry of Commerce

Moving into the 21st century, China continued to enjoy a steady growth in the construction of development zones. Take state-level development zones. At the end of the 11th Five-year Plan, there were 116 state-level development zones, their economic output having kept on expanding, the growth of their major economic indicators all in excess of the national average and their contribution to the national economy having steadily increased. Over the course of the 11th Five-year Plan, the total output value of state-level development zones increased at an annual rate of 23%, with its share of the national total having increased by 7%, the proportion of their industrial added value standing at 12%, the rate of their gross exports accounting for 16% and the percentage of their gross tax revenue standing at 6%. Compared with the levels at the end of the 10th Five-year Plan, these indicators had grown by 2%, 3%, 0.5% and 1.5% respectively. Moreover, the economic driving capacity of state-level development zones for local regions was strengthened, the gross value of production they generated accounting for more than 13% of the total of the cities in which they were located.

2. Influence of Development Zones on Remodeling Urban Industrial Space

For China, the original purposes of establishing development zones were to attract foreign capital and develop the high-tech and export processing industries. With the passage of time, however, development zones achieved more than this, becoming robust economic growth poles of local cities, the main platform for an export-oriented economy, the core area of innovation systems and the forefront of reform and opening up. In addition, they developed into the major driving force and key vehicle for urbanization.[①] Development zones were not only important venues where newly arrived peasants were expected to change their career and way of life, but the most significant regions that would spearhead the modernization of urban areas. Construction of development zones has enabled many cities to pool their massive industries and populations within a limited time period, and they have also played a crucial role in promoting local cities' industrial upgrading, optimization of urban spatial organization, improvement and elevation of urban functions, renewal and regeneration of urban infrastructure, and construction of new urban districts. Development zones, therefore, can be seen as important carriers or vehicles of China's urbanization.

The spatial relationship between China's development zones and the local cities has witnessed two stages of evolution.

(1) Development zones' 'isolated island' stage (1984-mid-1990s)

To moderate the highly probable impact and interference imposed by foreign-funded enterprises on China's economic system, development zones were established at the start in locations a short distance from urban areas. In fact, they were virtually 'isolated islands', spatially set apart from the local cities by roads, rivers and other geographic boundaries. At this stage, all development zones in China bore a resemblance to export processing zones in foreign countries in terms of functions. By taking advantage of China's inexpensive workforce and preferential policies, foreign-funded enterprises came to invest and establish operations in development zones, their scale of investment being relatively small and their technical merits inadequate. In general, the enterprises were remote from the economy of local cities because their raw materials and markets were both absent locally, which is why development zones established at that stage are now known as 'isolated islands'.

(2) Development zones merging with cities stage (mid-1990s-)

Beginning from the mid-1990s, development zones started to proliferate

---

① Zheng Guo. *Growth of Development Zones and Reconstruction of Urban Space in China: Implications and History* [J]. Modern Urban Research, 2011, (5). pages 20-24

both in number and in scale. Almost all cities rushed to plan and construct their own development zones. After 1998, when the guideline for constructing development zones was shifted from a previous reliance on inviting foreign capital to an emphasis on attracting both domestic and overseas capital while the focus of foreign-funded enterprises shifted from exports to both exports and the domestic market, the economic tie between individual enterprises and that between enterprises and local cities within development zones was bolstered when their growth pole effect started to come into play and their driving role in urban economic development was appreciably strengthened. In the meantime, as the expansion of urban infrastructure construction enabled urban areas to further extend and the overall layout of cities started to move from a monocentric to polycentric pattern, development zones and industrial districts of cities became increasingly connected to urban areas.

Thanks to its strong starting point, manufacturing industry in development zones generally represented the development trend of urban areas. At this stage, development zones took a lead in the spatial evolution of manufacturing industry in cities and had a clear and far-reaching effect on the industrial, residential and social space as well as social forms in urban areas. To begin with, the construction of development zones helped accelerate restructuring of urban manufacturing space and facilitated a fresh proliferation and concentration in the spatial structure of urban manufacturing industry, development zones having turned into a place where competitive urban manufacturing industries congregated. Second, the advance of development zones helped drive the suburbanization of the urban population and socio-spatial differentiation. At this stage, upscale communities dominated by affluent groups were attracted to development zones. Finally, due to the comparatively large scale of China's development zones and as a result of the expansion of land for industry that characterized China's urbanization at the time, development zone progress largely held sway over the reconstruction of the urban spatial pattern.

With the aggregation of industries, populations and diverse parameters of production along with the constant improvement in structure and function, development zones now increasingly border on urbanized areas in terms of density of population, level of facility and type of function. The visible and invisible 'boundaries' between development zones and other urban areas are breaking down and, in the long run, they will merge through unceasing amalgamation.

III. Development of New Urban Districts: Reconstruction of Industrial Space

During China's rapid urbanization, construction of new urban districts has become a priority and an effective measure to ease the pressure on population and industry in the downtown area and optimize the regional space of metropolises. At the beginning of the 21st century, when planning and construction of new urban districts was under way in many big cities in China, the formation of a more rational pattern of industrial division between new and old urban districts helped improve the industrial space.

1. Construction of New Urban Districts in China: Background

The history of new urban districts in China can be traced back to the building of satellite towns in the 1950s. Since these satellite towns were relatively small and contained few industrial sectors and ancillary facilities, they could play only a very limited role in addressing problems relating to the urban population and industry because they were of little attraction to residents.

Within the context of economic globalization and deepening of reform and opening up at the end of the 20th century, China's economy, society and urbanization entered a rapid and sustained phase of development. However, the over-density of the population and economic and social activities in metropolises gave rise to huge pressure on normal urban operation. Without reform of the prevailing urban structure, the further development of big cities would be constrained. In this regard, it became a key consideration for metropolitan governments to further expand urban development space, optimize urban structure, relieve pressure on population growth in old urban districts and boost the comprehensive competitiveness of their cities. This being the case, a growing number of big cities began to take the initiative to construct new urban districts in order to enlarge urban space. The purpose was to rationalize the layout and distribution of industries and populations. This meant relocating the population in downtown areas and moderating the pressure on the population and aggregated industries in city centers, while at the same time focusing on the urbanization of suburbs so as to arrest the probable flooding of the population into downtown areas.

Scholar Li Guiwen et al have reviewed the deep-seated factors explaining the rapid development of new urban districts in China since 2000.[①]

First, urban economic development has triggered demand for an expansion of urban space. Since the implementation of reform and opening up, urban areas have been spearheading the development of China's economy and this pattern of growth enables resource elements and populations to congregate in urban areas. Congregation and diffusion constitute two major manifestations in the development of cities. In highly developed metropolises, such as Beijing, Shanghai and Guangzhou, urban areas are no longer in a position to accommodate excessive populations and industries due to limited resources and space and therefore urban functions begin to extend outward and new urban districts have taken shape in the process of expansion and proliferation.

Second, the accelerated reform of land systems has changed the spatial pattern of urban industries. Since the reform and opening up was launched, the exercise of the system of paid use of land, coupled with the growth of the land market, has helped promote the efficiency of land use. The effect of land prices has made it possible for downtown areas to develop into places where commerce, trade, finance and other high-profit industries congregate, while activities such as industry and storage sectors tend to gravitate toward the suburbs where land is less expensive. These new urban districts in the vicinity of metropolises have become major areas that have facilitated a shift in functions.

Third, the reform of the housing system enables urban residents to choose where they would like to settle down. Since the second half of 1998, all towns and cities across the country have stopped the practice of allocating housing and replaced it with a free market in housing distribution. As house prices increased in central downtown areas, new urban districts have been attracting many residents with newly-built and reasonably-priced homes, thereby bringing about the rapid development of real estate and residential quarters in new urban districts.

Fourth, improvements in traffic and transportation have shortened the

---

① Li Guiwen, Zhang Xueyong & Zeng Yu. *Conditions for Construction of New Urban Districts in China – with Beijing, Shanghai and Guangzhou as Examples* [J]. Huazhong Architecture, 2011, (2)

temporal and spatial distance between new urban districts and downtown with the accelerated development of rail lines and bus rapid transit. By the end of 2005, 10 cities in China – Beijing, Shanghai, Tianjin, Guangzhou, Changchun, Dalian, Chongqing, Wuhan, Shenzhen and Nanjing – had put into operation urban rail transit networks. Moreover, networked rail transit in cities that shortens the commuting time between new urban districts and downtown has greatly helped strengthen the links between them and promoted the development of the former.

Unlike those industrial satellite towns established in the 1950s, the new urban districts constructed in China since the beginning of the 21st century have been on a larger scale, and boast more comprehensive functions and greater possibilities of 'balanced self-development'.

2. Optimization of Industrial Space via Development of New Urban Districts

(1) System of new urban districts in Beijing

Beijing is the capital of the PRC, and was among the first cities where satellite towns were built. Since the beginning of the 21st century, construction of new urban districts has been taken as a key initiative to decentralize urban residents and industries. In line with its master urban planning for 2004-2020, Beijing has laid out its urban spatial structure according to the design concept of 'double axis-two belts-multicenter' and thus brought into being 11 new urban districts to form a configuration that is typical of 'central city-new urban districts-towns' (see Figure 3-4). The central city, occupying an

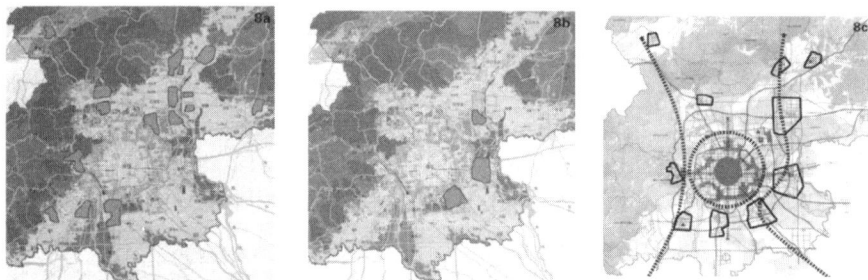

Figure 3-4 Distribution of new urban districts in Beijing
A. Distribution of the 11 new urban districts; B. The three new urban districts as key construction projects; C. Spatial layout of the new urban districts
Source: Beijing Municipal Planning Bureau

area of around 1,085 square kilometers, mainly focuses on political, cultural and economic functions. The new urban districts built on previous satellite towns enjoy relative independence and are responsible for decentralizing the population in the central city, aggregating new industries and shepherding regional development. Of the 11 projected new urban districts, Tongzhou, Shunyi and Yizhuang have been identified as priority development areas with a planned population of 0.7-0.9 million.

(2) Guangzhou: a polycentric and networked city

Prior to the reform and opening up, the development of Guangzhou, the third largest city in China, was primarily centered on its old urban district. Since the reform and opening up was under way, it has built the Guangzhou ETDZ, Nansha ETDZ, Guangzhou High-tech Industrial Development Zone and Guangzhou Science City, all of which had the attributes of early new urban districts. With Mount Baiyun and the Pearl River located within the city border, Guangzhou is fan-shaped, extending all the way to the east and the north. In 2000, the establishment of Panyu and Huadu as districts paved the way for the spatial growth of the built-up areas. In its new development strategy worked out in 2000, the pattern of its urban expansion was defined as a 'point-axis' model that featured radical development, in which a series of new urban districts would be constructed along the axes of extension toward the east and south. To date, the new urban districts that have benefited from all-round development have succeeded in decentralizing industries and population of the city, and have functioned as robust growth poles on the development axes as laid down in the city's strategic planning. Overall, they will apply themselves to promoting the way of urban expansion, accelerating the adjustment of urban spatial structure and boosting the regional comprehensive competitiveness of the city.

In line with the city's master planning outline for 2011-2020, the land for urban-rural construction will total 1,772 square kilometers and the permanent population will reach 18 million by 2020. The urban spatial layout will be polycentric and networked in structure, comprising 'one metropolitan area, two new urban districts and three sub-centers' (see Figure 3-5). The metropolitan area is identified as the major driver of key urban functions with priority on the development of modern commerce and trade, finance and insurance, cultural innovation, medical and health services, business and sci-tech information, headquarters economy and other modern service sectors. The metropolitan area should also feature an optimized layout of regions, high-end urban functions, protection of history and culture, and promotion of land-use efficiency and environmental quality. The two new urban districts are Nansha New Coastal City and Eastern New Landscape City, their primary functions being to improve comprehensiveness and coherence, enhance comprehensive service capacities, facilitate balance and coordination of residential, employment and public service facilities and their synchronous development with industries, and to attract residents and encourage congregation. The three sub-centers, located at Huadu, Conghua and Zengcheng, function as important vehicles of the overall urban-rural development, the role of which is to enhance comprehensive services, decentralize the population and functions within the metropolitan area, and drive the joint development of, and overall integration between, towns and incorporated villages.

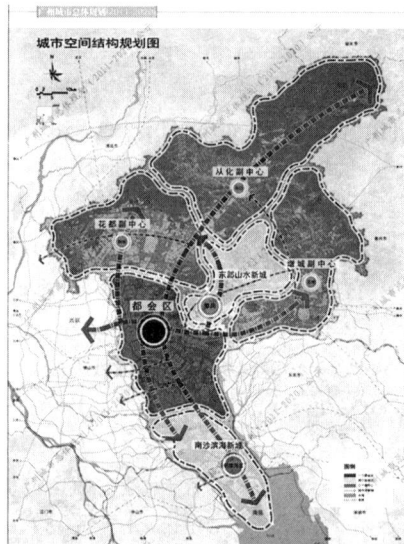

Figure 3-5 Planning map of the urban spatial structure of Guangzhou
Source: Guangzhou Municipal Planning Bureau

(3) New urban district in Ningbo City

The city of Ningbo has long been extending outward, with Sanjiang District as the center. The mode of construction, slow-paced, costly and tending to result in a highly compact old urban district and considerable disorder at the urban-rural fringes, can no longer meet the spatial requirement of the goal to develop Ningbo into an economic center to the south of the Yangtze River Delta. To make up the functional defects of the old urban district and mitigate the problems with the population, housing, traffic, the environment and others, the city government has decided to develop and construct a new urban district.

In line with the city's master urban planning for 2004-2020, Sanjiang District will focus on tertiary industry, production and residential areas, with the moderate development of high-tech or clean industries. The district will centre on the Yuyao, Fenghua and Yong rivers that run through the city. Along these rivers, a cluster of city-level centers of administration, commerce, business, culture and education will be established. The areas within the inner ring will focus on the preservation of the ancient town and the redevelopment of the old district; the district within the middle ring will center on the tertiary industry and residential areas; and the region between the middle ring and the outer ring will be devoted to clean urban industries and residences (see Figure 3-6). A new urban district will be developed and constructed in the east of the old urban district with the purpose of expanding urban development space, relieving pressure on the old district, decentralizing its population and industries, displacing some of the previous functions of the urban center and improving urban functions (see Figure 3-7).

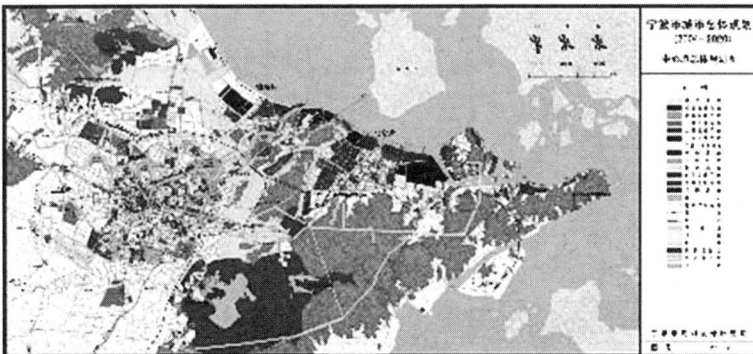

3-6 Master planning of Ningbo City (2004-2020): planning map of the central urban area
Source: Ningbo Municipal Planning Bureau

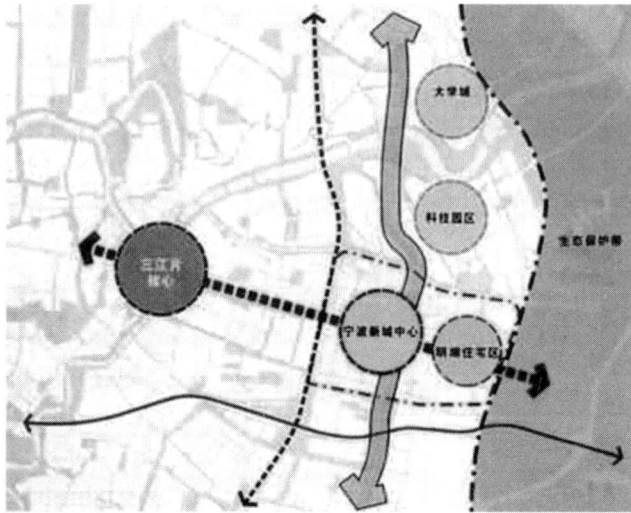

3-7 The new urban district in the east of Ningbo city and its connections with the old town
Source: Ningbo Municipal Planning Bureau

The new urban district is expected to mainly act as a center for administration, science, technology business, information, expositions, eco-leisure and residential homes, and will become the pivot of economic development in Ningbo. In line with this functional orientation, it will turn into a new urban district with a population of around 200,000-300,000, fully functional and relatively independent of the central city.

CHAPTER 4

Construction of Urban Infrastructure in China

I. History of the Construction of Urban Infrastructure in China

Urban infrastructure is essential for cities to sustain and develop. Urban traffic infrastructure, water supply, drainage, sewage treatment, gas supply, heat supply, power supply, telecommunications, landscaping, environmental health and flood control are closely related to the everyday lives of households. Actually, all economic activity in cities and the life of each and every resident cannot be sustained without them. Large-scale construction and development of urban infrastructure in China started with the implementation of reform and opening up in the 1980s. We may say that China's industrialization and urbanization have significantly promoted the progress of its infrastructural construction to the point that China now stands out as a great and powerful state in terms of infrastructural construction.

Infrastructure encompasses all public utilities or facilities in decent to good condition and they are indispensable for satisfying the needs of residents and the production of all trades and industries in the national economy. As the foundation of other social activities, infrastructural construction plays a crucial role in society at large. Infrastructure can be broken down into various types from different standpoints, the most commonly adopted method being their classification as economic and social infrastructure in terms of their components and supplies. As defined by the World Bank, economic infrastructure includes public utilities, public works and traffic facilities: public utilities consist of electric power, communication, water supply, environmental health, pollution discharge, collection and disposal of solid waste, and pipeline gas; public works refer to highways, railways, dams, irrigation facilities and canals for water drainage; and traffic facilities involve urban transportation, harbors, and air and water transport. Social infrastructure comprises human-generated facilities of culture, education, medicine, insurance and other sectors. This chapter mainly focuses on economic infrastructure.

1. Stage of Inadequacy before Reform and Opening Up

During the two decades or more after the founding of the PRC, investment in infrastructural construction was inadequate, not to mention the spiral of sharp decline that occurred during the Cultural Revolution. The share of infrastructural investment in capital construction investment was about 2% throughout the period. At the beginning of our founding, industry, heavy industry in particular, was given top priority in the nation's economic development plan, while urban development and investment in infrastructure were disregarded to the extent that the construction of infrastructure lagged far behind the development of industry and the urban economy. Inadequate and obsolete infrastructure exacerbated administrative monopoly in the sector, which in turn gave rise to inefficiency and inequity. In the meantime, laws, regulations and institutional policies connected with the planning, construction, operation and management of infrastructure were highly deficient and scant, while enterprises and public institutions engaged in infrastructure were desperately in need of a mechanism and motivation for self-development.[①]

2. Period of Recovery from 1981 to 1990

After the initiation of reform and opening up when governments at all levels and the society at large woke up to the fact that infrastructure played a fundamental role in social and economic development, infrastructural construction started to play a bigger role in economic and social development planning and fixed asset investment nationwide. At the same time, pilot reform was initiated in infrastructural investment, construction and the managerial system. During the decade, the aggregate investment in infrastructure reached 64.017 billion RMB, which was five times the

---

① Jiang Shijie. *Investment in Infrastructure and Progress of Urbanization* [M]. Beijing: China Construction Industry Press, 2010

total of the 25 years before the founding of the New China. Its proportion in total fixed asset investment increased from just 2-3% to 4%, China's infrastructural construction having thus begun to bottom out.[①]

3. Stage of Development from the 1990s to the Present Day

This stage witnessed a year-by-year increase in the share of social infrastructural investment, with remarkable achievements scored in infrastructural construction (see Figure 4-1). Considerable progress was made and a broad range of infrastructure was introduced for the first time in the country's history. Urban infrastructure was rolled out in a sustained manner that bolstered urbanization across the country.

Table 4-1 Development of urban infrastructure in China

Indexes	1990	1995	2000	2005	2010
Urban construction					
Built-up area (sq km)	12,856	19,264	22,439	32,521	40,058
Urban population density (people/sq km)	279	322	442	870	2,209
Urban supply of water, gas and central heating					
Aggregate annual water supply (bn m³)	38.23	48.16	46.9	50.21	50.79
Domestic water consumption (bn m³)	10.01	15.81	20	24.37	23.88
Domestic water per capita (tons)	67.9	71.3	95.5	74.5	62.6
Penetration of water supply (%)	48	58.7	63.9	91.1	96.7
Annual supply of manufactured gas (bn m³)	17.47	12.67	15.24	25.58	29.65
Household consumption (bn m³)	2.74	4.57	6.31	4.59	2.69
Annual supply of natural gas (bn m³)	6.42	6.73	8.21	21.05	48.76
Household consumption (bn m³)	1.16	1.64	2.48	5.21	11.72
Annual supply of LPG (mn tons)	2.19	4.887	10.537	12.22	12.68
Household consumption (mn tons)	1.428	3.702	5.323	7.065	6.339
Length of gas pipelines (1,000 km)	24	44	89	162	309
Penetration of gas supply (%)	19.1	34.3	45.4	82.1	92
Area of central heating (bn m³)	0,21	0.65	1.11	2.52	4.36

---

① Jiang Shijie. *Investment in Infrastructure and Progress of Urbanization* [M]. Beijing: China Construction Industry Press, 2010

Indexes	1990	1995	2000	2005	2010
Municipal facilities					
Year-end length of constructed roads (1,000 km)	95	130	160	247	294
Road lengths per 1,000 people (km)	31	38	41	69	75
Lengths of urban drainage pipes (1,000 km)	58	110	142	241	370
Density of urban drainage pipes (km/km^2)	4.5	5.7	6.3	7.4	9
Daily capacity of urban sewage treatment (mn m^3)				79.897	133.929
Treatment rate of domestic sewage (%)				51.95	82.31
Urban public transport					
Year-end number of operating public transport vehicles (1,000 vehicles)	62	137	226	313	383
Indexes	1990	1995	2000	2005	2010
Public transport vehicles per 1,000 people (standard vehicles)	0.22	0.36	0.53	0.86	0.97
Total length of rail transit lines in operation (km^2)					1,428.9
Urban landscaping and gardening					
Area of urban green space (1,000 hectares)	475	678	865	1,468	
Per capita area of parks and greenbelt (m^2)	1.8	2.5	3.7	7.9	11.18
Numbers of parks	1,970	3,619	4,455	7077	9,955
Area of parks (1,000 hectares)	39	73	82	158	258
Urban sanitation					
Delivering quantity of household refuse (mn tons)	67.67	106.71	118.19	155.77	158.05

Source: China Statistical Yearbook 2007; China Construction Yearbook 2011

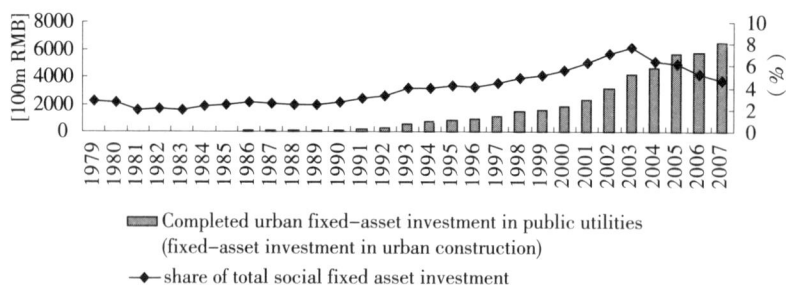

Completed urban fixed–asset investment in public utilities
(fixed–asset investment in urban construction)

share of total social fixed asset investment

Figure 4-1 Percentage of investment in urban infrastructure (1979-2007)
Source: China Urban Construction Statistics Yearbook

Beginning in 2003, the country took the initiative to multiply government investment in basic industries and infrastructure, and encourage foreign and private capital to invest in projects that would enhance the construction of basic industries and infrastructure. The appearance of cities, the progress in urban economic and social development, and the quality of life of urban residents across the country were significantly improved. Between 2003 and 2007, the aggregate investment in basic industries and infrastructure reached 18.2703 trillion RMB. This was 1.6 times the level of the 1978-2002 period, the average annual growth rate having increased by 24.9% compared with a 9.2% rise in the overall national economy in the same period.[1]

During the 10th and 11th five-year plans, built-up urban infrastructure across the country grew to a considerable scale. According to the National Bureau of Statistics, the accumulated total completion of investment in China's urban infrastructural construction during the 11th Five-year Plan hit 22.1 trillion RMB. By exploiting major international events, such as the 2008 Olympic Games and the 2010 World Expo, Beijing, Shanghai and other super-large cities further developed their urban infrastructure and elevated urban functions.

With the constant improvement to hardware construction in urban infrastructure, software-related elements were also being developed. Meanwhile, reform in the system and mechanism of infrastructure continued to flourish, the centerpieces of which were the market orientation and separation of government functions from municipal public utilities in the infrastructure sector. Over the past two decades or so, all economic enterprises and institutions have jumped at the chance to invest in, or construct and develop, urban infrastructure. Meanwhile, there has been a proliferation in the number of specialized enterprises engaged in urban infrastructure and municipal public utilities. Simultaneously, the central and local governments have all drawn up and implemented catalogues of laws and regulations on urban infrastructure and public utilities concerning investment, construction, operation and supervision, thus ushering in China's national and local legal systems for the construction of urban infrastructure and public utilities (see Table 4-2).

---

[1] Jiang Shijie. *Investment in Infrastructure and Progress of Urbanization* [M]. Beijing: China Construction Industry Press, 2010

Table 4-2 Laws and regulations related to drainage in Shanghai

Date of issue	Titles of laws, regulations and files	Contents	Notes
1995	Shanghai Municipal Administrations of Fees Paid for Drainage Facilities and Enforcement Regulations	Purpose, definition, application, competent authorities, collection and management authorities of drainage charge; computation, standard and way of charging	
1996	Regulations of Shanghai Municipality on Drainage Administration	Definition of drainage, drainage charge, supervision of the Water Supplies Bureau, reliability of districts and counties, duties of sewerage corporations, and accountability of governments at all levels and related departments in planning, construction, operation, management and maintenance	First issued in 1996 and amended three times in response to the reform of government's water affairs management system
2002	Provisional Regulations on the Management Liabilities of the City, Districts and Counties	Accountability of the Water Supplies Bureau in managing urban drainage inclusive of planning, supervision, approval, instruction and management of city and city-governed drainage facilities; competent departments at district and county levels responsible for planning, supervision, approval and reporting to higher authorities in managing city-owned and district-governed as well as district-owned and district-governed facilities	Adapted to the two-level coordinated management system between the city and subordinate districts
2011	Administrative Franchise of Shanghai Municipal Public Facilities	Franchising and authorized franchise through competition in operating and managing infrastructures	Exclusive of infrastructure in stock

II. Problems with the Construction of Urban Infrastructure in China

Although China has made impressive achievements in the construction and development of urban infrastructure and people have enjoyed ongoing improvements in their quality of life, we still have a long way to go in view of the mounting problems that confront us.

1. Asymmetry in Development

Despite the phenomenal progress in the development of urban infrastructure, China remains relatively behind in urban infrastructural construction considering the continuing acceleration of urbanization and residents' constantly growing demand for a better life. China is far behind highly urbanized countries and the world at large with regard to per capita indexes of most infrastructural facilities in light of the striking imbalance in the construction and development of its urban infrastructure. Such asymmetry refers to the disparities in regional distribution and the gulf between coastal regions and the interior. Second, it reflects the urban-rural disparity that exists due to the long-standing consideration that cities outweigh the countryside. Third, it relates to the fact that disequilibrium is found in the industrial structure of infrastructure and that the development of different infrastructural facilities varies considerably. For instance, in the 668 cities nationwide, about half of the built-up areas do not have a decent drainage system and are inflicted with inferior auxiliary facilities. This is particularly true in old urban districts where avenues are wide and a satisfactory plumbing system is absent, the penetration rate of drainage networks having stood merely at around 60%.[①]

2. Striking Financing Gaps

Studies by the Development Research Center of the State Council note that the most conservative estimate of investment in infrastructure for each increased urban resident will be 90,000 RMB. Findings by the United Nations Development Program show that investment in urban infrastructure in developing countries generally accounts for 3-5% of their GDP and the percentage will have to increase in line with an accelerating rate of urbanization. *Connecting East Asia: a New Framework of Infrastructure*, published by the Asian Development Bank, the Japan Bank for International Cooperation and the World Bank in 2006,[②] predicted that China's investment in infrastructure would reach approximately 7% of its annual GDP (see Figure 4-2). According to the estimate in the *Development*

① Jiang Shijie. *Investment in Infrastructure and Progress of Urbanization* [M]. Beijing: China Construction Industry Press, 2010

② ADB, JBIC & WB. *Connecting East Asia: a New Framework of Infrastructure* [M]. Beijing: World Bank Press, 2006

Report on China's Urbanization (2001-2002), an anticipated urbanization level of 70% in China by around 2050 will involve an investment of 40-50 trillion RMB in developing infrastructure, which means that an annual investment of 800-900 billion RMB will be needed. The financing of huge investment funds for infrastructure looms as a pressing issue to be addressed by the Chinese government.

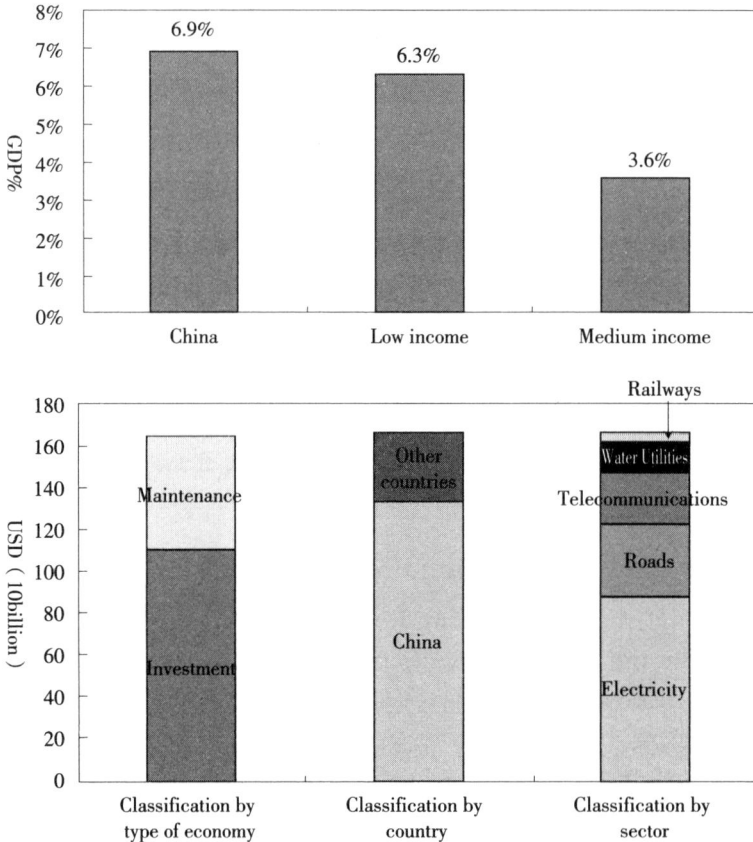

Figure 4-2 Prediction of demand for infrastructure investment in China
Source: ADB, JBIC & WB. Connecting East Asia: a New Framework of Infrastructure [M]. Beijing: World Bank Press, 2006

3. System to Be Further Improved

Since 1999, the Chinese government has gradually relinquished control of its urban infrastructure market and brought into being a framework of diversified capital by introducing the competitive market mechanism and improving the system and mechanism for urban infrastructure investment, construction, operation and management.[1]

In July 2004, the State Council issued the *Decision on Reforming the Investment System* that encouraged and guided social capital to participate in constructing for-profit public welfare and infrastructural projects in the form of, for example, individual proprietorship, joint venture, cooperation, joint management and project financing. In February 2005, the State Council promulgated the *Suggestions on Encouraging, Supporting and Guiding the Development of Individual and Private Sectors and Other Non-public Economies* in which non-public capital was allowed to engage in public utility and infrastructure industries. It was stipulated that the government would accelerate the franchise system, regularize bidding behavior, and bolster non-public capital to energetically participate in investment in, as well as construction and operation of, the urban supply of water, gas and heating, public transportation, sewage and refuse disposal, and other municipal public utility and infrastructure projects. This package of policies and regulations helped promote the reform of urban infrastructural construction and the institutional mechanism of investment and financing, thereby bringing into being the fundamental role of the market in allocating resources.

With the accelerated marketization of infrastructure and pubic utilities after the 11th Five-year Plan, problems such as lax government oversight arose along with alternative lines of thinking such as anti-marketization and de-marketization. However, the central government never changed its stance of driving the benign development of infrastructure and public utilities by bringing in the market mechanism, and instead it spared no effort in reforming and perfecting the institutional system of infrastructure and public utilities.

4. Deficiency in Maintenance

For quite some time, there has been a tendency to place a higher value on construction over maintenance with regard to urban infrastructure. Upon completion, many infrastructural facilities stay idle for a long time due to the absence of adequate regulations for maintenance. Several completed infrastructure facilities occasionally fail to be utilized on a sustained

---

① Liao Maolin & Huang Yuhua. *Reform and Development of Investment and Financing System in China's Infrastructural Construction [A]. in China's Urbanization within Three Decades (1978-2008)* [C]. Beijing: Social Sciences Academic Press, 2009

basis due to an acute lack of a mechanism to secure maintenance funds. Investigations found that the amount of public water supply facilities lying idle in some of China's municipal-level cities ranged from 20-50%. Of the 709 completed sewage treatment plants in China's 668 cities, only one-third are working normally, while one-third are under-utilized and the remaining one-third either operate only intermittently or remain idle. Inadequate maintenance of urban infrastructure will bring about inefficiency and a waste of infrastructure facilities, so much so that supplies of public services will be undermined. With the continuous acceleration of China's urbanization and the expansion of urban infrastructural construction, urban infrastructure facilities do require substantial maintenance. Provided that a stable and constant supply of funds for maintenance is absent and institutional arrangements for maintenance are unavailable, the operation of the infrastructure will be gravely affected to the point that even greater damage and waste will be caused.

III. Exploration into the Construction of Urban Infrastructure in China

1. Integration of Planning with the Market

Under a planned economy, infrastructure construction in China was controlled by the state and the government. Within the context of a socialist market economy, infrastructure construction and the development of municipal public utilities across the country was inseparable from the basic roles of government at all levels. Primary functions included investing part or all of the capital in infrastructure by using government funds, organizing and working out planning for urban infrastructure and industrial development along with the plan for implementation, formulating and improving the system, mechanism, laws and regulations for the marketization of infrastructure and municipal public utilities, arranging government bidding, implementing government procurement and transfer payments, coordinating public hearings, pricing municipal public services, and supervising and managing municipal public utilities.

In this regard, infrastructure and public utilities assume an organic and well-balanced combination of planning and marketing within the government-led framework that enables the government to play a basic and guiding role and puts to good use the market function of resource allocation so that enterprises will be able to compete effectively in a well-regulated market. China's experience has shown, time and again, that the government invariably plays the most crucial role where the market mechanism malfunctions, leaving the market and enterprises impotent in the infrastructure sector. When a favorable investment environment is created by the government to invigorate enterprises, the market and enterprises will further increase investment in, and development of, local infrastructure and public utilities to the extent that China's construction of urban infrastructure will gather pace and the development of urbanization and the regional economy will accelerate nationwide.

2. Integration of 'Soft Environment' with 'Hardware'

Since the central and local governments decided to accelerate the construction of urban infrastructure at the beginning of the 1980s, government sectors nationwide have all been keeping up with the times according to local circumstances. They not only gave preference to the construction of 'hardware infrastructure' but also woke up to the significance of driving an improvement of the 'software environment' in their efforts to pursue the principle of development that gives equal importance to both. Construction of the soft environment involves three aspects.

First, the emphasis on building up the external image of urban infrastructure has given way to a stress on improving the scope of public services. Today, policy priorities throughout the country have been shifted to how public service capacities of infrastructure can be improved rather than focused on the acceleration of infrastructure construction itself. The public disclosure of cost in water utilities is one example of government efforts to further the transparency of production and operation in public services.

Second, institutional establishment has been strengthened with the speeding up of construction of urban infrastructure, one of the major institutional orientations being the promotion of the function of market resource allocation. First, the reform of the financial investment system in the infrastructure sector has been carried out and the market has been progressively opened up with the introduction of the market mechanism in order that non-market capital will be invested in the construction of infrastructure. Second, the reform of the administrative system has been promoted in the field of infrastructure so that the role of the government will be transformed from administration to supervision of infrastructure and public utilities through separating enterprise from administration and the adoption of a franchise system in which the responsibilities of the government and enterprises in the investment in and construction and management of infrastructure will be clearly defined. In this way, construction and development of urban infrastructure will be stepped up with the gradual formulation and exercise of industrial policies, urban development plans, and laws and regulations that will help mobilize and motivate economic entities through guidance, management and regulation. Furthermore, the environment of market industrialization has been well cultivated in infrastructure so that all the various infrastructural enterprises will be energized to grow bigger and stronger. Government policies in this regard include the expansion of financing channels for infrastructural enterprises by encouraging them to be listed on the stock market, the elimination of unreasonable government administrative monopoly of enterprises by means of separating enterprise from administration, the encouragement of intra-industry mergers and integration of resources, the opening of regional markets and the promotion of cross-regional investment. The formulation and exercise of these policies has demonstrated that only market-oriented infrastructural enterprises will be able to develop wholesale and provide more and better public services for local municipal governments and communities.

Third, infrastructural construction and urbanization have been well integrated. Since infrastructural facilities in China are set up to serve both urban areas and rapid urbanization, infrastructure that is divorced from the development of cities is worthless and wasteful. In China's urbanization, therefore, the government must play a role in places where the market and enterprises are impotent so that government investment companies engaged in urban infrastructure will come into play. The increase in urban infrastructure investment has driven the revival of urban economic life and helped generate differential rents of urban land that will become the major source of revenue for local governments. As a result, the growth of the urban population and the local urban economy will be further quickened, to the extent that urbanization will in turn help promote the functions of infrastructure and the optimization of public services.

3. Integration of Innovation with Reality

Taking advantage of situations, acting according to circumstances, keeping up with the times and seizing the opportune moment to reform and innovate the institution, system and mechanism of infrastructure, and insisting on innovation in technology, management and concept are all pivotal to the construction and development of China's urban infrastructure. Construction of urban infrastructure, however, started at the primary stage of socialism that was falling behind economically and socially and was characterized by imbalanced regional development in which any innovative idea had to be realistic and pushed forward step by step according to real life conditions. For instance, the reform of Shanghai's urban infrastructure investment and financing system has stood the test of time because it did not materialize according to top-level design but was established after repeated trial and error along with the sustained deepening of reform in China's socialist market economy, the growing improvement of its financial and capital markets, and the mounting demand of its economic and social development (see Special Column 4-1). By contrast, some cities are blind to what is realistic in terms of speeding up infrastructural construction and expanding the scale of urban areas, resulting in investment bubbles in the infrastructure sector and the long-term waste of social and economic resources.

Special Column 4-1 Shanghai: urban construction and development[①]

Over the past three decades, the people of Shanghai, adhering to the ideological guideline of emancipating the mind and seeking truth from facts, and based on the realities of a country passing through the primary stage of socialism and with due consideration of what is distinctive in a super-large city, have acquired profitable experience and practices in urbanization.

1. Making urban construction the top strategic priority

Since the 1990s, urban construction has been given top priority for strategic development that is important for the overall reform and progress of the city. The municipal government has been focusing on the concurrent and mutual development of economic growth, social advance and urban construction along with the unified arrangement

---

① Chen Shijie, Feng Xiaomin & Luo Shiqian. *Urban Construction and Development in Shanghai* [M]. Shanghai: Shanghai People's Publishing House, 2004

and coordinated development of urban planning, construction and management, resulting in a significant increase in urban construction with a sustained growth in aggregate investment. Urban construction has created marked changes not only in the appearance of the city but also in its supply capacities and its multifunctional capabilities as well as in its overall economic activities. Studies suggest that urban construction was a major driving force behind the city's economic growth in the late 20th and early 21st century.

2. Scientific in planning and proactive in development

One of Shanghai's most important practices is to base urban construction and management on planning. The municipal government has insisted that urban planning is worked out in the first instance and, once this is done, specialized plans (including those of transportation, environment, water services, energy and information) will be able to relate to it so that a positive and proactive interaction between sectors can be achieved. The formulation of all plans along with the results of policy studies have played a guiding role par excellence in constructing specialized infrastructure.

3. Innovative, creative and pioneering

To substantially improve its inferior infrastructure, Shanghai has persisted in driving development by means of overall reform and innovation. The continuous intensification of the fundamental role of market resource allocation together with the constant resolution of relevant problems has lent powerful institutional support for rapid growth.

As regards the reform and innovation in urban construction and management, the highly-centralized urban construction system has gradually given way to the practices of 'two levels of government and three levels of administration' in urban areas and 'three levels of government and administration' in suburban counties. In both cases, the gravity of administration has shifted down.

In terms of the reform and innovation of public utilities, Shanghai has been pushing forward urban construction in a big way and in the process removed monopolized industries. From 1996-2000, Shanghai reformed the system, mechanism and fee scale of drainage, public transport, natural gas and water supply to form a market-orientated system of diversified investment and operation, and a comprehensive industrial management system.

Shanghai has all along been taking the lead nationally in the development of science and technological innovation. While forging ahead with large-scale urban construction, it has attached great importance to the role of scientific and technical innovation with the aim of improving the quality and efficiency of infrastructure construction by promoting scientific and technological progress. In the meantime, it has developed appropriate methods, standards and regulations and enhanced its modern urban administration by applying GPS information management, intelligent transportation systems, environmental biotechnology and other high-tech achievements to its urban and environmental management.

In terms of legal construction, Shanghai formulated and amended some 200 local laws and regulations that had significant bearing on urban construction and management between 1990 and 2004, of which around 90% were worked out based on the realities of the city. During the legislation process, stress was placed on the legislative program, preliminary investigation, adequate demonstration and all-inclusiveness. In operation, attention was paid to practicality, gradual accumulation and progressiveness in order to guarantee legislative quality and operability as well as the relative stability of local legislation. Insisting on administration and management according to the law, competent administrative departments were committed to promoting the effectiveness and efficiency of urban management with the help of legal and economic means.

Reform of both investment in urban infrastructure and financing systems is among the key government measures in its large-scale urban construction. By means of diversified and market-oriented investments and financing policies, such as inviting foreign capital, leasing land, issuing shares and bonds, collecting social funds, opening up the real estate market, making short-term loans from national financial institutions, and allocating social funds, Shanghai has addressed the problems with investment in urban construction and brought down the cost of financing, construction and operation. In this way it has significantly improved the economic efficiency and social benefit of investment.

4. Social participation and public support

The big expansion in urban construction in Shanghai is inseparable from the substantial support and assistance of society, one prominent aspect of which is diversified financing. Mindful of the overall interests and practical realities of their city, residents have contributed greatly to urban construction with their understanding and support. Given the sustained deepening of urban construction and growing extent of demolition in Shanghai, the government has had to enlist the understanding, support and cooperation of citizens. It adheres to the principles of wholeheartedly serving the people, helping to alleviate their hardships, doing what is good and pragmatic for their benefit, and providing them with timely help. In practice, it sticks to the belief that the public must be well informed when major reform policies are carried out so that they will offer support and engage themselves in the operation. With regard to reform proposals that involve wide public interests, the government calls on the people to contribute ideas and work to win their understanding and support. As for emerging problems in urban construction, particularly those that cause frequent arguments among citizens, it tries to assess the situation so that it will be able to provide timely guidance and prevent potential problems from occurring.

CHAPTER 5

Management of Urban Land in China

I. Property Rights of Urban Land

As the centerpiece of the land system and basis of agrarian relations, land ownership implies an economic form in which one owns land under certain social conditions. Accordingly, property rights of land, as the legal manifestation of land ownership, constitutes the legally protected exclusive and proprietary right of land owners that can be broken down into the right to use, the right to earnings, the right of disposition and so on. As is specified in the *Law of the PRC on Land Administration*, China practices the socialist public ownership of land, which involves ownership by the whole people and collective ownership by the working people. It further stipulates: "Land in urban areas of a city shall be owned by the state. Land in rural and suburban areas of a city shall be owned by a farmer collective, except for that which belongs to the state as provided for by law; housing sites and private plots of cropland and hilly land are owned by a farmer collective."

The land-use system that serves to stipulate the procedures, conditions and forms of land utilization is another key component of the land system. The right to the use of land is a legal manifestation that enables land owners to enjoy the right to use, manage and gain profit from land. The reform of the property right system of land in China mainly focuses on the institutional innovation of the right to the use of land.

After the PRC was founded, the system of land property in cities shifted from private ownership to state ownership. Before 1949, when private ownership of land was practiced, urban land in China accounted for a very insignificant share of the country's total territorial area and it was largely occupied by the bureaucratic bourgeoisie feudal landlords, national industrialists and merchants, self-employed laborers and foreigners. With the founding of the new China, municipal governments across the country took over the land previously owned by the Kuomintang government and confiscated extensive tracts of urban land occupied by imperialists and bureaucrat bourgeoisies. Official recognition was given to private land belonging to national industrialists and merchants, along with self-employed laborers and urban residents.

At the nascent stage of China's urban construction, therefore, there was a co-existence of state and private ownership of urban land. The owners of private urban land were not conferred the right to freely dispose of their own land until 1956. In the *Opinions on the Basic State and Socialist Reform of Current Private Urban Real Estate* issued on January 18, 1956, the Secretariat of the CPC Central Committee stipulated that all unused private-owned urban land and other real estate should be nationalized by appropriate means and that state-owned urban land should be allocated to land users free of rent by local governments[1] so as to bring into being the urban land-use system along with the overall nationalization of urban land ownership. In line with the system, the use of state-owned urban land would be free of charge, open-ended and non-liquid. The system of free allocation of state-owned urban land brought the integrated proprietorship and usufruct of land entirely under the control of the state.[2]

Despite the fact that the administrative allocation system of state-owned land was adapted to the development mode of the planned economy stage, growing problems became apparent: inefficiency of utilization, a severe waste of land resources, failure in economic realization of the ownership of state-owned land and an acute depletion of the rights to earnings and free disposition.

With the deepening of reform in China's economic system and opening up to the outside world, the national economic system was crackling with dynamic changes. A number of innovative initiatives were introduced because the previous system of land use had failed to keep up with the steps of reform and opening up. The institutional innovation of China's urban land use during the period largely found expression in

---

[1] Bi Baode. *Studies on the Real Estate Market in China* [M]. Beijing: China Renmin University Press, 1994, page 27

[2] Dong Liming. *Review and Prospects for Paid Use of Urban Land in China* [J]. Yunnan Geographic Environment Research, 1992, (12), pages 16-29

the establishment of the paid use system of urban land based on notional rent.

1. Charges and Taxes on Land Use

(1) Charges on land use

The reform of China's urban land-use system first took place in the land-use system for Sino-foreign joint ventures. In 1979, the State Council promulgated the *Law of the PRC on Chinese-Foreign Equity Joint Ventures*, which stipulated that the investment contributed by a Chinese party could include the right to the use of premises provided for the equity joint venture during the period of its operation; in case such a contribution did not constitute a part of the investment from the Chinese party, the venture should pay the Chinese government a fee for its use of the land. The *Provisional Regulations on Land for Construction by the Sino-foreign Equity Joint Ventures* issued by the State Council on July 26, 1980, specified that occupancy fees should be levied on land for Sino-foreign equity joint ventures, whether it was newly requisitioned land or the land of original enterprises. These laws, regulations and policies helped change the situation with the uncompensated use of urban land in China, thereby initiating the reform in the urban land-use system. In 1982, Shenzhen started to collect land occupancy charges and more than 100 cities across the country followed suit from 1998.

(2) Taxes on land use

In compliance with the *Tentative Regulations of the PRC on Urban Land-use Taxes* promulgated by the State Council on September 7, 1988, collection of urban land-use taxes would start from November 1, 1988. The central government would be responsible for levying taxes on domestic users of land while regional and municipal governments would take charge of gathering land-use taxes on foreign-invested enterprises as well as overseas companies' institutions based in China. With this, China finished establishing its legal system that featured paid or compensated use of urban land.

2. Establishment of the Urban Land Transfer System

Although the exercise of collecting charges and taxes on land users broke away from the previous system of uncompensated use of land and supplied valuable experience for the reform of the land-use system, it failed to touch upon the innovation of the land market mechanism. With the growing scale of urban construction, problems with the allocation of land resources raised government concern. As the tax rate standard stipulated was under par, the fees collected fell far short of meeting the demand of infrastructure construction. While land developers made easy and fast money, the ownership of the government as the representative holder of state-owned land failed to materialize economically. Moreover, collection of meager fees for the right to the use of land alone could not help promote the rational allocation of land resources and the efficient utilization of urban land. Although departments responsible for the administrative allocation of land strove to be impartial in their initial assignment, they still found that efficient use of land responsive to market signals was elusive due to the absence of necessary competition and economic levers coupled with a failure of the right to the use of land to enter the market for legal negotiation and mortgage. In this context, it was imperative to carry out a more profound and larger-scale reform in the land-use system.

Taking the lead in innovating the land-use system, Shenzhen tentatively separated the ownership of land from the right to use land. Based on the prerequisite that urban land is state owned, the government leased the right to its use by means of open bid and tender. On September 9 and 29 and November 1, 1987, the municipal government broke through the legal binding on the right to the use of urban land and became a national pacesetter in allocating land resources by means of the market when it leased the right to the use of three plots of state-owned land through agreement, open bidding and public tender. In November 1987, with the approval of the State Council, pilot reform of land use was conducted in Shenzhen, Shanghai, Tianjin, Guangzhou, Xiamen and Fuzhou, the essence of it being that the right to the use of administratively allocated land that had been free of charge, open-ended and non-negotiable was going to be paid, time-limited and negotiable.

This practical development entailed the modification of relevant laws. In April 1988, the National People's Congress amended the constitution by removing the previous stipulation that land was not negotiable and inserting "the right to the use of land may be negotiated according to law". Afterwards, corresponding modifications were made to the PRC's Land Administration Law, thereby creating the legal basis for the leasing and negotiation of the right to use state-owned land. In the *Interim Regulations of PRC Concerning the Leasing and Negotiation of the Right to the Use of State-owned Land in Urban Areas* issued in May 1990, the State Council expressly defined the leasing, negotiation, renting, mortgage and termination of the right to the use of state-owned land. The *Law of the PRC on Urban Real Estate Administration*, promulgated in 1994, explicitly stipulated the state-practiced system of using state-owned land under due compensation and terms of using the land according to the law. In 1998, the amended *Administration Law of the PRC* further stipulated that the right to the use of land might be leased by law, that the state introduced the system of compensated use of land owned by the state and that paid leasing should apply in use of land owned by the state by a construction unit. These issued and implemented laws and regulations have constituted the system of land-use rights composed of a package of legal documents consisting of the *Real Right Law of the PRC*, the *Land Administration Law of the PRC*, the *Law of the PRC on Urban Real Estate Administration*, the *Law of the PRC on Land Contract in Rural Areas*, the *Provisions on the Leasing of State-owned Construction Land Use Right through Bid Invitation, Auction and Quotation*, and others that have brought into being the basic institutional framework of the market operation of state-owned land as well as the land property right system with Chinese characteristics.

II. Utilization and Management of Urban Land

Administration of land use is a manifestation of national intervention for all the processes of land use so that the state will better organize and utilize land. Administration of land use in China mainly involves administration of land-use plans, land-use planning, land consolidation as well as purposes of land use. Since the reform and opening up was launched, China, based on its own national realities, has established the administrative system of land use singular to itself.

1. Protection of Cultivated Land

The protection of cultivated land is a top priority in land management and the centerpiece of land use administration. In March 1986, the Central Committee of the CPC and the State Council jointly promulgated the *Notice on Strengthening Land Administration and Curbing Unlawful Appropriation of Cultivated Land* in which the basic policy of the state was referenced for the first time: "Every inch of land shall be treasured and rationally utilized for protecting cultivated land." In August 1994, the issuing of the *Regulations on the Protection of Basic Farmland* by the State Council signified that protection of basic farmland was officially brought under the control of legal regulation. The *Land Administration Law of the PRC*, amended in 1999, established two policy frameworks for protecting cultivated land in China: a balance system of the total amount of cultivated land and a land-use control system. The introduction of the two policies signaled that the focus of land management had shifted from securing the supply of land for construction to protecting cultivated land, or from a batch-wise approval limit system (see Special Column 5-2) to a land-use control system.[①]

(1) Establishing a strict land-use control system

The land-use control system is extensively adopted in countries and regions across the world where the land management system is relatively well developed. In this system, the government, for the purpose of securing rational utilization of land resources in promoting the coordinated development of the economy, society and environment, works out land-use planning, stipulates the uses of land, defines the prerequisites for land use, and demands that all land owners and users utilize land in strict compliance with the uses and preconditions specified in the planning. The Chinese government hopes that the exercise of a land-use control system will provide strict protection for cultivated land.

(2) Intensifying the balance system of total amount of cultivated land

The balance system of the total amount of cultivated land, which is otherwise referred to as dynamic balance means of total arable land, is a central system designed to counteract the reduction of total arable land by adopting measures

---

① Land-use control system, the centerpiece of China's land management system, stipulates that governments at all levels are responsible for formulating the master planning for land use that defines the uses of land by classifying them into agricultural land, land for construction and unused land. The owners and users of land shall use the land in strict compliance with the purposes of use prescribed by the state. The government imposes a strict restriction on turning farmland into land for construction, controls the quantum of construction land and provides special protection for cultivated land. Structural adjustment of agriculture and development of protected agriculture will be promoted by making the most of barren mountains, waste hillsides, intertidal zones and other unused lands of low profit without occupying cultivated land, prime farmland in particular to secure an area of cultivated land adequate for the demands of social and economic development within a certain period of time. Articles 31 and 32 of the *Land Administration Law of the PRC* explicitly stipulate that the state fosters a system of compensation for the occupation of cultivated land. In the case of occupying cultivated land for non-agricultural construction, the units occupying cultivated land should be responsible for reclaiming the same amount of land in the same quality as that occupied according to the principle of 'reclaiming the same amount of land occupied'. Governments of all provinces, autonomous regions and municipalities shall strictly implement the general planning for the utilization of land and annual planning for the use of land and adopt measures that do not lead to a reduction in the total amount of cultivated land within their jurisdictions. When reductions occur, the State Council shall order land reclamation within a prescribed time limit to make up for the diminished land in the same quantity and quality, and the land administrative department of the State Council shall, together with the agricultural administrative department, examine and accept it.

Apart from these two measures, China also exercises strict control over the scale of urban land and strengthens the protection of cultivated land through the improvement of farmland quality and the establishment of detecting systems for the dynamic protection of arable land.

2. Planning and Enforcement of Land Use

In the *Land Administration Law of the PRC* issued in June 1986, people's governments at all levels were required to compile general plans for land uses. In accordance with the stipulation of this law, China restructured the classification system of land, worked out national general land planning for 2000, 2010 and 2020, formulated the top-down five-level overall planning system encompassing the state, provinces, cities, counties and townships, completed the optimal allocation of the scale, structure, spatial layout, intensity and time sequence of land use, realized the balance between varieties of land, protected arable land, promoted the development and utilization of inefficient and unused land resources, and satisfied the demand for construction purposes. In the meantime, it carried out in a comprehensive way the planning for the protection of prime farmland, for land consolidation, and for development and reclamation of land. It also formulated the annual planning for land use (inclusive of targets for non-agricultural construction) (see Special Column 5-1) and the control system of land uses.

Special Column 5-1 Management of land-use planning

By means of management of land-use planning, a macro-control measure adopted by the state to address all eventualities in land use, the state works out planning and issues control targets so that it can guide people to use land in a planned and rational way and in doing so it brings land use into the system of national planning management. Management of land-use planning mainly includes the formulation of plans, issuing of targets and implementation of plans. The plans comprise medium- and long-term plans for land use as well as an annual plan for construction land; the targets primarily refer to arable land for various construction purposes issued by the state each year as well as those of land for other uses; and implementation involves the exercise, inspection and summarization of plans. Put another way, local land administrations at all levels first propose the targets of land use before reporting, level by level, to the next superior administration. With balanced consideration, the national land administrations and planning departments draw out the plan in line with which the targets are allocated to each province before transmitting the control targets to governments at higher levels. In compliance with the control targets of land use, the local land administrations modify the previously suggested number of targets of land use before reporting once again to administrations at higher levels. With the approval of the central government, the planned targets are conclusively assigned to each subordinate government, level by level.

3. Management of Land for Construction

Land for construction refers to land exclusively used for specific project building and resource development by means of certain material input and engineering measures. Land for construction, according to its purpose of use, breaks down into land for agricultural construction and land for non-agricultural construction, of which the latter is further classified into land for state construction, land for construction of townships (towns) and land for construction by foreign-invested enterprises (FIEs) in accordance with the proprietorship, the source of investment and the uses of land. Land for urban construction chiefly consists of land for state construction and land for construction by FIEs.

Land for state construction refers to that used for developing a country's economy, culture, national defense and public utilities, including land for urban construction, industry and mining, transportation, irrigation and other specially-designated purposes.

Land for construction by FIEs refers to that used for production and engineering construction by Sino-foreign equity joint ventures, Chinese-foreign cooperative ventures and foreign-funded enterprises.

(1) Management of land for state construction

Land for state construction comes from two major sources: requisitioned land collectively owned in rural areas and allocated state-owned land. It can also be acquired by means of leasing or negotiation.

Land requisition is a process by which collectively-owned land is transformed into state-owned land according to law, responsive to the needs of economic and cultural construction, building of national defense, and the establishment of social and public welfare.

The allotment of the right to use land is an act in which a plot of land, with the approval of the people's government above county level according to law, is consigned to the land user for use after they have paid the required compensation and settlement fees, or the right to the use of the land is consigned to the land user for uncompensated use with the approval of the people's government above county level according to law.

Leasing of the right to the use of land is an act in which the state leases, within a term of years, the right to use state-owned land to land users who have paid the state leasing fees for the right to the use of land. Land users who have acquired the right to the use of land through leasing are entitled to the negotiation, rent and mortgage of the right to the use of land as well as other activities for business purposes within the prescribed time.

In agreement with the *Regulations on the Implementation of the Land Administration Law of the PRC*, the examination and approval of land for state construction involves the following procedures:

A. A construction unit proposing to use land for construction purposes shall apply to the land administration department of the local people's government at county level or above in the locality of the land it wants to expropriate by presenting an approved design assignment or other relevant documents such as preliminary designs or annual capital construction plans.

B. The land administration department of the local people's government at county level or above shall examine the application to use land for construction purposes and determine the boundaries of the area of land to be used, as well as arrange for the construction unit, the unit that formerly held the rights to the land and other relevant units to discuss matters of compensation and resettlement in relation to the expropriated land and report these particulars to the people's government at county level or above for approval.

C. After the application to the land for construction purposes is approved by the relevant people's government at county level or above pursuant to the statutory approval jurisdiction, the people's government at county level or above in the locality of the expropriated land shall issue a document of approval to use the land for construction purposes and the land administration department shall transfer the land-use rights in full or in stages, depending on the construction schedule.

D. Upon completion of construction, when the department in charge of the construction project arranges for relevant authorities to examine construction prior to acceptance of the project, the land administration department of the people's government at county level or above shall inspect and verify the actual use of the land (after completion of a construction project in an urban planning district, the administrative authority in charge of urban planning shall, in conjunction with the land administration department, inspect and verify the actual use of the land) and, subject to confirmation, land registration procedures shall be carried out and a land-use certificate for state-owned land shall be issued.

(2) Management of land for construction by FIEs

At present, the acquisition of land by FIEs mainly includes compensated transfer of the right to use state-owned land, allocation of the right to use land, utilization of the right to use state-owned land as the condition for cooperation as well as leasing of houses and premises.

A. Leasing of the right to use state-owned land

Leasing of the right to use state-owned land is an act in which the state leases the right to use state-owned land within a term of years to foreign-funded enterprises that have paid the state the leasing fees for land-use rights in full. The leasing of land-use rights is generally achieved by means of auction, invitation for bids or mutual agreement. In many places, it is stipulated that FIEs engaged in for-profit projects such as real estate development, commerce, tourism, entertainment and construction of luxury homes have to acquire land-use rights by means of leasing.

B. Allocation of the right to use state-owned land

With the approval of people's government above county level according to law, foreign-funded enterprises can enter into land-use contracts with the land administration departments of local cities and counties, pay land occupancy charges as stipulated, carry out land registration procedures and acquire certificates for the right to use state-owned land that they are not entitled to negotiate, mortgage or rent.

C. The right to use state-owned land as the condition for cooperation

As is stipulated by the state, a Chinese party, after going through land-use procedures in the land administration departments above county level, may have its plant, equipment and land-use rights evaluated in lieu of shares as the condition for establishing joint or cooperative ventures with foreign enterprises. When the right to use land is administratively allocated as the condition for cooperation, the Chinese party of the joint and cooperative venture shall pay land-use fees annually as stipulated.

D. Renting of houses and premises

When a foreign-funded enterprise rents houses or premises directly from state-owned or collective economic entities or from township enterprises or the army, it shall pay rent to the leasers annually in accordance with the provisions of their contracts.

4. Management of Land for Industry

To further economic progress, China has introduced its *sui generis* system and policies for development zones, making possible the centralized and efficient allocation of land for secondary industry. However, all places across the country, for the purpose of attracting investment, used to lease land at a low price and even free of charge to the extent that many inferior projects were launched blindly, land resources were squandered and a huge quantity of land assets were lost. For this reason, the State Council issued the *Decision on Deepening Reform and Intensifying Land Administration* in October 2004, which stipulated that conditions should be created for industrial land to be allocated or leased equally by means of invitation for bids, auction and price-listing so that the market-based allocation of land resources would be promoted. Before the promulgation of the policy, the practice of 'project approval prior to supply of land' was predominant in assigning land for industrial construction. That is to say, the scale of land use was determined in accordance with the land-use index for project construction or engineering design specification. In September 2006, the State Council issued the *Circular on Intensifying Land Control* in which the policy of 'land prior to project' was established when it stressed that leasing of the right to the use of industrial land must be exercised in line with the lowest price standard and that industrial land should be exclusively leased by means of invitation for bids, auction and price-listing. Beginning from 2007, with the implementation of the *National Standards for the Minimum Leasing Prices of Land for Industrial Purposes*, the minimum price standard for industrial land leasing was defined. On October 1, 2009, the Ministry of Land and Resources, with the aim to further carry out the *State Council's Approval and Forwarding of the Opinions of the National Development and Reform Commission and Other Departments on Restraining Overcapacity and Repeated Construction of Some Industries and Guiding Them to Embark on a Healthy Development*, promulgated a catalog of projects for which land was limited (supplement edition of 2006) and the catalog of projects for which land is prohibited (supplement edition of 2006) so as to promote industrial restructuring as well as the economical and intensive utilization of land. Accordingly, Shanghai and some other cities, in order to perfect the management system of industrial land, formulated and enacted a series of enforcement regulations and administrative standards, including the *Trial Measures of Shanghai City for Control and Management of Land-Use Scale in Approving Construction Projects*, the *Guide for Industrial Land Use in Shanghai City* (editions 2004 and 2006), the *Guide for Industrial Orientation and Layout in Shanghai, the Guideline for Supply of Industrial Land in Shanghai* (trial version), and the *Price Standards for Leasing Industrial Land in Shanghai*.

**Special Column 5-2 Multistory standard plants built in Shangyu
for enhancing the effective use of industrial land**

In its effort to press ahead with the public leasing of land for standard industrial plants and the construction of standard plants, Shangyu city has stood out as a trailblazer in the economical and intensive utilization of land. In order to break through the constraints of land on economic growth and set up a platform for small and medium-sized enterprises by means of intensive utilization of land, in 2005 the city decided to construct standard plants as the best solution to problems with industrial land. The government stipulated that all projects with a planning area below 10 mu (1.6 acres) and an investment of less than 10 million RMB would be settled exclusively with standard plants instead of an assignment of land. From 2005 to the end of April 2007, the city leased a total of 258 acres of land for standard plants, and finished constructing 1.4m square yards of multistory standard plants that attracted 145 small and medium-sized enterprises.

To drive the construction of multistory standard plants and encourage small and medium-sized enterprises to have access to them, the government has adopted incentives as follows: first, priority is given to projects related to standard plants; second, enterprises engaged in the construction of standard plants are rewarded and subsidized; and third, enterprises that have settled down in standard plants are rewarded and subsidized.

All standard plants engineered and constructed in Shangyu are above four floors with a plot ratio of more than 1.3 and a site coverage of at least 35%, the investment intensity having reached more than 1.35 million RMB per mu (about 800 square yards). The ratio of green space has been held within 15%, the proportion of living and administrative facilities has been controlled below 7% and the floor area of living and administrative facilities has been kept within 15%. The popularity of multistory standard plants has helped promote the intensive utilization of land.

Source: Li Feng & Qiu Jianyong. *The Win-win 'Project Number One' – Insight into the Rapid Construction of Multistory Standard Plants in Shangyu City* [J]. *China Land*, 2007 (6)

III. Management of the Urban Land Market

1 Current State of the Urban Land Market

China's land market currently comprises the market for leasing the right to use state-owned land and the market for negotiating the right to use state-owned land.

(1) Market for leasing the right to use state-owned land

In this market, the state transfers with compensation land-use rights to land users. At the market for leasing the right to use state-owned land, the land owner, namely the state, may lease land-use rights to organs, enterprises, public institutions or individuals by means of agreements, invitation for bids, auction and so on. What is transacted on the market is not the ownership or proprietorship of land but the use right within a given period of time. Moreover, rights are limited to land surface rather than underground natural resources, minerals, buried objects or hidden property. When the term of land-use rights expires and the contract is not renewed, the land owner shall reclaim the land-use rights together with above-ground structures. There are two means of market transaction for leasing land-use rights. The first is the long-term leasehold of land-use rights that meets the long-standing demand of land for which the tenure can be determined in line with the earnings and actual needs of the manufacturing industries and projects in operation. In China, the maximum terms of tenancy are: seven decades for residential land; five decades for industrial land; five decades for land for the purposes of education, science and technology, culture, public health and sports; four decades for commercial, tourist and recreational land; and five decades for commercial-residential land and others. The current maximum terms of leasing are legally stipulated by the State Council and specific provisions have been drawn up in individual places. The second means, which extends from one to 10 years, is the short-term leasehold of land-use rights that satisfies temporary or short-term needs.

Generally, a variety of provisions and qualifications will be attached to the leasing of land-use rights. These provisions and qualifications enable municipal governments to stipulate and carry out the overall design of social and economic development and land-use planning by means of legally-bound leasing contracts. Leasing contracts are covenants or agreements struck up between the land owner and lessees. Contracts should comprise the rights to which the lessees are entitled, the obligations they shall assume and the terms they must observe, including the duration of leasing, purposes of leasing, development types, building height, site coverage, ratio of floor area, minimum investment and requirement for public facilities. Any change in the purpose of land use must receive government approval and the parties involved will have to make good the stipulated price differences. The retransfer of land-use rights within a leasehold shall not be allowed until a change of registration is carried out in accordance with relevant provisions. The government is entitled to punish those breaching the contract.

The market for leasing land-use rights has three main features. First, though it is a market where land-use rights are transacted, the ownership of land is not lost after the buyer pays the premium and acquires the right to the use of land within a certain period of time while the seller receives the premium and loses land-use rights for the time being. Second, the land price is the purchase price of land-use rights within a given period of time, of which the basic components include absolute rent, differential rent and land interest on capital. Third, it is a market featuring monopoly and competition, the leaser of land-use rights being the state and the national department of land administration monopolizing land supplies at the market on behalf of the government. Land users are permitted to vie with one another through various competitive means for the right to use land.

(2) Market for negotiating the right to use state-owned land

The market for the negotiation of land-use rights is where the right to use land is negotiated between land users. If the former land user intends to transfer the land-use rights to another party, the duration of the new agreement shall not exceed the term of the contract struck between the former land user and the land owner. In this case, the negotiation of land-use rights will be considered illegal and punished according to law unless it is conducted under the supervision of the land administration department of the government.

During the negotiation of land-use rights, the former land user breaks off relations with the land owner through the transfer of overall land-use rights for a certain duration to a new land user. In doing so, relations between them and the land owner in terms of rights and obligations are simultaneously passed on to the new land user. Such a transaction follows the principle of 'priority of land over people', which means that a unit or individual is not only entitled to the rights and interests of land and housing estates but also assumes the liabilities and responsibilities regarding land disposal and real estate the moment they take over the land-use rights or real estate. In this regard, the exercise of 'priority of land over people' guarantees that the rights of the government and other units or individuals will not be negatively affected by repeated negotiations of land-use rights and real estate. In the final analysis, during the transfer or negotiation of land-use rights, the party involved shall pay the state value-added taxes on the land.

Negotiation of land-use rights has three main features. First, economic and legal relationships are more complicated since they involve relations between land users as well as economic and legal relationships between land users and the land owner. Second, the result of the transaction is a lateral flow of land-use rights, which helps to overcome the limitations of the longitudinal flow of leased land-use rights on the land market, eradicate land vacancy, promote the efficiency of land use and facilitate the rational allocation of land resources. Third, it is a well administered competitive market where competition for land-use rights exists on the supply side while potential users vie for the right to the use of land. In this light, the basis of price or leasing price of land-use right is increasingly brought under the regulation of the law of value and of land supply and demand.

The markets of leasing and negotiation of land-use rights that are reciprocally complemented and organically integrated constitute China's overall land market pattern.

2 Aspects and Modes of Urban Land Market Management

(1) Basic contents and modes in urban land market management

Land is a central factor of production and an important resource that can be controlled and regulated by the government. Based on its overall goals of social and economic development, the government intervenes in the urban land market by comprehensively applying economic and administrative means so that it can restrict land speculation, maintain the stability of the land market, optimize the management of land resources and distribute land revenues rationally.

A. Macro-management of the land market

By means of macro-management of the land market, the state, based on its long-term overall goals of social and economic development, intervenes in the urban land market through economic means (including industrial policies, finance and credit policies, and tax policies) and administrative measures (including plans and planning) so as to restrain land speculation, maintain the stability of the land market, optimize the allocation of land resources and distribute land revenues rationally. Macro-management of the land market comprises management of land market supply and demand, and control of land market prices.

B. Micro-management of the land market

Through micro-management, the state exercises unified regulation and management of the land market by applying legal and administrative means and measures so that it can ensure fair trade and competition between market entities and give play to the normal regulating functions of the land market mechanism.

(2) Regulation and management of land market supply and demand

As an important means to optimize the allocation of land resources and rationally distribute land revenues, regulation of land market supply and demand is conducive to the stability of land and housing prices as well as the adjustment and optimization of land-use structure.

A. Major contents of the regulation of land market supply and demand

i) Regulation orientation of land market supply and demand

The regulation orientation of land supply and demand involves opting for regulation goals and determining the operation orientation of regulating measures. The selection of regulation goals hinges on the development goals of the land market within a given period of time. In determining the operation orientation of regulating measures, the prevailing condition of the land market will have to be analyzed based on regulation goals. The operation orientation is roughly divided into two types: one is associated with the incentives adopted to stimulate the development of the land market, of which the operation is oriented upward and manifests as tax reduction and exemption, reduction of loan interest rates and so on; another has much to do with the measures taken to restrain the development of the land market, of which the operation is oriented downward and is evident in the control of loan sizes, the limitation of land supply and others. In general, the upward operation orientation is exercised as a regulating measure during the business cycle of the land market between depression and recovery, while the downward operation orientation is adopted when the land market is thought to be 'overheating'.

ii) Regulation time of land market supply and demand

To determine the regulation time of land market supply and demand, three parameters have to be taken into account: the decision-making time of regulation measures for supply and demand; the delayed time for the regulating effect of supply and demand; and the inertia of the regulating effect. The regulation of urban land market supply and demand must be combined with the improvement of the monitoring and warning system of the land market.

iii) Regulation intensity of land market supply and demand

The intensity or dimension of regulation is associated with a change in the variables that function as regulating measures. In this respect, four factors have to be considered: the extent of the economic fluctuation of land; the delayed time of the regulating measures from initiation to the moment when effect is generated; the scale of the inertia of the regulating effect; and the environment of regulation.

B. Measures for regulating land market supply and demand

– Development planning and formulation of land-use planning, notably annual planning, constitute the effective means to regulate the land market and determine the time for land to enter the market. Land-use planning functions as the key government measure to harness land supply, coordinate supply and demand, regulate and stabilize land prices and ultimately impose macro-regulation on the land market.

– Fiscal policies. Fiscal polices for the regulation of land market supply and demand include those of rent, tax and financial investment, and they play vital roles in regulating the speed of land market development as well as supply and demand dynamics. Tax policy functions in regulating land market supply and demand as follows: first, it regulates the land market by means of taxation in different operating links of the market; and second, it regulates the land market through tax relief. The policy of financial investment plays a role in directing financial investment by guiding social investment with financial investment so as to regulate industrial structure and regional disparities.

– Financial policies. Financial policies play a crucial part in the government's regulation of land market supply and demand. The regulatory functions of financial policies in regulating the land market fall into direct and indirect regulations. By virtue of direct regulation, the government, relying on the central bank, directly intervenes in the quality and quantity of land credit business through formulating land financial policies. Indirect regulation means that the state controls land market supply and demand by regulating the supply and demand of money by virtue of the interest rate, loan-to-value ratio and other financial levers.

(3) Macro-management and innovative management of the urban land market – the land reservation system

The land reservation system exists when the government is engaged in preliminary land development, consolidation and reservation in line with the overall planning of land use and urban planning through acquisition of the ownership and right to use land in its application of the market mechanism according to law so that it will be able to supply the land demanded in urban construction and regulate the management system and operating mechanism of the land market.

In terms of operation, the system of land acquisition and reservation primarily consists of land acquisition, land reservation and land supply.

A. Land acquisition

Land acquisition is an act in which land reserve institutions purchase or reclaim the right to use state-owned land within urban areas with the authorization of municipal governments and in accordance with land reserve plans. The procedures generally include application for acquisition, verification of ownership, consultation, expenditure measurement, submission and approval, compensation for acquisition, change in ownership and handover of land. In general, compensation for land acquisition is calculated according to the development cost of the land acquired. In cases where the right to use land is acquired through leasing, compensation should also include the sum for the previously paid leasing fees by land users though the leasing fees should be paid by the former land users for their actual use of the land.

B. Land reservation

Before it is leased to other land users, the land that has entered the reserve system shall be organized by land reserve centers for preliminary development, operation and management.

C. Land supply

With regard to land that has entered the reserve system, land reserve institutions are responsible for formulating supply plans and providing land for land users according to the needs of urban development and land market demand. In agreement with current provisions of land management, the supply of reserved land breaks down into leasing through invitation for bid, auction and price-listing and leasing by means of agreement.

In its effort to adapt to industrial restructuring, activate reserved urban land assets, optimize distribution of land resources and promote government regulation of the land market, the State Council promulgated in April 2001 the *Notice on Strengthening the Administration of State-owned Land Assets*. The notice stated that the governments of cities where conditions permitted should exercise a pilot system of land acquisition and reservation in order to strengthen the government's ability to regulate the land market. Governments at city and county levels could set aside some land revenues to provide credit aid for the acquisition of land and financial institutions. Subsequently, most cities across the country started to establish their own land reserve institutions and push ahead with the construction of land reserve systems. China's urban land reservation has three main features.

i) Market-based model

Land acquisition and reserve institutions, in accordance with the proposed plans for acquisition and government requirements, conduct evaluation of the land to be acquired and negotiate the acquisition price or gainshare with former land users before paying them the fees for acquisition, acquiring the land and carrying out the transfer procedures according to current provisions. Land reserve institutions are responsible for demolishing, consolidating and constructing supporting facilities before the land is leased to new land users by land administration departments.

ii) Government-led model

The scope of land acquisition is stipulated by the government's administrative laws and regulations. The land within the defined scope shall be purchased, reserved and developed by land reserve institutions commissioned by the government. Land administration departments, in line with the demand for land, are responsible for leasing the reserved land by means of invitation for bid, auction and price-listing.

iii) Combined mode of government leadership and market operation

This mode mainly applies to the acquisition and reservation of land appropriated during the reform of state-owned enterprises. The previously negotiated land that is publicly tradable with government approval, for which the land users have made good the leasing fees and readjusted the uses of the land in conformity with the overall planning, can either be acquired by land acquisition and reserve institutions or publicly traded on the land market.

CHAPTER 6

Management of Urban Communities

I. Evolution of the Urban Community Management System

It has been more than two decades since urban communities were first created. The practice has played a vital role in satisfying people's everyday needs, conciliating social friction during reform, upholding good social conduct and safeguarding ongoing reform. It has also been helpful in building a harmonious socialist society. In general, the urban community management system has witnessed two phases of development since the founding of the PRC.

1. Neighborhood Management under the Planned Economic System

(1) Evolution of residents' committees under the planned economic system

After 1949, the CPC quickly established the unit-based social management system in cities where an overwhelming majority of urban residents became members of individual units. The unemployed, those eligible for social relief, entitled groups, housewives and all others belonging to no unit were brought under the management of sub-district and residents' committees. This being the case, the unit-based system and sub-district committee system supplemented each other to constitute the general framework of the urban social management system. By virtue of the unit-based system and the sub-district committee system, the government brought about the classified management of urban residents. Both systems were accountable to the government, the former being in charge of the management of people belonging to units and the latter responsible for managing those related to no unit.

The sub-district committee system is a grassroots organizational form of social management with sub-district offices and residents' committees as vehicles. Sub-district offices and residents' committees took shape at the beginning of our founding when administration of the government in urban grassroots communities was dominated by sub-district governments. That is to say, sub-district offices or governments were then the primary-level urban regimes or basic government agencies established by the state as it took over cities based on those 'offices of takeover committees'. In 1953, Peng Zhen, in his capacity as mayor of Beijing, presented to the central government the *Report on the Funding and Organization of Urban Sub-district Offices and Residents' Committees* in which he suggested that urban residents' committees should be established. He said that residents' committees were self-governed mass organizations rather than polities or the 'feet' of political organizations. Though urban residents' committees were not governmental in nature, he continued, it was necessary to establish them as representative offices of cities or districts so that they could help alleviate the burden of district governments and police substations in assembling unorganized residents who belonged to no factory, enterprise, institution or educational establishment.[①] The report won central government approval and in 1954 the Standing Committee of the NPC formulated and issued the *Organic Rules Governing Urban Sub-district Offices* together with the *Organic Rules Governing Urban Residents' Committees* that defined the nature, position, function, responsibility, organizational structure, relationship with relevant departments and units, and financial resources of sub-district offices and residents' committees. From then on, the sub-district committee system in China's urban grassroots management was established.

Of particular importance was the germination of 'household committees', which were tantamount to residents' committees under the unit-based system. Since units had to be responsible for managing the livelihood of their staff and workers, most established their own living quarters that integrated the functions of dormitories and service facilities. Generally, all these living quarters had their household committees directly under the leadership of the units. As in the case of residents' committees, household committees used

---

① Wang Zhenyao and Bai Yihua. *Neighborhood Work and Construction of Residents' Committees* [M]. Beijing: China Social Sciences Press, 1996, pages 179-181

to be the lowest-ranked and self-governed social management organizations in cities prior to the implementation of reform. The difference was that they were merely management organizations within units since they did not acknowledge the leadership of, nor had any association with, the 'local' governments of the sub-districts where they operated.

(2) Changes in the role of residents' committees under the planned economic system
A. Changes in the role of sub-district offices

After the initial establishment of sub-district offices, their jurisdiction was not large, the people involved were not many and their tasks were relatively simple. In the *Organic Rules Governing Urban Sub-district Offices* issued in 1954, it was stipulated that sub-district offices had three tasks: handling neighborhood affairs designated by the governments of cities or districts, guiding the work of residents' committees, and reporting residents' opinions and demands to local governments. In actual fact, sub-district offices only played supplementary roles in social management because those they served were merely limited to the aged, the sick and the disabled beyond the unit-based system and their duties were restricted to areas such as household policies, relief, the urban environment and sanitation.

Since the 1990s, urban sub-district offices have strengthened their functions and gradually assumed a role bordering on government. Currently, sub-district offices undertake at least 10 tasks: first, development of the 'sub-district economy'; second, management of cities in areas such as urban environment and sanitation, municipal facilities and urban landscaping; third, civil affairs concerning public welfare undertakings, consolation and relief, and marriage registration; fourth, community services such as services for the elderly and disabled, mental health services, services of benefit and convenience to the public, and folk customs reform services; fifth, management of the population involving family planning, labor and employment, and the transient population; sixth, governance of social security such as law popularization, civil mediation, security and safeguarding, and maintenance of social order; seventh, socialist cultural and ethical construction, including the development of culture, education, scientific activities, sports and healthcare in communities; eighth, public administration and undertakings assigned by district governments; ninth, supervision of the work of community committees and reporting to the local government residents' opinions and demands; and tenth, reinforcement of party building in communities.

B. Changes in the role of residents' committees

The *Organic Rules Governing Urban Residents' Committees* promulgated in 1954 made palpable the role of sub-district committees: offering public welfare services related to residents; reporting to local governments or their representative offices the opinions and demands of residents; motivating residents to respond to government policies and abide by the law; overseeing public security; and mediating in disputes between residents. In the late 1980s, the role of sub-district committees increased slightly. In line with the *Organic Law of Urban Residents' Committees of the PRC* issued in 1989, sub-district committees were obliged to assume the following duties: first, propagating the constitution, laws, regulations and state policies, safeguarding the legitimate rights and interests of residents, guiding residents to perform their obligations according to law and protect public property, and carrying out activities of socialist cultural and ethical construction; second, conducting public affairs and welfare for residents in their residential areas; third, mediating disputes between residents; fourth, assisting in the maintenance of social security; fifth, assisting people's governments or their representative agencies in performing their duties in public health, family planning, consolation and relief, adolescent education and other affairs that have a bearing on the interests of residents; and sixth, reporting to people's governments or their representative agencies the opinions and demands of residents and bringing forward their own advice.

(3) Features of sub-district committees under the planned economic system

The sub-district committee system that took shape in the era of the planned economy and which featured a 'strong state and weak society' was supplementary to the unit-based system in function and therefore had many properties *sui generis*, of which the most peculiar were its being controlled solely by the government and its being auxiliary or subsidiary in organizing and managing urban residents.[1]

---

[1] Lei Jieqiong. *Urban Grassroots Community Organizations in Transition – Studies on the Grassroots Community Organizations and Development of Communities in Beijing* [M]. Beijing: Peking University Press, 2001, pages 35, 197-198

A. Absolute control by the government

As in the case of the unit-based system created in the planned economy, the state exercised rigid and even absolute control over sub-district offices and residents' committees, particularly in terms of finance and personnel appointment and displacement, to the extent that relevant laws and regulations only existed nominally. The *Organic Rules Governing Urban Sub-district Offices*, promulgated in 1954, stipulated that directors, deputy directors and secretaries of sub-district offices should be assigned exclusively by municipal districts or people's committees of cities without sub-districts. In fact, the key leadership of sub-district offices set up after 1958 were all designated by higher authorities. It was stipulated in the *Organic Rules Governing Urban Residents' Committees* that each residents' team should elect one committee member, and candidates for directors and deputy directors should be mutually nominated among committee members. In reality, however, all committee members, including directors and deputy directors, were appointed by the street committee or by internal appointment. As with finance, it was specified in the *Organic Rules Governing Urban Sub-district Offices* that all office expenses and staff salaries of sub-district offices should be appropriated by people's committees of provinces or municipalities. It was also stipulated that all incidental office expenses and extra subsistence allowances of residents' committees should be appropriated by people's committees of provinces or municipalities. In this way, through their absolute control of personnel appointment and financial power, superior governments exercised control over sub-district offices and residents' committees.

B. Auxiliary in functions

After the mid 1950s, the Chinese government primarily exercised control over and coordination of society by means of the unit-based system. Sub-district offices and residents' committees came into being because some residents who belonged to no unit had to be brought under management, which is why we now believe that sub-district offices and residents' committees were auxiliaries of the unit-based system. The system was characterized by a number of peculiar features. First, the primary targets of sub-district offices and residents' committees in management were the aged, the sick, the disabled, housewives and others who belonged to no unit. All these vulnerable groups were among the non-labor forces in cities and largely marginalized in government management. Second, residents' committees initially were only responsible for maintaining social order and security, doing cleaning, mediating disputes and conflicts, and other work. Since their activities were non-productive and non-political, sub-district offices and residents' committees were naturally auxiliary and secondary compared with those units that assumed significant roles in politics, the economy, culture, education, mobilization and management.

Since sub-district offices and residents' committees were auxiliary in nature, they constituted urban grassroots organizations that played crucial roles in maintaining urban order, mobilizing residents, providing services of benefit and convenience to the public, developing the community economy, and increasing employment in the context of a planned economy. With the deepening of reform and the transformation of society, this primary-level management system became more outdated and there were calls for pressing reform and innovation when its defects increasingly came to light.

2. Community Management under the Market Economic System

(1) Evolution of community management system

The construction of urban communities was the natural continuation of social services in a new context. Since the late 1980s when community services thrived in China, calls grew for enhancing the construction and development of communities. With the advance of the economy and society, and deepening of reform, the integration of government administration with community management and the combination of government functions with enterprise management prevailing in the planned economy could no longer keep pace with the times. The organizational structure of society was transformed in China and the functions of social organization structurally changed in a big way with the breakdown of the unit-based system when 'unit men' became 'social men' or 'community men' and functions such as social services and management were splitting off enterprises and government sectors. As the one and only type of management mechanism, the sub-district organization system could no longer satisfy the demand of multi-functional communities. In this context, reform of the urban community management system was becoming imperative.

At the beginning of the 1990s, China brought forward the idea of community construction and started pilot projects in a number of cities.

In December 2000, the General Office of the CPC Central Committee and the General Office of the State Council jointly forwarded the *Ministry of Civil Affairs' Opinions on Promoting the Nationwide Construction of Urban Communities* in which community was defined as a social group of people who inhabited a certain region. It further noted that the scope of urban communities generally referred to the administrative regions whose scale had been readjusted with the reform of the community system. The promulgation of the document marked the overall start of urban community construction across the country.

After 2002, the construction of urban communities in China entered a phase of constant improvement and deepening. It was stated in the *Report of the 17th CPC National Congress and the Decision on a Number of Major Issues on Building a Harmonious Socialist Society* passed at the Sixth Plenary Session of the 16th Central Committee of the CPC that urban communities should be built into social groups that are harmonious and well civilized, with ordered management and perfect service. It was an idea that highlighted the overall goals of community construction with Chinese characteristics. In the given context, ordered management refers to perfect organization, specific responsibility and rational mechanism in management. In communities, party organizations must play leading roles, the democratic consultation system and all systems of democracy must be sound and standardized, and residents should be the masters of their own destiny in management of grassroots society, economy, politics, culture and other public affairs so that a dynamic self-governing system of residents under the leadership of the party would be created. The security system must be improved, the network of mass prevention and governance and the mechanism for addressing social conflicts must be complete, government administration and self-management of communities should be connected effectively, and government administration according to law and self-management of communities by law must be integrated so that communities are well ordered and residents enjoy their life and work to the full. 'Perfect service' means that communities should be equipped with public facilities and varied services so that they could offer their residents diversified and personalized services. 'Harmonious and civilized' means that residents should have faith in science and be committed to learning, that cultural and ideological progress should be promoted, that learning families and organizations should be widely established, that residents should willingly abide by laws and disciplines, that families and neighbors should be well-mannered and respectful, that scientific, healthy and civilized life style should be universally formed, and that residents should foster the consciousness of social morality and awareness of environmental protection.

(2) Basic framework of China's urban community management system

According to the *Ministry of Civil Affairs' Opinions on Promoting the Nationwide Construction of Urban Communities* jointly forwarded by the General Office of the CPC Central Committee and the General Office of the State Council, governments at all levels should take on leadership, civil affairs sectors should play leading roles, departments should cooperate and coordinate, residents' committees should sponsor and organize, social forces should supply support and the public should participate intensively so that the integrated framework for community construction would be brought into being. Based on these practices, the current community management of China has taken shape.

A. Leadership of party committees and governments

To strengthen their leadership in community construction, government departments of all provinces and cities and their representative agencies (sub-district offices) have established coordinating organizations of community construction to be responsible for the routine work of communities within their administrative regions.

B. Regulation by civil affairs departments

The Primary Political Authority and the Management Division subordinated to the Ministry of Civil Affairs, the competent functional department in charge of construction of communities, are jointly responsible for community construction, their primary obligations being conducting investigations, formulating regulations, directing and coordinating, and inspecting and supervising.

C. Relevant departments as competent entities

Community management is a systematic project that entails cooperation and coordination of all related sectors. Take the practices of district-level governments. Generally, steering committees in charge of community construction are set up at the levels of district committees and governments. The top leaders of district committees, governments, people's congresses and political consultative conferences assume the posts of directors and deputy directors, while the key leaders from more than 20 sectors including organization and publicity departments of district committees, bureaus of civil affairs, finance and urban administration of district governments constitute the members of steering committees. In this light, they are both collective decision-making agencies and collective authorization institutions. Community construction offices subordinated to steering committees are based in civil affairs bureaus that supervise the implementation of obligations of all government departments and coordinate relations between competent departments on behalf of steering committees. This system design allows the interactive mechanism governing each department to take form (see Figure 6-1).

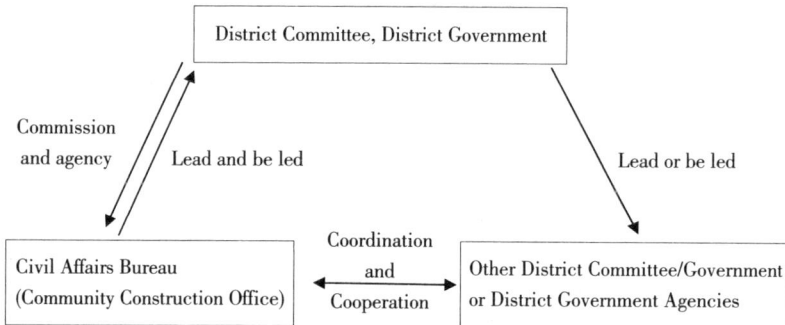

Figure 6-1 Interaction between government sectors in community management
Source: Ding Maozhan. *Reform of China's Urban Community Management System* [M]. Beijing: China Economic Publishing House, 2009, page 52

D. Neighborhood communities as organizers

Residents' committees, within the authorization of the national constitution and laws as well the decrees and regulations of the government and in compliance with the rights and obligations stipulated in the *Organic Law of Urban Residents' Committees of the PRC*, exercise authority in the discussion, coordination, service, supervision and management of community affairs, and conduct democratic self-governance of communities under the leadership of community party organizations and with the guidance of district governments, sub-district offices and various competent sectors.

E. Extensive participation of social forces

The construction of communities is a systematic project that calls for the engagement of government and non-government organizations as well as the wide participation of community residents and social forces. As is pointed out in the *Ministry of Civil Affairs' Opinions on Promoting the Nationwide Construction of Urban Communities*, construction of communities entails maximum resource sharing, joint development and extensive participation of organs, groups, the army, business organizations, government institutions and other forces within communities.

(3) Progress towards a community management system – orientation of reform

With the advance of society and the economy in China, the demands on improving the community management system are getting more pressing. Since 1991, when the Ministry of Civil Affairs proposed the idea of community construction, China's community management system has undergone continuous progress and improvement. Their functions having been constantly expanded, urban communities that have already developed into places of congregation for diversified social groups, confluences of various interests, footholds of multi-faceted social organizations and pivots of the party's government of society have been playing increasingly significant roles in satisfying public demand, integrating interests, mediating social conflicts and maintaining social stability. However, with the progressive drive of reform and opening up and sustained growth of the socialist market economy, social management is becoming more challenging, with profound changes in China's economic system, social structure, interests pattern and people's ideology. As a consequence, it is imperative that urban management abilities should be strengthened, social stability should be safeguarded and social harmony should be promoted through reforming the community management system.

The ultimate goal of innovation in the community management system is to establish a robust and reliable foundation for building a harmonious socialist society based on the existing system by bringing into being a modern governance structure. In this structure, community units act in close coordination and community residents participate extensively with community party branches as the core, social self-governing organizations as the base, community service stations as the pillar, and community social organizations as the supplement by means of integrating social resources and attracting extensive participation of social forces. In this way, a new pattern of community governance adapted to the socialist market economy will be constructed to further bring into being a community governance system and operating mechanism in which the regulation mechanisms of government and society interconnect, the functions of government administration and social self-governance are complementary, and the forces of government management and social synergy interact.[①]

II. Urban Community Services in China

Community services in China reflect Chinese characteristics since they have been established by integrating welfare and social services based on the country's realities of social security. At the start, community services took shape and developed with the advocacy of the government and civil affairs departments. At the 16th National Congress of the CPC, the principle of 'expanding community services in order to make life easier for the people' was written into the party's political report for the first time in its history. In April 2006, the State Council promulgated the *Opinions on Strengthening and Improving Community Services* in which it was pointed out that a community system should be set up that adapts to the socialist market economy and covers all community residents with diversified service principals, perfect service functions and relatively high service quality and management level so as to raise people's living standards and quality of life. It was the first official document issued by the State Council in the development of China's community services that energetically gave full expression to the state's concerns with the public's right of a basic livelihood.

1. Properties of Community Services in China

Community services in China aim to deliver public, welfare and convenient services to all community members, including community residents and units within communities. The aim is to satisfy the mounting physical and cultural needs of community members under the leadership of the party and government by relying on the support and participation of non-governmental organizations, related government sectors and their representative agencies as well as self-governing mass organizations, by mobilizing community

---

① Ding Maozhan. *Reform of China's Urban Community Management System* [M]. Beijing: China Economic Publishing House, 2009, page. 52, Chart 2-1

forces and by pooling community resources. In this light, community services in China include free or inexpensive public and welfare services, and involve inexpensive and paid services that are convenient and beneficial to community residents.

In the era of China's planned economy, community services used to feature a top-down supply model operated by the government alone. With the transition of society and the economy, community services began to assume some new properties in their cooperation and integration with the government, society and market. First, service principals tended to be diversified. While the government was the main provider of community services, a number of non-governmental organizations, self-governing mass groups and private enterprises had begun to participate in the manufacture and supply of community service products. Second, the objects or targets of service were varied, encompassing residents, special populations, vulnerable groups and units within communities. Third, the properties of services were varied, including public and welfare services such as social care, relief and assistance, as well as services convenient and beneficial to the public. Fourth, the types of service multiplied with the co-existence of government administrative services, social mutual services and market-based services.

2. Community Services in Today's China

Driven by government administration, China's community services have been progressing since the mid 1980s and playing pivotal roles in promoting economic development, sustaining social stability and uplifting the living standards and quality of the public.

(1) Preliminary progress in construction of community facilities

By the end of 2010, there were 84,689 urban communities countrywide, which had established 30,021 comprehensive community service stations, 3,515 neighborhood community service centers and 693,000 public convenience service outlets, along with numerous community health centers or stations, community cultural centers and other specialized community facilities.

(2) Constant expansion of community services

Labor and employment, social security, subsistence relief, cultural entertainment and other public affairs have become accessible to communities.

The enrollment and registration system of community service volunteers has been exercised extensively and voluntary mutual services have boomed. The construction of supermarkets, vegetable markets, breakfast stands and other commodity networks has been highlighted. Household services, estate management, elderly care and pre-schooling, food distribution, repair services, waste recycling and other projects have made life easier for residents and helped improve their quality of life.

(3) Sustained increase in community service staff

Members of residents' committees have been elected according to law, full-time community staff have been publicly recruited from society and a multitude of qualified urban and rural residents have joined in community services. Moreover, a growing number of residents have become volunteers active in community services and played important roles in community construction.

(4) Continuous promotion of community service models

Relying on community service centers and stations, many places have put into practice one-stop services and in the meantime promoted the informatization of communities so as to satisfy the varied needs of residents as efficiently as possible by means of modern information technology. Some places have invigorated their own community services and the service capacities of social organizations through government purchase of services, the establishment of funded projects, supply of subsidies for projects and participation of social organizations, enterprises and public institutions as well as residents in community management and service.

(5) Initial formation of community service system environment

The state has issued laws and regulations on securing the rights and interests of the aged, the under-aged and the handicapped and has promulgated policies on community health, social assistance, labor and employment, culture and education, community service facilities and others. Policies and measures have been adopted for promoting community services across the country, laws and regulations for community services have been steadily perfected, party committees and governments of all levels have been lending weight to community services, and community residents have been increasingly identifying themselves with community services.

Despite the fact that considerable progress has been made in the construction of China's community service system, several hurdles have yet to be cleared. With the speeding up of economic development and urbanization in China, communities have already turned into places where various social groups and conflicts congregate. Problems confronting current urban community services in China include a scarcity of service facilities and an inadequate number of places for services in some communities. The contents of community services need to be enriched and disparities between supply and demand are acute. Talented personnel engaged in community services need to be strengthened and the quality and structure need to be improved. The community service system and mechanism in need of unified planning should be optimized. Insufficient investment, lack of coordination and redundant construction are pronounced. The integration of resources is inadequate and the mechanism of social participation is to be perfected. In this light, to address the problems with the system and mechanism is central to the development of community services in China.

3. Prospects for Urban Community Services: Transform Government Functions and Develop NGOs

(1) Transformation of government functions as the prerequisite for developing urban community services

The historical development and administrative characteristics combine to determine the crucial role of the government in community services and the practice of government-led community services has constituted the inevitable form of community services in China during the process of development. That is to say, the Chinese government has been playing a significant part in promoting the initiation and growth of community services and it would be impossible for China to have achieved such progress in community services within a short time without the drive and intervention of the government. However, with the transition of China's economy and society, problems experienced by the government in community administration, such as overreaching itself and being absent, are constantly exposed, so much so that they have already harmed the sound development of community services. The limits of government capacity have given rise to the inefficient operation of community agencies and failed to meet the diversified and specific demands of residents in a timely manner. The government has now been confronted with various conflicts in community services and stunned to realize that it has to press for the transformation of its functions so that its role and capacity will be well coordinated. With the transformation of functions, the 'unlimited government' will be translated into a 'limited government' so that its limited functions in community services will be given full play. In the meantime, diversified community service principals should be fostered to assume the functions yielded by the government.

(2) NGOs as structured vehicles in transforming government functions

The Chinese government has been working to give full play to NGOs and turn them into the leading suppliers of community services. In April 2006, the State Council promulgated the *Opinions on Strengthening and Improving Community Services* (hereafter referred to as the *Opinions*) in which it claimed that NGOs should be fostered in the community services sector, particularly those providing services for the aged, minors and the handicapped along with those applying themselves to the public good, charity and mass-oriented cultural and sports activities. Conditions should be created for NGOs to start operations and, where conditions permit, the right to use some community service facilities could transfer to NGOs, places and office equipment required for operation should be supplied and qualified staff should be recruited for them through competition so as to strengthen coordination between service organizations. Volunteer service in communities should be standardized, an incentive mechanism for volunteers should be established and participation of mass organizations composed of people from all walks of life in communities as volunteers should be bolstered. The *Opinions* further noted that NGOs should be supported and given full play in undertaking community services. Residents should be encouraged to set up various charitable organizations, mass-oriented cultural and sports groups and popular science societies as well as organizations that provide services for the aged, the handicapped and the poor. The promulgation of the *Opinions* demonstrated that the government was lending increasing weight to the role and position of NGOs in community services in its advocacy and was shoring up NGOs as the main supplier of services.

(3) Fostering, development, administration and supervision equally underscored as the basic principles for managing community NGOs

Fostering and development means encouraging and bolstering the growth of NGOs in a way that is conducive to social progress. By reinforcing administration and supervision, illegal NGOs and those violating the law will be investigated and cracked down on, according to the law. Only the integration of fostering and development with administration and supervision can promote the healthy growth of NGOs. Take Shanghai as an example. Based on its actual realities, Shanghai worked out a hub-like system for the management of NGOs. The 'hub-like system' is essentially a management vehicle set up between government sectors and NGOs, acting as a service center for community NGOs that is responsible for organizing services for, and management of, NGOs within communities in aspects of party building, operations and security. These service centers for NGOs have been established at the levels of sub-districts (towns) and districts and perform the following duties in managing NGOs registered according to law within the jurisdictions: establishing archives for party members employed by NGOs within the jurisdictions; carrying out party building and effectuating overall coverage of all community NGOs in terms of party construction; integrating the human resources of NGOs within the jurisdictions and reinforcing dynamic management; underwriting insurance for endowment, health and unemployment for NGO staff; conducting proactive evaluations and surveys on newly-established NGOs within the jurisdictions and writing opinions and suggestions after assessment; organizing professional training and consulting services associated with NGOs, providing them with information and holding seminars and symposiums; offering various paid intermediary services; and forewarning illegal NGOs and assisting relevant departments in investigation. The staff required in service centers should be employed by means of open recruitment in combination with internal assignment based on the principle that full-time personnel should outnumber part-timers. The funds of service centers are guaranteed with financial subsidies by means of government-purchased services along with other adequate subsidies from party membership dues. Budgets must be reasonable and expenditures should conform to regulations. Offices of service centers are provided largely by sub-district committees. By means of hub-like management, effective administration of and full services for NGOs have been achieved, at least in communities when the responsibilities of fostering, development, management and supervision have been carried out well. In summary, the hub-like system of management has provided an operating platform of socialized administration for promoting the transformation of government functions, improving social management modes, reinforcing the ruling foundation of the party and strengthening the self-development of NGOs.

Special Column 6-1 'Service circles within a quarter' established in Chaoyang district in Beijing aimed at promoting the well-being and satisfaction of citizens

By constructing 'service circles within a quarter' as a support, Chaoyang district in Beijing succeeded in improving community services, satisfying public demand, mobilizing social participation and strengthening the building of harmonious communities.

By the beginning of 2011, Chaoyang had set up 119 'service circles within a quarter'. During the construction of 'service circles', government functional departments, community service stations, volunteer organizations, units based in communities, enterprises and individuals all played full roles. The district, in its effort to do well in community public services, services for public good and virtual services, lent powerful support to the building of 'service circles within a quarter'.

First, a catalog of community public services has been formulated to buttress such services. The catalog functions as a 'basic menu' that gives community residents free access to all basic public services delivered by the government. At present, item 97 of the catalog has already been exercised at the grassroots level.

Second, volunteer services have been well promoted to support services for the public good. The city's first 'public savings center of volunteers' has been established in the district with sub-centers set up in sub-district offices and varied service stations put up in communities and business buildings. Relying on the website of the 'public savings center of volunteers', the district has integrated resources of different sectors and established a real-name database of volunteers. And by means of deposit or saving of time, spiritual incentive and others, the district, in its call to 'work as volunteers if you have spare time and asking volunteers for help when you have trouble', has set up platforms for exchange of volunteer services and image display.

Third, regional service resources have been integrated to support convenience services in communities. Socialization has constituted the central principle of community services. Insisting on pursuing social benefit with economic efficiency as the means, the district has brought together the resources of social units based in communities and has tried to constantly enrich the contents of service. The district has been working to intensify the opening of the public service facilities of schools, the army and other social units to residents. Today, 83 schools, colleges or universities have opened their sports facilities to society and more than 160 units have opened their canteens, conference rooms, sports grounds and sports facilities to residents. In this way, problems with public recreational and sports activities have been addressed. In addition, all sub-district committees have been integrating banks, post offices, hospitals and other social units within their jurisdiction and encouraging them to deliver services for residents.

Fourth, information technology has been applied to support community virtual services. The district has been giving full play to modern information technology as it promotes the informatization of community services. It has coordinated all hotline resources of the district government and promoted the systematization of consultation, complaints, community services and monitoring of public livelihood by further improving the functions of hotlines, community service networks, SMS and MMS. In addition, all sub-district committees and communities have set up their own 'virtual communities' so that they may satisfy the individual demands of residents.

Fifth, social organizations have been fostered to promote professional services. Social organizations within communities are important coordinators of community services. Coordinating committees of social construction have been set up in all the 23 sub-districts, and coordinating committees of public affairs have been established in all communities. The third-party coordinating agencies of social construction have been put up as platforms for people from all sectors of society to express their views and participate in social construction. The district has also established social work offices together with professional agencies and institutions of higher education and participated in community services by means of service purchase and project operation.

III. Self-governance of Urban Communities

The long-term goal of community construction is to achieve self-governance of communities by residents. As is stated in the *Ministry of Civil Affairs' Opinions on Promoting the Nationwide Construction of Urban Communities* jointly forwarded by the General Office of the CPC Central Committee and the General Office of the State Council in November 2000, self-governance of communities by residents shall be exercised under the leadership of the party and the government. Put another way, self-governance shall be practiced at the levels of self-governance, self-service, self-election and self-supervision, and its aim is to realize democratic election, decision-making, supervision and management.

1. History

Self-governance of communities by residents in China means neither federalist autonomy nor collective self-rule in an absolute sense; nor does it border on absolute local autonomy. Self-governance organizations in China's communities are subject organizations in communities, namely community committees of residents whose members are generated through democratic elections and are responsible for the management of daily affairs. Community committees of residents are in nature mass self-governing organizations through which community residents exercise self-governance, self-education, self-service and self-supervision under the leadership of the party.

In line with the Constitution promulgated in 1954, the state worked out and passed the *Organic Rules Governing Urban Residents' Committees* in which it was stipulated by law for the first time that residents' committees were "mass self-governing organizations of residents" and thereafter construction of residents' committees was launched across the country. After 1958, particularly during the Cultural Revolution when several grassroots self-governing organizations of the masses were demolished, including residents' committees; democracy at the primary level got bogged down in the crisis. It was not until after the reform and opening up was under way that the development of democracy at the grassroots level was restored. On January 19, 1980 when the state reissued the *Organic Rules Governing Urban*

Residents' Committees passed in 1954, the urban grassroots self-governing system started to resume development. Based on the *Organic Rules Governing Urban Residents' Committees*, the *Organic Law of Urban Residents' Committees of the PRC* was passed by the Standing Committee of the NPC. Thus far, the primary-level self-governing system in cities was brought under the protection of the law.

2. Basic Framework

(1) Leadership of the party as the core

At present, party organizations have been established in all communities, including community party committees and general party branches, under which are party branches. The establishment of party branches in residents' committees marks the most striking difference between democracy at the grassroots level in China and that in western countries. China's choice of its system is justifiable in that it guarantees the exercise of self-management, self-education and self-service of residents without deviating from the overall direction of socialist development. As far as residents' committees are concerned, the establishment of party branches in residential quarters facilitates implementation of the party's mass line so that the committees will better exercise residents' self-governance under the leadership of the party.

(2) Construction of residents' committees as the pivot

It is stipulated in the *Organic Law of Urban Residents' Committees* that urban residents' committees are self-governing organizations of the masses through which community residents practice self-governance, self-education and self-service. The framework of the community residents' self-governing system comprises: community party branches – the center of leadership; residents' representative conferences of communities – the core of procedure for decision-making; community committees of residents – both executives and decision-makers during the adjournment of residents' representative conferences of communities. As the leading organizational carrier of residents' self-governance, it does not transform the grassroots and self-governing nature of residents' committees, nor does it change the dominant role of residents' committees in residents'self-governance.

Institutionally, the framework of residents' self-governance of communities gives prominence to the role of residents' committees as key organizational carriers. As far as institutional construction is concerned, the conference system of residents' representative assemblies, residents' meetings and others are established and perfected along with the setting up of financial and auditing systems. Take Shaojiu Community in Beijing's Donghuamen sub-district, for example. Today, more than 70 community systems of every description have been established here. In the meantime, the community has set up residents' groups, volunteer teams and other organizations with the assistance of the residents' committee. As regards operational mechanism, the election system of residents' committees has been improved. For instance, in the general election of residents' committees conducted in Beijing in 2003, almost every sub-district had a pilot direct election by means of which residents' committees were elected at residents' representative conferences and subject to their supervision. During the pilot election reform exercised by Jiudaowan Residents' Committee, Dongcheng district, Beijing, the will of the residents and the tenet of self-governance was highly regarded in choice of election model, nomination of preliminary candidates, determination of official candidates and germination of the residents' committee. Moreover, the conventional performance evaluation system has been transformed and some indicators for performance appraisal with residents' committees as the subjects of evaluation have been canceled. Instead, residents have become the subjects of appraisal and their satisfaction has been taken as the yardstick for evaluating the actual performance of residents' committees.

(3) Serving all residents as the focus

Functionally, the systematic framework of residents' self-governance has generated new features in promoting the traditional role of residents' committees:

A. Macroscopic planning

In their efforts to satisfy residents' demands, most communities across the country have worked out their unified planning of development and set down their short-, medium- and long-term goals and tasks of development.

B. Decision-making

Residents' meetings and representative conferences are held to discuss and work through major issues and matters of pubic interest in communities.

C. Organization and management

Since residents' committees offer services for all, they have to organize and call on residents to conduct self-management, self-education and self-service as it is impossible for them to address the many thorny issues on their own.

D. Coordination and communication

Residents' committees are devoted to both create a harmonious and peaceful community environment and coordinate between resident representatives and the government or property management companies for the interests of all.

E. Supervision of communities

Social workers are invited by residents' committees to report on their performance at a given time and suggestions will be made based on the exercise of their work.

In general, the role of residents' committees is to wholeheartedly comply with the will of urban residents and provide services for all community residents.

3. Case Study: Innovative Self-governance of Weifang Sub-district, Pudong New District

After continuous exploration for more than a decade, Weifang Sub-district in Pudong New District succeeded in finding a new way to implement residents' democratic self-governance that featured 'four selfs', as follows:

(1) Self-election of residents' committees

As early as 1999, Daoyuanzhu Residents' Committee in Weifang Sub-district achieved success in a pilot 'direct election'. The practice was further assumed by 14 residents' committees in 2000 and 'mass-election' was adopted in all Weifang's 27 residents' committees as of 2006. By means of 'mass-election', those enthusiastic in community services and strong in social mobility and practice came to the forefront and their participation was manifested in the rights of grassroots residents to self-manage their own communities. This showed that residents' committees had become more trustworthy self-governing organizations that work to represent, safeguard and promote the interests of the masses.

(2) Self-decision on major issues

Residents' committees as channels for delivering public opinions and places where conflicts of interest are mediated and resolved are closely related to many major issues in residents' public life. With the coordination of committees, the self-governance of residents is achieved through consultation. Take Yiju Community in Weifang Sub-district, for example. The primary-level government once invested heavily in its own initiative to improve the living environment of the community. The endeavor, however, failed to be recognized by all residents. Families with private cars called for a widening of roads in communities, while people without private cars were set against it. Confronted with this dilemma, the sub-district committee eventually managed to win the approval of all by soliciting opinions from all sides before working out proposals and inviting every resident to participate in the making of the final decision.

(3) Self-organization of mass organizations

Weifang Sub-district now has 200 cultural organizations self-organized by residents that hold regular activities covering sports and fitness, culture and art, education and reading, and popularization of science. These various events have attracted extensive resident participation and helped promote the cultural progress of communities and residents' skills.

(4) Self-management of communities

Residents of communities are actively engaged in volunteering and participation in the self-governance of communities. The attachment of residents to their communities has increased and many residents are racing to enter into community services. By 2011, Weifang Sub-district Committee had established 27 volunteer service stations, 37 model units engaged in volunteering, around 100 volunteer teams and more than 10,000 volunteers.

CHAPTER 7

Protection of Urban Historical and Cultural Heritage in China

I. Protection of Urban Historical and Cultural Heritage in China: Past and Present

Broadly, cultural heritage is either tangible or intangible. Intangible cultural heritage includes drama, music, folklore and festival ceremonies, while tangible cultural heritage contains both movable cultural relics such as antiques, calligraphy and paintings and immovable cultural antiquities such as ancient ruins, architecture and cave temples. Immovable cultural relics, such as ancient sites, towns, neighborhoods or villages and famous cities of historical and cultural value are accounted for in the *Law of the PRC on Protection of Cultural Relics*, and are equivalent to 'cultural heritage' that has been internationally recognized, are actually referred to in a broad sense. For those engaged in urban planning in China, ancient sites, towns, neighborhoods or villages and famous cities of historical and cultural value are frequently identified with historical and cultural heritage and, barring those intangible and movable relics, they could be recognized as cultural heritage in a narrow sense. In this chapter, both 'cultural relic' and 'cultural heritage' are used in the narrow sense.

1. Before Reform and Opening Up

China boasts a wealth of cultural heritage as it has 5,000 years of history and is home to 56 nationalities. Due to historical reasons, however, protection of China's cultural heritage started much later than in Europe. From the late 19th century to the early 20th century when imperialist powers invaded China, some scholars and missionaries from Europe and the US arrived, many of them with the aim of plundering antiquities and wealth. Protection of cultural relics in China began in the 1920s when archeological research began to thrive. In 1922, Peking University established its institute of archeology and archeological academy, the first institution for academic research of heritage protection and preservation in China's history. In June 1930, the then government promulgated the *Law on the Protection of Antiques* and soon after issued the *Detailed Regulations Regarding the Law on the Protection of Antiques*. In 1932, the Central Committee of Heritage Preservation was established. Due to political unrest and warfare, however, many cultural relics were neglected across the country at a time when laws and regulations were only in nominal existence.

After 1949, faced with the massive destruction and considerable losses of antiques during wartime, the Chinese government issued a package of decrees, set up central and local administrations, established archeological institutions and worked out various measures for the protection of cultural relics. By the mid-1960s, the system of protection for China's cultural relics took preliminarily shape. During this period, the government focused primarily on the protection and preservation of individual ancient architectural structures including buildings, historical sites as well as scenic spots and places of interest. In March 1961, the State Council published the *Provisional Regulations on the Protection and Control of Cultural Relics*. In the meantime, it brought out the first 180 key historical sites under state protection and implemented a protective system in which cultural relics and historic sites were designated as 'sites of cultural and historical value'.

The Cultural Revolution that started in 1966 wreaked havoc upon the laws and regulations of the country and it was only natural that protection of cultural relics would suffer huge losses.

2. After Reform and Opening Up

Historical preservation and urban planning administration was revived after 1978. In 1982, the State Council published a second group of key historical sites under state protection when, in February of that year, the first 24 famous cities of historical and cultural value under state protection were made known. The protective system of historical cities in China was now under way. In November 1982, the *Law on the Protection of Cultural Relics* was promulgated. In January 1984, the State Council issued the *Ordinances on Urban Planning*, in which it was stipulated that protection of cultural relics and historic sites should be heeded, while national styles and local features should be well preserved and protected in urban planning. In 1986, the State Council listed another 38 famous cities of historical and cultural value under state protection, having further stipulated that ancient architectural complexes and towns, neighborhoods or villages of historical and cultural value should be protected and that all provinces could bring out their own local famous cities of historical and cultural value. The protection of cultural heritage in China expanded from places where historic buildings and architectural complexes were located to certain urban areas and beyond. The system for protecting famous cities of historical and cultural value was therefore established and the graded protective system of China's historical and cultural relics took shape (see Special Column 7-1).

Special Column 7-1 Graded protection of historical and cultural relics in China

Historical and cultural relics under protection in China, unlike those in other countries, break down into three types: sites protected for their historical and cultural value; towns, neighborhoods or villages of historical and cultural value; and famous cities of historical and cultural value. With regard to sites protected for their historical and cultural value, the principle of preserving the historical contours of the original places applies. In protecting towns, neighborhoods or villages of historical and cultural value, the overall style and exterior appearance of architectural structures should be kept intact, although internal alterations or modifications are permitted in the latter case. As for famous cities of historical and cultural value, construction is allowed in places where no tangible or intangible historical and cultural relics are found provided that the overall layout and features of old towns or cities are preserved during construction. The graded or differentiated protection of historical and cultural relics congruent with the prevailing situation in China helps address any conflicts between preservation and construction.

With the booming growth of the urban economy and a

marked rise in real estate after 1990, many towns, neighborhoods or villages of historical and cultural value were demolished, the protection and preservation of historic environment having been confronted with new predicaments. In response, the Ministry of Construction and the State Administration of Cultural Heritage jointly set up the Committee of Experts on the Protection of Chinese Famous Cities of Historical and Cultural Value in March 1994 so as to strengthen supervision and technical consultation in protecting famous cities and assist local governments to better protect and manage famous cities of historical and cultural value. Moreover, with the aim of improving and promoting the protection of historical and cultural heritage according to law, the State Administration of Cultural Heritage promulgated the revised *Law on the Protection of Cultural Relics* in 2002, the Ministry of Construction issued the *Code of Conservation Planning for Historic Cities* in 2005, and the State Council published the *Regulations on the Protection of Famous Historical and Cultural Cities, Towns and Villages* in 2008.

II. Protection of Urban Cultural Relics and Historical Sites in China

1. Methods and Principles

Cultural relics and historical sites include sites of ancient cultures, ancient tombs, ancient architectural structures, cave temples, stone carvings, murals that are of historical, artistic or scientific value, and important modern and contemporary historic sites, material objects and buildings that are related to major historical events, revolutionary movements or famous personalities and that are highly memorable or are of great significance for education or for the preservation of historical data. As is stipulated in the *Law on the Protection of Cultural Relics*, the Chinese government implements protection of various important historical sites and other immovable cultural relics recognized by the state as sites of historical and cultural value in terms of their historical, artistic or scientific value. Today, there are 60,000 county-level famous historical sites, 7,000 provincial key cultural sites and 1,268 sites of historical and cultural value under state protection across the country.

The *Law on the Protection of Cultural Relics*, as the legal basis for the national protection of cultural relics and historical sites, has set down the principle for historic preservation. It gives priority to the protection of cultural relics, attaching primary importance to their rescue, and making rational use of and tightening control over them, the purpose of it being to preserve and carry on the overall historical value and message. All protective measures exercised shall be in compliance with the principle that the original state of historical and cultural relics shall remain unchanged.

2. Laws and Regulations on Protection of Urban Architectural Heritage

According to the *Law on the Protection of Cultural Relics*, ancient architectural structures are among the key cultural heritage to be protected. As is stipulated in Article 17, no construction of additional projects or operations such as blasting, drilling or digging may be conducted within the area of protection for a historical and cultural site. However, where under special circumstances it is necessary to conduct construction of additional projects or operations such as blasting, drilling and digging within the area of protection for such a site, its safety shall be guaranteed, and the matter shall be subject to approval by the people's government that formerly verified and announced the site and which, before giving approval, shall ask consent of the administrative department for cultural relics under the people's government at the next higher level; and where construction of additional projects or operations such as blasting, drilling and digging are to be conducted within the area of protection for a major historical and cultural site protected at the national level, the matter shall be subject to approval by the people's government of the relevant province, autonomous region or municipality directly under the central government, which, before giving approval, shall ask consent of the administrative department for cultural relics under the State Council.

On the basis of the actual need for the protection of cultural relics and with the approval of the people's government of the relevant province, autonomous region or municipality directly under the central government, a certain area for control of construction may be drawn up around a site protected for its historical and cultural value. No construction of a project in an area for control of construction may deform the historical features of the site protected for its historical and cultural value. No facilities that pollute the sites protected for their historical and cultural value or their environment may be put up within the area of protection for these sites or the area for control of construction, and no activities that may adversely affect the safety and environment of these sites may be conducted. Where there are already facilities that pollute the sites and their environment, they shall be brought under control within a specified time limit. When choosing a place for a construction project, the construction unit shall try its best to avoid the site of immovable cultural relics and where it is impossible to do so under special circumstances, it shall do everything it can to protect the original site protected for its historical and cultural value. Where it is impossible to protect the original site or the site needs to be moved to another place or dismantled, the matter shall be reported to the people's government of the relevant province, autonomous region or municipality directly under the central government for approval; where a site protected for its historical and cultural value at the provincial level needs to be moved to another place or dismantled, consent of the administrative department for cultural relics under the State Council must be obtained prior to approval. No major historical and cultural sites under state protection may be dismantled; where such a site needs to be relocated to another place, the matter shall be reported by the people's government of the relevant province, autonomous region or municipality directly under the central government to the State Council for approval.

On top of that, specific provisions have been made for the rights and obligations in protecting historical architectural structures in Article 21 of the *Law on the Protection of Cultural Relics*: users of state-owned immovable cultural relics shall be responsible for their repair and maintenance; and the owners of the immovable cultural relics not owned by the state shall be responsible for their repair and maintenance. Where the immovable cultural relics not owned by the state are in danger of damage and the owner cannot afford their repair, the local people's government shall offer the owner assistance; and where the owner can afford their repair but refuses to perform their obligation to do so as required by law, the people's government at or above county level may make emergency repairs and the expense incurred shall be borne by the owner. In the meantime, in repairing, maintaining and removing immovable cultural relics, the principle of keeping cultural relics in their original state shall be adhered to. Moreover, in compliance with the stipulation in Article 22, where immovable cultural relics are totally damaged, the ruins shall be protected and the damaged relics may not be rebuilt on the original site.

3. Keeping Intact the Original Forms of Historical Construction

In 1982, the principle of keeping cultural relics in their original state was written into the *Law on the Protection of Cultural Relics*. It made clear that this principle shall be adhered to in repairing, maintaining and removing immovable cultural relics. In line with the principle, 'four preservations' shall be adhered to in repairing and maintaining ancient buildings: preservation of the original state, preservation of architectural structure, preservation of construction material and preservation of technology. Not unnaturally, the principle helps secure the authenticity and integrity of historical constructions. As ancient architecture is evidence of history, the preservation of intact historical space and cultural memory helps people trace back to the remote past and place themselves in the genuine context of bygone days.

The principle of keeping cultural relics in their original state requires a series of measures to vouch for the preservation of historical architectural structures. First of all, it is crucial to respect history. We must think highly of the positive contributions of all historical ages to the construction of ancient architectural structures and conduct careful identification and remove traces of repair by later generations in an attempt to restore them to the state of the known historical time. Second, importance should be attached to the preservation of originals. Reinforcement of original structures should be focused on preservation, while eliminating hidden perils in repairing original structures. Third, historical features must be preserved. Authenticity should be retained as much as possible and traces of modern intervention should be reduced. Fourth, evaluation and research should be strengthened. Value estimates and assessment of the current condition of structures should be conducted and substantial measures for preservation and repairs should be worked out to prolong the life of historical buildings. Fifth, technical innovation should be promoted. New techniques and materials should be applied to reinforce the structures of ancient architecture based on scientific research and experiments. Sixth, intangible cultural heritage must be protected. In repairing and maintaining ancient buildings, traditional craftsmanship, techniques and materials should be used so that technical historical skills will be preserved and passed on.

Special Column 7-2 Protection of the Potala Palace in Lhasa, Tibet

The Potala Palace in Lhasa is among the largest and best-preserved palace-style architectural complexes in the world. In 2002, the palace witnessed the launch of a second round of a comprehensive preservation and maintenance project.

In line with the principle of following the original design, maintenance staff first carefully surveyed and studied the texture and all components of the palace before starting repair work. Since the overall structure of the palace could be divided into different parts that were inconsistent with one another in terms of construction time, function and technique, it was necessary for them to have each part individually surveyed, mapped and analyzed before working out a plan for maintenance and preservation. They also studied the construction materials and traditional craftsmanship peculiar to Tibet. While integrating traditional techniques with modern technology, they applied new techniques and materials to reinforce the palace so as to make up for the weaknesses of traditional materials and techniques and promote the inheritance, perfection and development of preservation techniques of cultural relics (see Figure 7-1).

Figure 7-1 Preservation and maintenance of the Potala Palace completed (Photographed by reporter, F Bbu Zahi, of Xinhua News Agency)

III. Protection of Historical and Cultural Street Districts in Chinese Cities

1. Definition and Principles

As is stipulated in the *Law on the Protection of Cultural Relics* promulgated in 1982, towns, neighborhoods or villages with an unusual wealth of cultural relics of important historical value shall be verified and announced as famous places of historical and cultural value. In the *Regulations on the Protection of Famous Historical and Cultural Cities, Towns and Villages* jointly drawn up by the Ministry of Construction and the State Administration of Cultural Heritage (draft for examination and approval), historical urban districts – towns, neighborhoods or villages of historical and cultural value – are defined as places of considerable scale with relatively rich historical remains, cultural relics, and modern and contemporary historical sites and buildings that authentically and perfectly reflect the traditional style and local features of a certain historical period. The definition has highlighted 'traditional style' and 'considerable scale' and thus marked the distinction between urban districts of historical and cultural value and sites of historical and cultural significance in terms of scale.

Three principles have been worked out for protecting urban districts of historical and cultural value. The first is protecting authentic historical remains, which is tantamount to protecting cultural relics and historical sites. The second is protecting the overall exterior style and features, which is distinct from the protection of cultural relics and historical sites. It means that internal restructuring and renovation are permitted and that the focuses of protection also include architectural environment and others that are separate from the relics and the sites proper. The third is preserving and giving play to the original usability. In other words, what is preserved should also include the social and cultural activities and functions the relics and sites assume so that they will stay active and their lives will be prolonged.

2. Outline of Planning

First, the scope and dimension of a protection area for the control of construction around a site protected for its historical and cultural value shall be determined. A historical urban district shall simultaneously satisfy the requirements of three established criteria for urban districts of historical and cultural value in terms of scope of protection: historical authenticity, true to life and integrity of style and features. Historical authenticity means that a certain quantity and proportion of authentic physical or substantial entities such as historical architectural structures that bear historical information should markedly dominate the ambience or atmosphere of a historical urban district. The quantitative criterion for historical authenticity is largely based on the time when the structures within the historical urban district were established. In general, the proportion or floor area of ancient architectural structures within China's historical urban districts that manifest the time of traditional buildings of distinct styles and features should reach around 50%. By true to life, it means that historical urban districts are not only places that used to be residences, but places that are and will be playing their roles as natural and organic components of social life. There are two criteria for judging true to life, the first being the measurable retention rates of former residents and the second the qualitative retention rates of original lifestyle. That is to say, an urban district of historical and cultural value should be a place where traditional culture and lifestyle are strikingly distinctive and have been best preserved in the city or district. Put another way, the retention rates of original traditional lifestyle should be the highest in the district. Today, the population retention rates in China's historical urban districts will have to be as high as around 60% so that the style and structure of social life within the districts will be kept intact and, meanwhile, the original residents retained will be satisfied in terms of current national residential standard and modern standard of living.

Integrity of style and features as a criterion can also be defined. First, the style and features within reach of a historical urban district should be essentially consistent with the visible environment, relatively integrated and preservable. Second, an urban district of historical and cultural value should be adequate in scale. In determining the scale, two aspects should be taken into account: the scale of the historical urban district should not be much too large in delimitation because it is the place where construction of a project is banned and the historical features are to be renovated and preserved; in the meantime, the area delimited should not be much too small considering that there should be relatively integrated features and a comparatively complete structural system of social life within the district. In this light, the proportion of historical features and architectural structures satisfying the criteria should stand at about 50%, and not less than 30%. Poorly located buildings and those with inferior features should account for about 20% of the total and no more than 30%. In addition, an urban district of historical and cultural value should be limited in size, the suggested area for the key zone to be preserved being 15-30 hectares with a total area of around 30-55 hectares.

Second, measures for preserving and renovating historical structures shall be worked out. For identified sites protected for their historical and cultural value or those to be identified as such according to planning, measures specific to sites protected for their historical and cultural value shall be exercised. For historical buildings whose original styles and features are better protected, the appearance of the originals shall be preserved though additional facilities that are much needed in modern life may be included in the renovation. For those suffering serious internal damage, the internal structure could be replaced while preserving the historical appearance. New buildings that are sympathetic to the historical environment could be kept unchanged. For new buildings such as huge modern constructions that clash with the historical styles within an urban district of historical and cultural value, renovation should be conducted, for example by restructuring façades, removing some floors or complete dismantlement.

Third, requirements for preserving and renovating environmental factors or elements of historical urban districts shall be formulated, including maintenance of roads and revetments and protection of mature trees.

Fourth, municipal facilities shall be renovated and reconstructed within historical urban districts to help address problems with the likes of rainwater and sewage systems, power supply, telecommunications and firefighting.

To wrest tighter control over vandalism of urban districts of historical and cultural value, the Ministry of Construction published the *Measures for the Administration of Urban Purple Lines* in November 2003 in which the purple lines were delimited for historical urban districts within national famous cities of historical and cultural value, historical urban districts listed by the people's governments of provinces as well as historical constructions recognized by people's governments above county level. It was stipulated in the Measures that the purple lines should include key districts under protection and peripheral zones where any construction is controlled. Architectural structures protected within the purple lines should not be dismantled; newly constructed or reshaped buildings should not be built in the traditional layout and style of a historical urban district; and gardens and greenbelts, rivers and lakes, roads, and mature and precious trees reserved according to planning should not be vandalized.

3. Successful Cases in Recent Years

Since the system for protecting historical street districts was established in China, considerable progress has been made in the preservation and renovation of historical street districts. Here are some successful cases.

(1) South Avenue in Pingyao

Located in Pingyao County, Jinzhong City, Shanxi Province is the Old Town of Pingyao, one of the famous state-level towns of historical and cultural value that enjoys a history of more than 2,700 years. In 1977, when renovation started with South Avenue that runs through the center of town, all overhead electrical cables and telecommunications lines were relocated underground and all asphalt roads were restored to stone paving along which residents were encouraged to run stores and hold exhibitions of folk art. After renovation, the original historical style and features of the district were well preserved, and the economy thrived with the development of tourism (see Figures 7-2).

Figure 7-2 Vista of South Avenue in Pingyao after renovation (Photographed by reporter, Fan Minda, of Xinhua News Agency)

(2) Lijiang

The Old Town of Lijiang in Lijiang City, Yunnan Province, is among the second group of famous towns of historical and cultural value approved by the state. Making use of funds appropriated by the state for preserving and protecting historical urban districts, the government has reconstructed the drainage and lighting in the district and restored its original historical style and features, which in turn has helped promote the preservation of the old town and its economic growth (see Figure 7-3). Today, the Old Town of Lijiang and the Old Town of Pingyao, both well-known tourist attractions in China, have succeeded in their application for world cultural heritage status.

Figure 7-3 Vista of the Old Town of Lijiang (Photographed by reporter, Lin Yiguang, of Xinhua News Agency)

(3) The Old Street of Tunxi in Huangshan City

The Old Street of Tunxi in Tunxi District, Huangshan City, Anhui Province has been identified by the Ministry of Construction as a pilot urban historical district under state protection. During the renovation, the government has funded infrastructure improvements while residents have paid for finishing their own storefronts. After renovation, it has become a must-see for those visiting Mount Huangshan, and tourism around the street has developed rapidly (see Figure 7-4).

Figure 7-4 The Ole Street of Tunxi in Huangshan City (Photographed by reporter, Wanglei, of Xinhua News Agency)

(4) The Old Street of Wuzhen in Tongxiang City

Situated in Tongxiang City, Zhejiang Province, Wuzhen is a time-honored town whose historical style and features have been well preserved. Since 1999, when a specialized institution was set up in Tongxiang, policies have been drawn up[①] for the renovation of the environment and

---

① Tongxiang City has established a specialized institution for the protection and development of Wuzhen, namely the Management Committee of Protection and Tourism Development of Wuzhen Town. The policies it has formulated include the *Management of Housing Relocation for Protection and Tourism Development of Wuzhen Town*, the *Management Ordinances for the Protection and Development of Wuzhen Town*, and the *Opinions on Speeding up Protection and Tourism Development of Wuzhen Town*

144

architectural structures in the district in a planned way, resulting in the successful restoration of the original historical style and features. During the renovation, old materials were used to replace or repair old houses, streets and bridges so as to reproduce the original features of the old street. All overhead electrical cables and telecommunications lines have been relocated underground and flush toilets have been installed along the street. Today, the Old Street of Wuzhen is enjoying rapid development (see Figure 7-5).

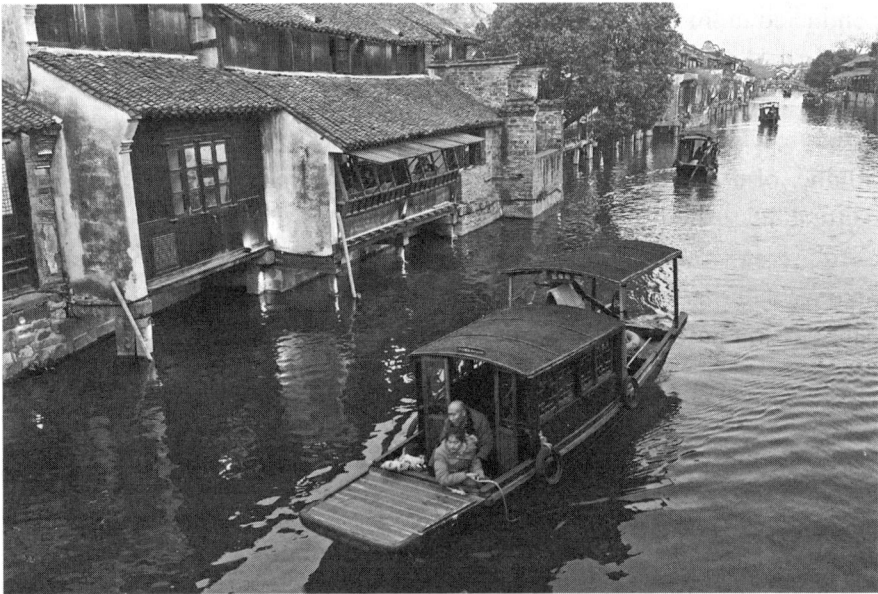

Figure 7-5 The Old Street of Wuzhen in Tongxiang City (Photographed by reporter, Tanjing, of Xinhua News Agency)

IV. Protection of Historical Cities in China

1. Definition and Criteria for Selection

(1) Definition of historical cities

According to the stipulation in Article 8, Chapter 2 of the *Law on the Protection of Cultural Relics* published in 1982, cities with an unusual wealth of cultural relics of important historical value or high revolutionary memorial significance shall be verified and announced by the State Council as famous cities of historical and cultural value.[①] A concept native to China, 'famous cities of historical and cultural value' is slightly distinct from the way things operate in foreign countries. In effect, the concept does not mean preservation of a city at large. Besides, the contents and scale of protection are determined by means of urban planning.[②]

(2) Criteria for selection

Selection of famous cities of historical and cultural value in China is primarily conducted in line with three criteria. First, the city chosen must have a long history with a wealth of well-preserved cultural relics and historical sites, as well as significant historical, scientific and artistic value. Second, the current structure and style of the city should retain historical features with a known number of districts representing the city's traditional properties. Third, the cultural relics and historical sites should be largely distributed in downtown or suburban areas, and protection and fair use of this historical and cultural heritage will positively affect the city's make-up, layout and formulation of construction policies.

2. Features of Historical Cities in China

Famous cities of historical and cultural value in China have the following two features:

(1) Large in number

There are now 101 famous cities of historical and cultural value under state protection in China promulgated by the State Council: 24 in 1982, 38 in 1986, 37 in 1994 and two in 2001. In this regard, China boasts the largest number of famous cities of historical and cultural value in the world. For instance, there are only four famous cities under state protection in the UK. Unlike China, however, the UK focuses on preservation and protection of conservation areas, cultural relics and historical sites. Statistically, there are as many as 500,000 nationally listed architectural structures[③] and 8,000

---

① *The Law of the PRC on the Protection of Cultural Relics*, Article 8
② Wang Jinghui. *The Role of Urban Planning in Cultural Heritage Protection: Interaction between Urban Planning and Protection of Cultural Relics* [J]. *China Cultural Heritage Scientific Research*, 2006, (1)
③ The practice of cultural properties being nationally listed is widely adopted for the preservation of history in western countries

conservation areas in England alone.

(2) Complex in type

Based on the distinct factors that constitute history, nature, human geography, urban material elements and urban functional structures, the 101 famous cities of historical and cultural value under state protection can be broken down into seven types: cities as ancient capitals characterized by a wealth of historical remains and features; cities with traditional styles and features that have retained intact architectural complexes of one or more historical eras; cities of scenic attraction in which the natural environment plays a decisive role and the dynamic integration between architectural structures and natural environment constitutes their pronounced distinctness; cities of regional and ethnic features located in ethnic places and manifesting unique characteristics, ethnic customs, regional cultures and peculiarities of their own due to the effect of geographical diversity, cultural environment and historical change; cities significant in modern and near modern history that are distinguished by a certain historical event or by their historical constructions or architectural complexes of a certain period; cities with special functions, of which at least one used to be extremely significant in history and constitutes their present distinctness; cities that have a wealth of cultural relics and widely dispersed historical sites to constitute their traditional features.

3. Principles and Contents of Protection

(1) Principles of protection

The formulation of principles for protecting famous cities of historical and cultural value aims to protect cultural heritage in cities and promote the growth of the urban economy and society in order to constantly improve the living and working environments. Cities are organic entities in which tens of thousands of people live and work. For the development of the economy and facilities, and for the betterment of people's living standards and the realization of modernized cities, the wealth of historical and cultural resources should be exploited to the full by protecting famous cities of historical and cultural value so that they will be given full play in boosting the development of the urban economy, society and culture.

(2) Contents of protection

Three aspects have to be taken into account in protecting China's famous cities of historical and cultural value: the first is the protection of historical and cultural sites as well as regions of historic significance, of which the protection areas can be delimited; the second is the protection and preservation of historical arrangements and features of ancient cities by means of working out catalogues of management measures and standards of control in urban planning; and the third is inheritance and the carrying forward of fine historical and cultural traditions, which entails the efforts of competent departments and sectors of urban planning as well as the common concerns of the public.

Special Column 7-3 Overall protection of the Old Town of Suzhou

It is remarkable, at an international level, that the site of the Old Town of Suzhou in Suzhou City, Jiangsu Province has never changed since it was founded more than 2,500 years ago. Covering an area of 14.2 square kilometers, the Old Town of Suzhou was the first in China where global or overall protection was practiced. The historical layout and features of the town have been well preserved over the years. Compared to the 1980s, the skyline of this time-honored town has remained unchanged. In 2003, when the master planning of the city was once again modified, 29 historical sites were delimited and the *Provisional Regulations on the Compulsory Contents in Urban Planning* were formulated, in which measures for protecting the overall style and features of the old town were stipulated with regard to the height, color, form and size of constructions. The government took the national lead in its application of an urban purple line by means of which it worked to incorporate the protection of the old town and cultural relics into the compulsory contents of its master urban planning. On October 26, 2012, another initiative for protecting the old town was brought out by the government when the Suzhou Conservation Area of the National Famous City of Historical and Cultural Value was officially established. The government's persistent efforts to protect and preserve the Old Town of Suzhou provide a cherished example for the overall protection of historical towns or cities across the country.

In protecting famous cities of historical and cultural value, global views and comprehensive protective measures combine to constitute the tenet and attributes of the effort and in the meantime help create conditions for protecting cultural relics and historical sites while promoting the development of urban construction. The measures to be taken include determining social and economic development strategies suited to the protection of historical cities, working out a rational urban layout and orientation of development in protecting old towns and developing new districts, and improving the functions of old towns in protecting their spatial patterns and visual corridors between key cultural landscapes so that the cultural relics and historical sites will be highlighted. In non-historic or recently developed regions within a famous city of historical and cultural value, limitations of taste and appropriateness also apply to new construction projects in consideration of the city's overall pattern. For a famous city with profound historical and cultural heritage, historical traditions should be highly regarded and promoted.

Special Column 7-4 Hangzhou: the win-win development strategy in constructing new urban districts while protecting the old town

One of China's seven ancient capitals and well-known for its West Lake and other places of interest, Hangzhou was among the first group of famous cities of historical and cultural value to be put under state protection. Since the reform and opening up, it has been identifying the establishment of a famous city of historical and cultural value as well as protection of cultural heritage with primary productive forces. It has coordinated the twin goals of protecting the famous old town and constructing new districts in its urbanization and found the optimal balance point. Based on its principle of 'constructing new districts while protecting the old town', the city government has been focusing on protecting its old urban district because it is clear that the West Lake, the layout of the old district shaped like a waist drum and the outline known as 'a city enshrouded in cloudy hills on three sides' will be well protected in its effort to keep intact the old town.

As it builds new districts, the government is focused on construction, industry and relocating the population from the old town to new districts. With the construction of Qianjiang New City, Hangzhou has left behind the 'age of the West Lake' and entered the 'era of the Qiantang River' in its burgeoning urban development. Over the past decade or more, the overall layout and scale of the new city along the Qiantang River have taken shape, during which time a huge number of people and industries have aggregated in the new urban area. As the pressures and burdens on the old town moderated, the government has scored win-win achievements in its effort to protect the old town and promote the economic development along and across the Qiantang River.[①]

---

① Wang Guoping. *Cities: Where to Go*? [M]. Beijing: People's Publishing House, 2010

Chapter Follow-up Questions and References

Chapter 1

Questions

1. How does China's urbanization relate to that of the world?

2. How does the historical development of China's urbanization differ from that in your country? And why?

3. What are the Chinese government's policies with regard to the country's urbanization?

Bibliography

1. Chu Tianjiao & Tan Wenzhu. *Urban Planning and Management in Rapid Urbanization* [M]. Beijing: People's Publishing House, 2012

2. Zhou Ganzhi. *A Probe into Urbanization with Chinese Characteristics* [J]. Urban Planning International, 2009, (S1)

3. Li Jingwen. *Major Trends of Development in China's Urbanization: Rise of Urban Clusters and Their Demand for Investment* [J]. Innovation, 2008, (3)

4. Gao Xincai, Zhou Yi & Xu Jing. *On the History of China's Urbanization* [J]. Academic Exchanges, 2010, (1)

Chapter 2

Questions

1. What should we do to address the relationships between the 'rigidity' and 'flexibility' in urban-rural planning within the context of rapid

urbanization?

2. How should we bring into effect urban-rural planning so that diversified capital would be brought in to urban construction?

3. What effect have different political and economic systems generated in the administrative system of urban-rural planning and its operating system?

Bibliography

1. Chu Tianjiao & Tan Wenzhu. *Urban Planning and Management in Rapid Urbanization* [M]. Beijing: People's Publishing House, 2012

2. Dong Jianhong. *History of Cities in China* [M]. Beijing: China Architecture & Building Press, 2004

3. E. Howard, *Garden Cities of Tomorrow* [M]. Translated by Jin Jingyuan. Beijing: the Commercial Press, 2002

4. Geng Yuxiu. *Management of Urban Planning* [M]. Shanghai: Shanghai Science and Technical Literature Press, 1997

5. Li Dchua. *Principles of Urban Planning (third version)* [M]. Beijing: China Architecture & Building Press, 2001

Chapter 3

Questions

1. What effects does economic globalization have on the spatial layout of urban industrial structure?

2. How does the government-led construction of new urban districts attract diversified capital?

3. How can we do a good job of addressing the relationship between developing new urban districts and promoting the functions of old urban districts?

Bibliography

1. Chu Tianjiao. *Evolutionary Trend of the Structure of Manufacturing Industry in the Yangtze River Delta* [J]. World Regional Studies, 2010, (3)

2. Contemporary Shanghai Research Institute. *Research on Urban Development in Contemporary Shanghai* [M]. Shanghai: Shanghai

People's Publishing House, 2008

3. Wang Fengyu & Zhu Xiaojuan. *China Development Zones Development Review and Strategic Thinking* [J]. Yunnan Geographic Environment Research, 2006, (4). page 96

4. Yu Hongjun & Ning Yuemin. *Outline of Urban Geography* [M]. Hefei: Anhui Science and Technology Press, 1983

5. Zheng Guo. *Growth of Development Zones and Reconstruction of Urban Space in China: Implications and History* [J]. Modern Urban Research, 2011, (5). pages 20-24

Chapter 4

Questions

1. What phases of construction of urban infrastructure has China gone through? And what are their main features?

2. How should the financial problems in China's urban infrastructure be best addressed? And what innovative initiatives should be adopted in reforming its systems and mechanisms?

3. What enlightenment and inspiration can we draw from the construction of urban infrastructure in China?

Bibliography

1. Liu Xuexin. *Risks in Market-based Reform of China's Infrastructural Industry* [M]. Beijing: Science Press, 2009

2. Jiang Shijie. *Investment in Infrastructure and Progress of Urbanization* [M]. Beijing: China Construction Industry Press, 2010

3. Gao Jian & Wang Xiongjian. *Leverage of Investment Strategies in China's Urban Infrastructure on Economic Growth* [M]. Beijing: Peking University Press, 2009

Chapter 5

Questions

1. What are your thoughts on China's property rights system?

2. What means or measures do you think are applicable to the regulation of land market supply and demand? How should regulatory policies

for land market supply and demand be best coordinated with fiscal and financial policies? And in what way could a satisfactory regulation effect be achieved?

3. How can the utilization efficiency of urban land be enhanced?

Bibliography

1. Bi Baode. *Studies on China's Land Market* [M]. Beijing: China Renmin University Press, 1994

2. Chu Tianjiao. *Patterns of Land Negotiation and Their Standardization* [J]. Shanghai Economic Forum, 2002, (4)

3. He Fang. *Development and Innovation of the Land System with Chinese Characteristics* [J]. Shanghai Land Resources, 2012, (3)

Chapter 6

Questions

1. What effects could different economic systems have on urban community management?

2. What more efforts do you think China should make in its transition from community management mode to community governance mode?

3. What should the party do to promote the sound development of residents' self-governance and strengthen its leadership?

Bibliography

1. Chen Xian, et al. *Community Economy and Services* [M]. Shanghai: Shanghai University Press, 2001

2. Cheng Yushen. *Studies on the Development of China's Urban Communities* [M]. Shanghai: East China Normal University Press, 2002

3. Lin Shangli, et al. *Community Organizations and Construction of Residents' Committees* [M]. Shanghai: Shanghai University Press, 2001

4. Lu Hanlong. *Organizational Construction of Community Services* [J]. Quarterly Journal of the Shanghai Academy of Social Sciences, 2002, (2)

5. Ma Xiheng & Liu Zhongqi. *Governance of Urban Communities: with Reference to Construction of Shanghai into an International Metropolis*

[M]. Shanghai: Xuelin Publishing House, 2011

6. Peng Bo. *Changes in Contemporary China's Urban Communities* [M]. Beijing: China Social Publishing House, 2007

Chapter 7

Questions

1. How have the ideas and concepts of protecting urban cultural heritage in China evolved?

2. What are the means by which urban cultural heritage in China have been well protected?

3. What new practices has China promulgated to protect its urban cultural heritage?

Bibliography

1. Ruan Yisan, Wang Jinghui & Wanglin. *Protection of Historical Cities: Theory and Planning* [M]. Shanghai: Tongji University Press, 1998

2. Shan Jixiang. *Retaining the 'Root' and 'Soul' of Urban Culture: Exploration and Practice of China's Cultural Heritage Protection* [M]. Beijing: Science Press, 2010

3. Wang Lin & Wang Jun. *Formulation of Planning for Protecting Urban Historical Districts* [J]. Urban Planning, 1998, (3)

4. Wang Jinghui. *Protection of Historical Sites: Theory and Applications* [J]. Urban Planning, 1998, (3)

5. Robert Riddell. *Sustainable Urban Planning* [M]. London: Blackwell Publishing Ltd, 2004

6. Stephen M. Wheeler. *Planning for Sustainability* [M]. London: Routledge, 2004

责任编辑:洪　琼
版式设计:顾杰珍

图书在版编目(CIP)数据

中国城镇化/楚天骄等 著.—北京:人民出版社,2016.12
(中国故事丛书/冯俊主编)
ISBN 978－7－01－016467－0

Ⅰ.①中…　Ⅱ.①楚…　Ⅲ.①城市化-研究-中国　Ⅳ.①F299.21

中国版本图书馆 CIP 数据核字(2016)第 166851 号

中国城镇化

ZHONGGUO CHENGZHENHUA

楚天骄　王国平　朱　远 等著

人民出版社 出版发行

(100706　北京市东城区隆福寺街 99 号)

北京汇林印务有限公司印刷　新华书店经销

2016 年 12 月第 1 版　2016 年 12 月北京第 1 次印刷
开本:710 毫米×1000 毫米 1/16　印张:19.25
字数:280 千字　印数:0,001-5,000 册

ISBN 978－7－01－016467－0　定价:50.00 元

邮购地址 100706　北京市东城区隆福寺街 99 号
人民东方图书销售中心　电话 (010)65250042　65289539

《中国城镇化》一书的英文部分由刘全福(Liu Quanfu)翻译